THE SOVIET SYSTEM OF GOVERNMENT

THE SOVIET SYSTEM OF GOVERNMENT

FIFTH EDITION, Revised

JOHN N. HAZARD

THE UNIVERSITY OF CHICAGO PRESS

CHICAGO & LONDON

The University of Chicago Press, Chicago 60637
The University of Chicago Press, Ltd., London

ISBN: 0-226-32193-2 (clothbound) 0-226-32194-0 (paperbound)
LCN: 79-16827

87 86 85 84 83 82 81 80 54321

PREFACE TO THE FIFTH EDITION

Communists believe in the efficacy of institutions. With them they expect to be able to restructure society to foster the values they have chosen to respect. While all activists show confidence in institutions as a means of achieving what they have come to idealize as a good society, the Communists of the Soviet Union declare that their attitude toward institutions is qualitatively different from attitudes in the non-Communist world. Their task is to create a new society, new in every way. They have no intention of protecting a long-established nineteenth-century social structure. They expect to experience the need to try various political experiments, but these will always be related to achievement of their predetermined goal. There is no desire to explore various goals through experimentation; only to search for appropriate institutions likely to help them achieve a goal of whose desirability they have no doubts.

This book focuses on institutions, institutions manipulated by the avowed Marxists of the Soviet Union to achieve the goal they call communism. In spite of their declared intention to break completely with the past in creating a new society, history has shown that no people has ever succeeded in making such a sudden break. There is always a past in history which makes itself felt, and Russian history provides no exception. Soviet institutions, although designed to create a new type of society, were not conceived on a blank page on the night of November 7, 1917, when the Winter Palace in Petrograd fell. The institutions which the Communist leader, V. I. Lenin, chose to use for governing when his party and its political partners seized power were already in place. The structure of the new state, the "soviet," was already meeting in the capital, ready to become the symbol legitimating the new regime with the working masses. The Communist leadership already had its disciplined activist instrument of guidance, tempered in the revolutionary struggle that had been seething since the turn of the century.

The decades during which the soviets and the Communist party had matured had been important in creating attitudes toward a desirable form of government. These attitudes had become so fixed in the minds of those who led, that experts helping to draft the first Constitution of 1918 were unable to persuade those leaders even to consider alternate forms of government. History had left its imprint, and the soviet system, as it had evolved during the years of revolution, became fixed in the basic law.

Sixty-odd years of experience since 1917 have not changed the leadership's determination to preserve the Communist party and its mass arm, the soviets. Although sharp criticism is leveled at times at past mistakes, the dominant contemporary soviet leaders show no desire to abandon their governmental structures to try something new. This conservative attitude helps to explain the new U.S.S.R. Constitution of October 7, 1977. Its major effect is preservation of the well-established forms which have developed since 1917. The Constitution does for the state apparatus what revision of the Communist party rules did for the party structures in 1966: it reaffirms the determination to avoid change.

Readers may ask why Soviet leaders now sense the need to reaffirm structures in a new Constitution. Why was it not desirable to continue in force the 1936 Constitution, reserving for later years any updating that might be necessary to meet unexpected events as the last decades of the twentieth century unfold? It is expected to be a period of great change, with the introduction into the Soviet economy of the scientific and technological revolution; a period when political change can be expected to follow economic change. The answer to this question is not easy to find, primarily because the Communist party has succeeded over many years in keeping secret from the West the policy debates that occur within it. Westerners do not know for certain what groupings or factions have come to the fore, in spite of a party rule against the forming of factions. They know, however, that there are differing views among the top leaders because the increasingly large numbers of persons leaving the Soviet Union for the West disclose such varying views. These reports gain credence from the vocal opposition to the Soviet model that has emerged among Communists in Italy, France and Spain, and among the professed "scientific socialists" of Africa. Clearly, Soviet structures are not universally acclaimed even by those who accept Marxist goals and look to the Soviet Communists for inspiration.

From these various sources, Western analysts have sometimes concluded that the Communist party leaders now dominant are determined to conserve the institutional Communist party and Soviet state structures that have emerged in sixty years of practice, and that they face some opposition from both a Right and a Left within the party, each of which seeks some measure of change in institutions, the better to serve Communist aims. The Right is thought to include those who think the leadership has strayed too far toward liberalization of attitudes; too far toward relaxation of the discipline which Stalin had required; too far toward rigid formalities that hamper flexible application of governmental power. The Left is thought to argue that the center has not gone far enough in liberalizing the system. In a measure, they want more emphasis upon "legality"; more emphasis upon humanism in the governing process; more opening of the gates of censorship so as to permit penetration into Soviet specialist circles by renovating Western ideas designed to reap the full benefits of the scientific and technological revolution.

While it now seems unlikely that any group would go so far as to restore to the political stage the fraternal parties of socialists and agrarians which shared in the early months of Lenin's government, and whose counterparts still function in a supportive position in Poland and Hungary alongside the Communists, it is possible that some recognition of "interest groups" might be favored by the liberalizers.

If it is true that pressures are being felt by the dominant group of leaders within the Communist party, it is possible that 1977 was chosen as the year of the new Constitution in order to strengthen the hands of those who resist institutional change. It is a document designed to make radical innovation difficult, if not impossible. It is a document designed to "freeze" Soviet political structures for decades to come against inroads proposed or to be proposed by the generations now ascending the ladder of political power.

While structural change seems to have been set aside for the

life of the new Constitution, there is one area of potential development of the political process which is in the news. This is the
area of "public participation" in government. It is heralded by
the new Constitution as an aim of the Soviet state's policy makers, and it is implemented by various provisions such as the
referendum, the right to petition, and the public discussion of
drafts of law. The question arising in the minds of some Western
students of the Soviet system is whether broad segments of the
population can be drawn into the governing process without affecting the system of élite government which has characterized
the first sixty years, and whether "public participation" means
broad or only limited participation in the process of implementing Communist party policy. Materials in this book are designed
to provide a basis for reaching conclusions to this question. Assured answers cannot be expected, because the accidents of history often upset the best of forecasts. Yet the broad design of
contemporary leadership is clear: to the extent that a constitution
can achieve their purpose, they want to preserve the structures
that have stood the test of time, and "public participation" must
fit into the current pattern as a strengthening adjunct, not as a
force for change.

A word needs to be said in explanation of the last chapter. The
book ends, as have prior editions, with a chapter entitled "The
Peril Points." This chapter was originally inspired by a sense
that forces rampant in the United States during the late 1950's
were trying to establish counterweights to Jeffersonian democratic institutions by preventing wide-ranging discussion of
policy through public pillorying, if not eventually outright censorship, of those who disagreed with them. The campaign was so
artful that many did not realize its subversive character until it
was turned on some of the most respected figures in the nation.
The point of the last chapter is that Soviet experience can have
lessons for democrats in other lands. Communists have demonstrated that it is possible to structure institutions of government
along lines of Jeffersonian democracy and to turn these institutions to the achievement of goals over which there can be no
debate.

Although the 1950's have passed into history, the perils of
those years occasionally recur, and sometimes in unexpected
quarters. New York police, while off duty, tried to silence a great
newspaper by preventing its delivery trucks from reaching

newsstands because they disliked its editorial policy regarding the police's position in collective bargaining then in process. Students have howled down speakers in prestigious universities in spite of the arguments of noted liberal educators who have tried to show that however hateful a message may be, the way to oppose it is not by preventing its presentation by formal or informal censorship, but rather by counterargument. The American Civil Liberties Union has found it increasingly necessary during the last decade to put its lawyers into the courts to defend the right of speakers to present positions which others would like to suppress by closing avenues of communication to their proponents. The civil libertarians are trying to reassert Winston Churchill's noted aphorism that democracy has only one institution to defend: the means to express ideas.

Study of the Soviet system of government is, therefore, not without lessons for others, although its forms have been influenced by a historical experience peculiar to the Russian Empire and the U.S.S.R. Much of the leadership in developing countries and also in Western Europe is now considering the suitability of the Soviet model to their needs. Some are accepting it in various degrees; some are rejecting it as unsuitable; but a great many are studying it. It is the purpose of this book to facilitate that study so that Westerners, and particularly North Americans in Canada and the United States, may draw their own conclusions from the facts.

J. N. H.

CONTENTS

CHAPTER 1

IN THE NAME OF DEMOCRACY

A "socialist democracy," unlike any system yet seen upon the earth, is the promise of Soviet leaders to their own people and to the world. Political forms utilized for generations by Americans, Englishmen, Frenchmen, and Scandinavians—and held up as models by many leaders of Asia and Africa creating new states—in Soviet minds serve a useful purpose, but only in transition. Soviet politicians claim to offer more, both in abundance of production and mass participation in government than Jeffersonian democrats can possibly provide. Their sixty years of experience has moved these politicians to argue that manipulation of power by the educated few in the interests of the many can bridge a gap between the conventional democratic right of the people to choose policies and men and their traditional inability to do so wisely. Communists believe themselves standing upon the threshold of a new life capable of proving, if it has not done so already, that the Soviet system of government is the best in the world.

No Soviet author argues that the system has yet achieved perfection. It is seen to be in an early stage, to be preparing the way, but the Communists boast that the base has been laid for mass participation in the governmental process through activities of a new kind. To them their system is inspired by the tribal communism of the ancient past brought up to date. It is one in which deep social conflict stimulated by sharp contrast in property holdings has abated; a system in which the masses are overcoming ignorance and the political apathy it breeds; a system in which all people talk out problems in harmony to reach a consensus; a system without triumphs of a majority over a minority in contests of voters; a system in which leaders, constantly re-

1

freshed by new men chosen from the masses by the leaders themselves, guide the people like the tribal leaders of old to wise decisions. This is the essence of "socialist democracy" in its ideal form.

The realization of the ideal depends, as in all systems, upon the character of the leaders, and these combine in their persons often unrecognized influences springing from both the historical environment and the traditions of political thought in which they were reared. None are left in positions of power who have more than a youth's impressions of the Russian Empire from which the Soviet Union was created. The heritage of the leaders of today is a taught tradition rather than a personal recollection, but this teaching is not without influence. Perhaps it holds greater sway over contemporary Soviet minds than the personal experiences of their elders, which often provided conflicting impressions.

Fixed impressions have been gained from teachings of parents and the teachers of the early Soviet schools: impressions of the widespread poverty of the past, of the limited opportunities for education, of the corruption of political institutions, of the pressing need for reform in 1917. From the Marxist texts read in childhood leaders have gained a belief that man has at last discovered the factors that make for social development and can with this knowledge manipulate social forces so as to achieve a goal called "communism."

The taught tradition of political thought and the leaders' perception of their environmental heritage have sometimes combined to create a fixity of purpose which brooks no interference, but at other times two currents have created mixed attitudes. It is from this confusion that contradictions have arisen, often baffling to foreign observers seeking to understand the sources of motivation of Soviet policies. A few examples may indicate the points at which there have been manifestations of fixity of purpose, the points at which there has been flux, and the likelihood of evolution of policies in a foreseeable pattern in the years to come.

The Influence of History and Political Theory

The heritage of Russian history as taught in the schools of the first decade of Communist rule and the Marxist political theory interpreted by early teachers have combined in the minds of contemporary Soviet leaders to create a primary aim: to raise the standard of living. History's contribution to this aim was Russia's poverty, notably in the villages and the mill towns from which the families of current leaders came, or about which those who were educated men of the great cities read or heard on periodic visits outside the capitals. Political theory's contribution was to teach that poverty need not be the curse of man. Marxism held out to its adherents a promise of a society in which every citizen might obtain satisfaction of his needs if capitalism were destroyed and if the working classes were to seize power. This was the message given by the early Communists to the students of Russia, and their pamphlets were distributed and have since been redistributed in millions of copies as the primary textbooks of the Soviet schools.

Russian history and Marxist political theory combined in the early nineteenth century to create a second fundamental urge: to devise a political system unlike that of the Tsars. Yet no one was sure what it should be. The heritage of Imperial Russia and Marxist political thought provided no base for a single answer. Peasant tradition of the time offered a model of village democracy in which every villager had his say, after which the village elders decided on the basis of discussion what ought to be done. Here was the voteless consensus, formulated in concrete terms by heads of families, and this system had widespread appeal. Yet this approach was by no means satisfactory to those of the intellectuals, known as the "intelligentsia," who looked to England or France for models and thought in terms of parliaments, political parties, elections, and votes.

Russian history provided neither type of political formation an opportunity to test its theories at the national level. It was cruel, especially to the Western-oriented intellectuals. Until 1906 the Tsar allowed no parliament. He established severe limitations upon freedom of speech and of the press, upon freedom of movement, upon the right to form trade unions and co-operative associations. The statutes even created legal inequality of citizens. The situation became so tense that many of the nobles, who were the privileged class, felt it necessary to Russia's future to petition the Tsar for reform at the turn of the century, but he was reluctant to act. Not until the serious unrest and riots of 1905 did he feel impelled to promise a parliament, and even then in his first plan he withheld the vote from the entire working class until severe disorder forced him to grant it.

The reforms following what has been called the "Revolution of

1905" left much to be desired by those hoping for development of democratic institutions on the English or French models. The Prime Minister and his cabinet could not be forced to resign by a vote of lack of confidence; the Tsar retained a veto over the acts of his parliament, dissolved it on various occasions when its activity frightened him, and in the interval between parliaments governed by decree, as he had before 1906. In consequence the forces craving democracy on the English model were weak in experience when the collapse of Imperial power near the end of the First World War created the opportunity for a second great revolt. There was agreement to end forever the principle enunciated in Article 4 of the Fundamental Law of the Empire, which read: "To the Emperor of all the Russias belongs the supreme autocratic power. To obey his commands not merely from fear but according to the dictates of one's conscience is ordained by God himself." Still, there was an experience that was only skin deep with a system that the intellectuals hoped to create in its stead. The great mass of the people hated their rulers, but their expectations of reform were limited to their experience with village democracy, which did not correspond to that in the minds of those with education. In this fact lay perhaps the major influence upon the experiments with political institutions which were to follow.

The history of the year 1917 only intensified the demand of the masses for complete change. While the Provisional Government, under important influences created by the intellectuals who hoped to implant an English-type system, assumed power with the abdication of the Tsar and struggled to make progress in the direction of its dreams, it met with serious obstacles. It was still conducting a very unpopular war with the German Emperor, and the country was in economic chaos. Under constant pressure from the center and left, the government tried to introduce reforms, but it was unable to meet the growing hunger for radical change, especially from the peasantry. The masses had tasted blood in 1905 and again in March of 1917. Under the leadership of the left they revolted yet again in November, 1917, to establish what they hoped would be a new system of government that would cope first of all with the pressing economic needs of the times and do so under policies associated with what was to most the hazy concept of "socialism."

Marxist political theory contained much preaching about the desirability of democracy, but it also contained within it the seeds of the negation of democracy. These seeds were to be found in the important role assigned by the theory to "leadership." This factor was taught as essential to the achievement of communism. Marx and his collaborator, Friedrich Engels, had no confidence in the political preparation of the general public for the task of building the kind of society they had planned. Although they wrote for a public in western Europe in which there were already large numbers of sophisticated people, they expected that only a relative few would understand what they were recommending and that still fewer would have the determination and stamina to try to put the Marxist program into effect. The authors of the program expected the great mass of the people to accept passively the inevitable continuance of the capitalist system. They expected that the mass would not rise in revolt against the system unless it were led by the few who were willing and able to take the trouble to understand what had to be done. They called for leadership of the masses toward the goal of communism. They were not content with the mere liberation of the masses from capitalism, to be followed by popular determination of political goals.

Marx's Concept of Democracy

Marx was not preaching democracy in the sense in which it is understood in the countries that have long experienced it, yet he claimed to be a democrat. Such a claim was necessary to win adherents, for democracy was on the lips of all as the aspiration of humanity. Marx held out the goal of economic abundance, which he assumed to be the primary desire of mankind. He seemed honestly to have thought that his analysis of history had discovered the forces that made for social progress, and he counted on the effective manipulation of these forces to achieve economic abundance.

Having assumed that mankind sought abundance and that his analysis of the forces that could provide it was correct, he took a step that has been popular also with other figures in history. He assumed that his system was democratic because it was designed, and in his view it was certain, to achieve maximum benefit for the general public. For him, "democracy" became synonymous with his plan to save the world; it did not mean a mechanism of government to be used by a majority to decide what it wants to do.

Marx was optimistic that if his plan could be introduced and the general public taught to appreciate its virtues, there would come a time when a leadership with the authority required to enforce its decisions would become unnecessary. He did not live to outline his dream of this final period, but his colleague Engels described it as the ultimate "withering away of the state." As Engels conceived of the final stage of government, it was to be a time in which the general public, satiated in its economic needs by the socialistic organization of the economy and trained over the years to understand its duties toward the community, would accept the rules that had been devised to achieve the goal. At that point no police, no courts, no army, no force of any kind would be necessary to restrain dissenters. There would remain only the administrators, and even these might be ordinary citizens taking their turn at the desk. These administrators would channel the flow of goods so as to achieve efficiency of production and distribution and the creation of the cultural media necessary to satisfaction of the mind as well as of the body.

The ultimate goal of a society without institutionalized compulsion looks utopian to students of government in the Western world, and it came during Stalin's declining years to look utopian to Soviet politicians as well. They satisfied their consciences by pushing its achievement so far into the future that it was not an active consideration in their planning. Only after Stalin's death was there imaginative consideration of means through which to reflect the process of withering. But even with the renewed interest in application of theory, this obscure Marxist concept still is of little more than theoretical concern to Soviet authors and approaches rejection in practice. There has been no rejection, however, of the basic theme of "leadership."

For the Russian Marxists the necessity of leadership had even stronger appeal than for those Western workmen who first accepted Marx's plan of action. The Russian Marxists believed that although the masses of Russian peasants and workmen were demanding the right of self-government during the early twentieth century, they were, generally, completely unprepared to govern. In this view, the working masses thought only of what could be gained by self-government: a full stomach, clothes, decent housing, and the essential home conveniences. Few of them were literate, and the Russian Marxists did not expect them to understand how their hopes could be realized.

To Vladimir Lenin, who came forward at the end of the nineteenth century as the most dedicated and vigorous of the Russian school of Marxists, the first task was to spread the new ideas among a limited few whom he planned to organize thereafter into a hard core of dedicated leaders. Lenin had no plan to invite the masses to share in the determination of goals. In his view this was unnecessary, for the goals had been already determined by Marx. Lenin saw his task as the preparation of leaders to execute Marx's plan and not that of preparing thinkers to devise new plans. Lenin called upon the masses to follow those who had mastered Marx and who demonstrated the skill and training necessary to achieve Marx's goals. Lenin was astute enough to know that leaders cannot overthrow governments without masses behind them. Masses were necessary, but their place was to afford weight and not to share in the decision-making process. He and his small body of colleagues were to be the vanguard.

In order to win their confidence in his leadership, Lenin analyzed the mass desires of the Russian people and of the minority peoples who lived on the fringes of the Russian Empire. He knew that the minority peoples wanted to be free of domination by the Great Russians, who had been the core of the Tsarist system of government. He knew that the peasants wanted to be rid of the landlords and to have sole control over the use of the land. He knew that the workmen wanted to be free of the discipline required by factory owners and managers. He knew that by 1917 the soldiers had become tired of war and wanted to go home. It was by playing upon these yearnings that he hoped to win the support of the masses for his plan.

Lenin sought also to win the allegiance, or at least the neutrality, of the educated men. Many of them had been increasingly active in pressing the Tsar to make concessions leading to a constitutional monarchy. Some were prepared for socialism, but few would have accepted Lenin's concept of government had he disclosed it to them. Most of the educated men sought the democratic determination of goals by democratic procedures. They considered that the means were as important as the ends. They would not accept Lenin's order of emphasis.

Lenin had his fixed ideas of leadership, but he could not swim against the current of history. He had to talk like a democrat in the traditional sense, both before the Russian Revolution and for some months after it, to win the loyalty of the various forces on which he relied for success. Yet he held tenaciously to his belief in a special type of leadership that would not be subject to dismissal by any majority vote of the general public. He enlarged his relatively small group of colleagues, whom he had first helped to organize in 1903, and created an elite to lead. The group came to be known as the "Communist party." He created behind the party a political police, to single out the enemies of his party's program when these enemies became sufficiently threatening. He demonstrated in practice after the Revolution that his view of democracy was quite different from that of many of those from other political groups who had fought with him to overthrow the Tsarist system of government.

The Leadership Circle is Narrowed

Lenin took the Marxist germinal idea that mankind requires leadership, at least for a time, to guide it toward the goal of communism, and he interpreted it to mean that voices seeking to lead in directions other than his and his party's must be silenced. His development of the Marxist idea of leadership was in the direction of monopoly, restricted to those who had accepted the Marxist goal and who were dedicated to its achievement. Lenin did not go so far as to suggest that he alone had the right to determine policy even for his own party. Although he demanded for himself the loyalty of his colleagues and used political maneuvers to outwit those who opposed his views, he supported the role of the Central Committee of the party as the maker of policy. He may have thought of himself as the first among equals, but he seems not to have desired to assume a role of dictator to all.

Lenin showed his fear of personal dictatorship as the possible outgrowth of what he had done by preparing a political testament on December 25, 1922, only nine days after his second stroke. He called upon his colleagues to avoid a split in the party between Leon Trotsky and Joseph Stalin. He said of Stalin that he had concentrated enormous power in his hands and that it was not certain that he always knew how to use that power with sufficient caution. He said of Trotsky that he had proved in his struggle with the Central Committee that he was distinguished not only by his exceptional abilities but also by his too far-reaching self-confidence and a disposition to be too much attracted by the purely administrative side of affairs.

Lenin had good reason to fear the emergence of a personal dictator, as subsequent events were to show. He had created a mechanism that made personal dictatorship possible, although he had not used it to establish himself. When he died, in January, 1924, there was no device that could be used by the rank and file of the party to hamper the rise of a personal dictator, and there was waiting a man without Lenin's particular willingness to impose self-restraint upon his ambition.

A triumvirate of Lenin's heirs was intrusted by the Communist party with the task of guiding the destinies of the country. Trotsky was omitted from the triumvirate as the result of the maneuvers of those who feared his assumption of power. Gregory Zinoviev, Leo Kamenev, and Stalin became the official leaders, and they described themselves as a "collective leadership." Stalin seems to have accepted the idea of sharing power with two colleagues only because he was not yet strong enough to do otherwise, but he soon exhibited the qualities that Lenin had feared. He began to push his colleagues from the triumvirate. By the beginning of 1926, Stalin and the machine he had created through his position as Secretary General of the Communist party had established control over the party. Collective leadership was no more, and it was not to be restored until after his death in 1953.

Stalin utilized the opening that Marxist political thought, as developed by Lenin, gave him to justify his personal assumption of power. Yet he had also to consider the stream of Russian history and the desire of the masses for democracy, and he needed also to reduce his enemies abroad and to expand Soviet influence among foreign leftist groups. To win adherents to his system, he had to espouse democratic principles and even to take steps that might be interpreted as leading to the ultimate realization of a government in which the people shared in policy-making and in the choice of leaders.

Stalin seized the propaganda initiative in declaring his regime the most democratic the world had ever seen. He drafted a new constitution in 1936 that opened elections to all and that created a type of parliament more nearly like that known in the West than the one created by the Congress of Soviets at the time of the

Revolution. He included within the constitution what he called a "bill of rights," which went considerably beyond the statement of rights adopted soon after the Revolution. He eliminated from the laws the discrimination in securing employment and schooling that had previously operated against those whose background had not been peasant or worker.

At the very moment that professedly "democratic" forms were being developed in an effort to please the masses, there were being established counterweights to prevent any possible use of the forms to influence policy or to select leaders. This was Stalin's way of trying to resolve the conflicts caused by the fusion of democratic yearnings arising from the frustrating Russian historical experience and of his version of the Marxist political concept of leadership. On the one hand, he was trying to satisfy the historic, although inexperienced, craving of the people for democracy, and, on the other hand, he was trying to make certain that no one would challenge his authority to decide what was good for the peoples of the U.S.S.R.

Stalin's Heirs Introduce Reform

Stalin's heirs, on his death in March, 1953, seem to have recognized the danger of a successor's assumption of dictatorial power. They soon indicated their appreciation that Stalin had pushed too far the concept of leadership developed by Marx and expanded by Lenin. Lenin had made Marx's idea concrete by establishing a monopoly party, which was to be led, in turn, by a Central Committee. Stalin had created the role of personal dictator over the monopoly party and over its Central Committee.

To meet hostility toward his assumption of dictatorial powers, which is now revealed to have been widespread but unspoken during Stalin's declining years, Stalin's heirs reverted to the expedient adopted in the crisis caused by Lenin's death in 1924. They called for the re-establishment of collective leadership within the Communist party. They indicated their determination to permit no single man to hold all reins of power and to claim all-embracing knowledge. The renunciation of Stalin's type of personal dictatorship received world-wide publicity when the Communist party met in its twentieth congress in February, 1956. Stalin's system was denounced as the "cult of the individual." The official history of the Communist party, in which facts had been distorted to prove Stalin a genius and to vilify all those who disagreed with him as enemies of the people, was ordered withdrawn and rewritten. Stalin's heirs said "Never again!"

The principle of collective leadership faced difficulties within a short time. By June, 1957, some of the members of the collective were intriguing to oust the man who had come through the first years after Stalin to lead the group, namely, Nikita S. Khrushchev, because they disagreed strongly with his plans for heightened regional authority within the economic structure rather than the centralism that was characteristic of Stalin's time. Khrushchev utilized the position he had been able to establish within the Communist party among the provincial leaders and he persuaded the army's chief to strengthen his hand in ousting three of Stalin's former close associates from power, leaving himself the major force among those who remained. Then he completed the process by dismissing the army chief in November, 1957. He had become temporarily supreme, but his power was by no means as all-embracing as had been Stalin's, and in this lay his eventual undoing. Times had changed, partly as the result of his own denunciation of Stalin. When he attempted to foster programs of a wide variety of previously untried patterns of structural change both within the party and the state apparatus, his colleagues conspired against him and ousted him by vote of the Central Committee on which he had previously relied to make his own ascent. With that vote in October, 1964, began a new era in the political life of the U.S.S.R. Collective leadership, albeit with a prominent place given to the party's Secretary General, Leonid I. Brezhnev, was created in a new form without a figure like Lenin or Stalin or even Khrushchev at the helm. In a sense the party that led the Soviet state to its fiftieth anniversary no longer was personified by one man either for Soviet citizens or for the world. In this fact lay a major measure of the transformation of Soviet society from the image created by the colorful world figures who had gone before.

Democratic Forms Subject to Counterweights

The Soviet political apparatus can be understood and contrasted best to that of Jeffersonian democracy when it is described as incorporating Western democratic forms counterweighted with the controls established as fundamental to socialist democracy. Such an approach, while relatively novel in Stalin's time when some Western political scientists thought it helpful to analyze the Soviet system as an autocratic or totalitarian machine masked in democratic phraseology, is now widely adopted in Europe and North America. It offers certain pedagogical advantages.

First, it facilitates exposure of the Soviet system in terms understandable to every student of Jeffersonian systems. To portray the Soviet government as one of institutions of completely unfamiliar form can lead to disbelief among beginning students when their subsequent research discloses Soviet references to institutions with familiar names. When the Soviet system provides "elections" in which all citizens are permitted to vote without restrictions, these institutions stand out in their stark difference only if examined as the forms they purport to be, subject to restraints preventing their functioning as a means of choosing among candidates. When parliamentary sessions are held to enact legislation, their special character can be observed more easily by pointing out the controls that exist on what Westerners would expect to be their function than by denying that there is a parliament.

So long as peoples of the world are attracted to the Soviet system as a new form of democracy improving upon institutions which have functions of specific content in Jeffersonian terms, the claims need to be met directly with an explanation of the controls which deprive them of their familiar functions.

Second, it makes credible the fact that change can occur within the Soviet system without amendment of the constitution or of the institutional structure. Had Stalinism created institutions of a wholly new type, the new moderation and increasing mass participation in government which has occurred since his death would have been inconceivable without revolutionary change. The evolution which has been noted the world around since his death has been possible because institutions offering the prospect of activity more closely approximating that of Western systems were available to be put to other purposes than those for which they were originally conceived. Still, there are limits to that evolution established by currently existing controls, and the student of politics cannot overlook them and the extent to which they are fundamental to the system if he wishes to gauge the potential within the system for even further change.

Third, emphasis upon the forms and the counterweights permits a student to draw a moral from a study of the Soviet system.

The moral is that forms, even when democratic, provide no assurance that the function they perform will automatically result in giving the people an opportunity to express their will. The counterweights are as important as the forms, for astute politicians can devise ways of perverting democratic forms so that the mass will remain confident that it is in no danger of losing its voice while it has in fact lost, or is in process of losing, any real influence on leadership. This is of great importance, not only in new states that begin their lives with Jeffersonian forms which to many inexperienced citizens seem impervious to subversion, but also to citizens of states of long traditions in democracy, because in times of crisis there are always those who urge that the exercise of democracy is a luxury that cannot longer be enjoyed.

The pages which follow will make abundantly clear that the Soviet system of government is not easily characterized. It speaks in the name of democracy of a new type, and some forms familiar to Jeffersonians exist within the system, although currently counterweighted to prevent their functioning as Jeffersonians would expect them to do. Since Stalin's death the counterweights are being lifted in varying degrees, but the Communist leadership has evidenced its fear on repeated occasions of the free flowering not only of political ideas, but also of creative literature and art. Even students in the universities pressing for release from the formulas of Marxian orthodoxy have been chastised when their protests have become strong enough to attract the attention of the outside world.

Obstacles to unhampered self-expression still remain. The nature of the primary obstacle, however, is not an institution but an idea. So long as those who rule the U.S.S.R. lack faith in the capacity of the general public to choose policies wisely, democracy in the Jeffersonian sense can hardly be born. The leadership idea as currently interpreted is the primary barrier to evolution to the stage of the Western welfare state. To be a democrat as understood in the Anglo-American world, and also in that part of the world under the influence of traditions of the French Revolution, one must share with Edmund Burke his faith that, although the people may make mistakes, "in all disputes between them and their rulers, the presumption is at least upon a par in favor of the people."

Soviet leaders since Stalin have shown remarkable aptitude for extension of public participation in the governing process, but they cannot bring themselves to conceive of a socialist democracy as viable without incorporation of the leadership concept. The first sixty years ended with a Soviet system lacking much of its initial stage of militant communism, but doctrine remained unshaken on the point of leadership. The Soviet political manual in vogue a decade earlier called the system one of "directed democracy."

The chapters that follow will indicate such change as has occurred since Stalin's death and the possibilities for change that still remain. In doing so they will necessarily expose the very real limitations that "directed democracy" contains in comparison with Jeffersonian democracy. They will also suggest the problems Soviet leaders may expect to face during the years to come if they conclude, as their doctrine has envisaged since the publication of the Communist Manifesto in 1848, that it is time to permit all to share in the process of determination of policy and selection of leaders.

CHAPTER 2

THE HARD CORE OF THE SYSTEM

The people cannot yet be trusted to govern themselves. This is the creed of Communist party leaders, the principle that they have extracted from Marxist political theory as developed by Lenin and Stalin. Leadership is essential, and it must be a special kind of leadership. It must guide the people toward a specific goal, not in response to their present wishes but by molding them so that their wishes coincide with those of the leaders.

A description of the Soviet system of government must begin differently from an account of North American or West European democracy. The latter would focus upon the operation of instruments through which the public expresses its will. Western political scientists are now centering their attention upon pressure groups, upon parliaments and their committees, upon law which enables the individual to speak his mind without fear of retaliation. Soviet parliamentary institutions and pressure groups work differently, for these serve as focal points from which the influence of leaders is radiated throughout the populace. Only informally do strata with specific interests exert influence upon policy formulation. The key to the functioning of the Soviet system is the leadership group. The 1977 Soviet Constitution (Art. 6) reaffirms this fact. Study must begin, therefore, with the Communist party.

While the Communist party is called a "political party" in textbooks from the U.S.S.R. and from elsewhere abroad, it is so different from Western political parties that some Westerners have suggested that another term be invented for it. A look at the characteristics of the Communist party as a political organization will both indicate its distinguishing elements and help to suggest the features of Western political parties that are essential to preservation of intra-party democracy and of a political party's function in a democratic system of government.

The key terms in any characterization of the Communist party are "centralized structure" and "discipline." Armies, too, are structured centrally and require discipline of the troops. In considerable degree the Communist party is patterned on an army. It has its officers, from the level of the general staff down to the platoon, and their command is law. Yet the Communist party would not attract members if it were structured completely on army lines. A twentieth-century political party must attract and hold its members on a basis other than that of a military draft or of a system of military discipline and punishment. Ever since the American and French revolutions, too many people, even in Russia, have dreamed of democracy and of mass determination of policy to be attracted to a political party without a show of these.

Thus the leaders of the Communist party have been faced with a more difficult task than the organizers of an army. They have found it necessary to provide a mechanism through which the rank-and-file members appear to have the opportunity to choose their own leaders and to influence policy. Having created this mechanism in a form susceptible of democratic use, they have felt it necessary to devise a subtle system of counterweights to prevent an overturn of their leadership and an adoption of policies contrary to their desires. The Communist leaders have devised a name for this system of mass participation subject to counterweight control. They have called it "democratic centralism."

The Formalities of Communist Party Structure

How is the system operated? The democratic feature comprises two elements, the first of which is the choice of officers. Party members at the level that would be called a platoon in an army are given the formal right to elect every year their second lieutenant, who is called, in the Communist party vocabulary, "secretary of the primary party organization." In the large organizations this secretary is aided by an executive bureau, also elected formally each year. The party members in the primary organization, who may be as few as three or as many as three hundred, also are given the formal opportunity to choose delegates at intervals to attend periodic conferences of delegates from primary party organizations within a geographical area corresponding to a county or a large city. These conferences meet seldom, being required by the Communist party rules to convene only at two-year intervals. When the delegates meet they choose from their number a smaller group, called a "committee," to meet every three months. This committee proceeds to select its executive bureau, including several secretaries, who must be confirmed in office by the provincial committee. One of the secretaries is designated "first secretary," and, in practice, it is he who runs the bureau and the affairs of the committee in general.

The large conference of delegates from the party organizations within the various counties and large cities also elects a delegate to attend periodically, at intervals of two or three years, a superior meeting called a "provincial conference," or, in the small republics not divided into provinces, a "republic congress." Khrushchev tried an experiment between 1962 and the time of his ouster in 1964 of duplicating party conferences at the provincial level: one for agricultural direction and one for industrial direction. Too much overlapping of functions and confusion of authority resulted. In the few cases of very large cities, such as Moscow, the party conference of delegates from below brings together only delegates from the ward party conferences of the city, the wards being in the position of counties within the party structure. Such party conferences in the very large cities have the same rights within the party hierarchy as provincial conferences and are represented directly in higher party agencies rather than through the provincial conference of the party organization in the province in which the very large city is located geographically.

When the provincial party conference meets, its delegates take steps similar to those taken in the various county conferences. They choose their own "committee," which, in turn, selects an executive bureau including several secretaries. The provincial committee meets only every four months, but its executive bureau is on call at all times. The provincial party conference in each of the four larger republics also selects a group of delegates to proceed, at five-year intervals, to the capital of the republic within which the province or very large city is situated. Again the same procedure is followed in the choice of an executive body: the republic congress chooses a committee, called in this instance a "central committee," and the central committee then chooses an executive bureau including several secretaries. The delegates to the republic party congress also name a group of delegates to proceed to the quinquennial all-Union congress in Moscow.

To this pattern of ever higher party bodies leading up through the republics to Moscow, an exception is provided by the largest republic, that comprising the Great Russian ethnic element of the population. In this large republic, called the Russian Soviet Federated Socialist Republic, stretching from Leningrad across Siberia to Vladivostok, there is no republic party congress. The various provincial party conferences send their delegations directly to the all-Union meeting in Moscow. Khrushchev introduced as a co-ordinating committee for the provincial conferences a "bureau of the party's Central Committee," but it was abolished in 1966 as unnecessary, since the Central Committee's Presidium and Secretariat had been performing the function on a parallel basis.

The pattern of the co-ordinating bureau was extended in 1962 to some of the non-Russian areas as part of Khrushchev's party reform, but there was a difference. While the party Central Committee's bureau for the Russian Republic co-ordinated provincial party organizations, the bureaus created in 1962 and 1963 for Central Asia and Transcaucasia co-ordinated the work of party organizations in several republics. This made superfluous the Republic organizations in the Uzbek and Kazakh Republics, where the only function had been previously the co-ordination of provincial party activities within the Republics. Perhaps because of this the regional co-ordinating bureaus were abolished in January, 1965, soon after Khrushchev's ouster.

The all-Union meeting in Moscow, composed of delegates from republic party congresses and from the various provincial conferences of the Russian Republic, is called "The All-Union Communist Party Congress." It is of very large size. It has always been large, and since 1961 has been increased threefold with a change in ratio of delegates to party members. At the twenty-fifth congress of 1976, 4,998 delegates represented the 15,694,187 full and candidate members. Being large, its importance seems to outsiders as more symbolic than real, for no floor debates or divided votes occur. Still, the congress has utility. For the leadership, it periodically legitimates its role by providing public evidence of rank and file support. For the delegates, it provides an opportunity to see and meet leaders; to gain orientation in political, economic and social problems by listening to reports; to share experience with peers during corridor and hotel conversations; and, perhaps most importantly, to sense the exhilaration of being recognized as an important cog in a machine proclaimed from the congress tribune as infallible and invincible. This experience can contribute to morale when the delegate returns home to find often frustrating tasks requiring party guidance for solution.

The All-Union Communist Party Congress chooses by vote its own "committee" to conduct the policy-making function between congresses. It is called the Central Committee of the Communist Party. As named in 1976 at the twenty-fifth congress, it numbered 288 members and 139 alternates, the latter having no vote but enjoying the right to attend meetings. Vacancies among the voting members are filled from the alternate panel. The congress also names a "central auditing committee" to monitor finances.

The Central Committee chooses its steering committee from its own members, in accordance with party tradition dating from pre-revolutionary Russia. As Political Buro its task was then, and remains today, direction of highest policy. The group was originally small, but in 1952 Stalin changed its name to "Presidium" and increased its membership to 25 members and 11 alternates. On his death, his heirs reduced it to its previous size, and in 1966 restored its original name. Its membership began to grow in 1956, reaching 16 members and 6 candidates by the twenty-fifth Communist party congress in 1976, but dropping to 13 and 9 respectively in late 1979. It is the key policy making institution of the party.

Ostensibly to provide rotation in positions on the executive bodies at each level within the party, the 1961 rules introduced a requirement of rotation in office, and established a compulsory ratio of renewal for the executive bodies at each level subject to exceptions for persons with special qualities. Khrushchev seems to have feared stultification through aging and lack of assurance of reinvigoration through the election procedure. In 1966 the compulsory ratios were removed, as beginning to have a negative effect on the work of the primary party organizations, but the principle of rotation was reaffirmed.

Also introduced as change in 1966 was the re-creation of the All-Union Party Conference, abolished in 1941 at a time when Stalin evidenced his determination to rule with a minimum of participation by the party rank and file. In its revived form it meets on call of the Central Committee whenever needed to bring together top personnel of the Republic party organizations and of the provincial organizations in the Russian Republic. In structure it is a Party Congress but is organized on a smaller scale. Possibly the trebled size of the Party Congress in 1961 made desirable reinstitution of a smaller but demonstrably more representative group than the Central Committee, to discuss and popularize new policy positions between the quinquennial sessions of the full Congress. Whatever the purpose of the amendment, party conferences have not been called since its adoption.

What has been a considerable staff or "apparatus" serves the Central Committee as a secretariat, headed by a "General Secretary" and including a varying number of "secretaries"—in 1978, ten. Although this staff has been reduced under resolution of the twentieth party congress after Stalin's death, it seems still to number about one thousand. It is divided into sections, each headed by a secretary or some member of the Central Committee. Several of the secretaries are also members of the Political Buro, and they wield much more power than might be supposed from the example of secretarial positions elsewhere. Each section has the task of compiling information for the formulation of policy papers. Since Stalin's death they have called increasingly on the experts from the state apparatus which they parallel, and this has permitted reduction in the size of the party "apparatus." They also see to execution of party policy decisions by lower party organizations once they have been adopted, and for this purpose they establish analogous sections in Republic party committees and even at local party levels.

Though no rule establishes the number or names of these sections, it has become known that they include sections for party appointments and for propaganda and agitation. Additionally, they supervise the major branches of the economy: heavy industry, military industry, light industry, finance and trade, transportation and communication, and agriculture. They also see to science and culture, public education, courts and prosecutors, work among women, military affairs, foreign affairs, Komsomol and trade union relations with the party, state security, and party schools. When some new problem becomes critical, a section is created for the time necessary to prepare a solution.

Controls within the Party

The creation of a hierarchy of party agencies is an attempt to meet the desire of the rank and file to share in the selection of its leaders. Share they do, yet there are controls so that this selection cannot result in the overturn of the leaders. It is in the formulation of these controls that Lenin, and subsequently Stalin, showed skill in manipulating democratic forms for their own purposes.

One measure of control is inherent in the nature of this very hierarchy. Because there are no direct elections of top Communist party officials, a wave of mass discontent over party leadership would have to exist for several years and sweep almost the whole country to be reflected in the top echelons. The rank and file can influence only the choice of their committee and of their delegate to the next higher party conference. By their committee they are insulated even from selection of the party secretary, who in practice controls the destiny of a primary party organization. Top party officials are chosen by the small Central Committee of the party, and this in turn can be reconstituted only once in five years by The All-Union Party Congress. Even this opportunity has been withdrawn in the past, because party congresses were postponed for long periods of time during which the leaders did not account even formally to representatives of the rank and file, except at rare intervals.

A second measure of control lies in the nominating and electing procedure within the party. Nominations are prepared by the first secretary at the level of the primary party organization and by the executive bureau at higher levels. These individuals can, and usually do, assure their own election by placing only their own names on the ballot. Until 1939 the rules of the Communist party under which operations within the party were conducted provided that voting upon the nominations should be by a show of hands. Clearly this method of voting, which has been subject to abuse wherever it has been tried, permitted the executive bureau to determine its enemies and subsequently to take measures discriminating against them, if not ousting them from Communist party membership. In 1939 the rules were amended, on the recommendation of Stalin, to introduce secret voting for the executive bureau and for delegates to the higher party conference. It was further required that the vote now be on each name separately rather than on a whole slate. This amendment prevented the secretary from pushing through an unpopular delegate by including his name upon a slate which had to be accepted or rejected as a whole.

The 1939 change in voting procedure seems to have been made as a result of pressure from party members upon Stalin for relaxation of the very strict controls that had tended openly to negate the presence of democracy within the party not only in the eyes of Communist party members within the U.S.S.R. but perhaps even more importantly in the eyes of those who were being wooed by Communist parties in France, Italy, and elsewhere. Stalin conceded the secret ballot probably because of his growing confidence in the effectiveness of his Communist party machine. He had been developing discipline in this machine during the seventeen years of his control over its heart, namely, the general secretariat of the party, and he had completed in 1938 a purge of his most powerful opponents within the party. By 1939 he could afford to appear to be democratic, since he could be sure of the results even when the ballot was secret.

Stalin also may have felt by 1939 that a secret ballot for the various secretaries of the primary party organizations would be a good way to test their political effectiveness. While he could be sure that the rank and file had learned the lesson of the preceding seventeen years, a lesson dramatized by the purge trials of 1936, 1937, and 1938 in which expectable penalties for dissenters on basic issues had been made clear, he could not be sure that his party secretaries at the levels of the primary party organizations and above were not making enemies unnecessarily by being completely arbitrary and unresponsive to demands which should not be ignored. The secret ballot gave Stalin some opportunity to find out from the rank and file itself which party secretaries were so tyrannical that they would be voted against. According to announcements in the Communist party newspapers of the time, there occurred some overturns in the local secretaryships, overturns that the party press hailed for clearing out local party officials who had become drunk with power.

The secret ballot has not, however, created a bar to the influence at lower levels of the General Secretary of the party. Waves of changes among the provincial party secretaries accompanied Khrushchev's consolidation of his power as he prepared for a test of strength with other members of the collective leadership. These changes fortified him for his victory over his opponents in the Presidium in the crisis of 1957 when the Central Committee, composed in large measure of men owing their positions to him, put Malenkov, Molotov, and Kaganovich off the Presidium. His control position did not, however, save him in 1964, when the Central Committee called him to give his defense and then voted his ouster. Possibly, his subordinates within the party had already undermined his authority by making appointments which he had no time to verify, or his innovations in party rules had become so novel and disruptive of tradition that even his friends thought it time to oust their aging leader, and he had no other force to use to retain power.

Selection of Party Members

A third measure of control, in addition to the intraparty measures of the multi-stepped system of elections and the self-nominating procedure adopted for these, lies in a careful selection of candidates from among those who express their desire for party membership. Not every applicant is admitted to membership. In 1978 the total party membership constituted only about 9 per cent of the adult population of the U.S.S.R.

The small number of members in the Communist party is the result of a selection system devised to eliminate from consideration all but those most devoted to the cause of the party—those who can be expected to be willing and able to accept party discipline. The selection process is placed within the authority of the primary party organizations, which are established at places of employment such as factories, government offices, collective or state farms, divisions of railways, large department stores, universities, and army units. The Communist party leaders have indicated their feeling that those who know a person at work know a great deal about him because the good and the bad in a man or a woman appear more clearly at work than in social activities. Application for candidate membership must be filed, therefore, with the primary party organization at the applicant's place of work, and he is judged by those who in party thinking know him best.

An application must be accompanied by recommendations from three persons who have been members of the Communist party for at least five years. These are not lightly given, because those who recommend and vouch for a candidate are subject to penalties, including loss of their own Communist party membership, if he proves to be a serious misfit within the party. If the applicant is under 23 years of age, he can be admitted to membership only if he comes up through the Communist youth league and has the endorsement of its county or city committee.

When an application has passed the scrutiny of the primary party organization to which it is delivered, it is reviewed by the district committee of the county or big-city Communist party conference to which the primary party organization concerned sends a delegate. If this superior, and presumably more reliable, body approves the recommendation of admission made by the primary party organization, the applicant has passed the first barrier. He is not yet a member of the party, for he must prove his worth during a period of trial.

During a candidate's period of trial, which is currently established at one year, he is subjected to rigid tests in the form of duties such as propagandizing with party doctrine groups among whom he circulates. If he shows himself to be well disciplined and effective, he is admitted to full membership by the primary party organization in which he has been a candidate, but only after repeating all the steps required for his original admission to candidacy. If, after one year, discussion within the primary party organization concludes that a candidate has not proved himself worthy of membership, and if the county or city party committee agrees, he is dropped from candidacy and returns to the ranks of non-party people from which he came.

During World War II, this selection system was ignored in an effort to bring into the party men with proved leadership qualities. Refugees from the U.S.S.R. have since reported that desirable soldiers were pressed to accept membership and that recommendations were arranged for them by the party secretaries. The same procedure was applied to men and women in industry or in agriculture between 1962 and 1966, during which time 2,755,074 members and candidates were added, but the twenty-third congress reaffirmed the rule of careful selection and demanded that lax admission policies be abandoned. For admission, the 1966 rule requires that two-thirds of the members present at the meeting of the primary party organization passing upon the matter cast their vote affirmatively. The principle of careful scrutiny of membership applications has been maintained by subjecting persons admitted through exceptional procedure to a subsequent review. If the new member indicates after admission that he is below standard, he is expelled. Many soldiers admitted on the field of battle during the war were expelled in later years when they showed themselves lacking in desire or capacity to make the theoretical studies required of party members.

Reports of refugees also indicate that careerists have sometimes slipped through the selection process for new members. With the passing of the years and with the increasing favoritism shown party members in the allocation to them of positions of power and prestige, the desirability of party membership has been enhanced. It no longer attracts persecution as it did in pre-revolutionary times nor does it require self-denial as it did during the 1920's. In consequence, ambitious opportunists have crept into the party, with the result that members are not today always as dedicated as party rules would have them appear. This is especially so of the more youthful ones.

In its formalized selection of members the Communist party reveals one of the primary distinctions between itself and the mass political parties familiar to the student of politics in the United States and in many other countries. In the West, parties other than the Communist party generally provide no such process for the selection of members. In most parties there is required no more than a declaration of membership, and there is no obligation to perform duties or to accept any form of discipline. Even representatives of these parties within the various parliaments or congresses of the West generally consider themselves free to oppose their leaders if they think that a decision has been unwise.

Limitations on Expression of Opinion

The extent to which opinion may be expressed on matters of policy has come to be a measure of a democratic system of government, and the designers of the Communist party have found it necessary to provide a semblance of honor of this measure both to hold the loyalty of party members and to attract outsiders into the ranks. Again, however, there seems to have been a problem of providing a means for popular expression of opinion and at the same time of devising a counterweight. The party leaders seem to want to be sure that expressions of opinion will never result in the adoption of a policy before the highest officers of the Communist party have had an opportunity to consider its prospective influence upon the course of events.

In defining democratic centralism, the rules drawn up by the Communist party leaders and adopted formally by The All-Union Communist Party Congress establish the outlines of the control mechanism. Every party member is given the formal right to express his opinion within the group to which he belongs, whether it be his primary party organization or a higher-level conference to which he is a delegate. This right is widely advertised by the Communist party press as indicative of the democratic character of the Communist party.

Having given the formal right of free speech to party members within their organizations, the draftsmen of the party rules provided a counterweight. The rules declare that members shall not be permitted to form a voting bloc, known in party parlance as a "faction," within the organization to which they belong. This restriction means that while a member is permitted to rise in his place and speak his mind at a party meeting, he may not have consulted with friends in advance to solicit their support of his views so that his speech will not be the solitary one on the subject he espouses. Nor may he have bargained with others to vote for his project in exchange for his subsequent vote in favor of some project dear to their hearts.

The effectiveness of this counterweight to free speech will be obvious to any American who contemplates the working of any organization to which he belongs. It will quickly be evident in any group that a single voice carries no weight unless it be that of an unusually persuasive speaker or of one with political power within the organization. Even the persuasive speaker will be voted down if his colleagues are in no mood to listen. Minorities have been effective in tempering policies only when they could organize into groups which threatened to grow and become majorities, or if they were able to manipulate themselves with such skill that they held positions of balance of power, promising support to one or the other side of an argument in accordance with the willingness of the one or the other to support their causes. Soviet politicians seem to have put their finger on the key to a minority's strength and to have locked the door and thrown away the key. They can champion democratic forms within the

Communist party without fear that any minority will become unmanageable.

There is yet another formal counterweight to the democratic right of free speech guaranteed to individual members within the party. It lies in the obligation established by the rules that when a decision has been taken, it is binding upon all those who shared in it, even if they voted against it on the floor. They are not permitted to argue for its reversal until it has been tried to the satisfaction of the leaders. The decision is binding upon them until opened again for discussion.

Discipline for Party Members

Discipline within the Communist party is enforced in two principal ways, by persuasion and by punishment of violators. Persuasion plays a part greater than is often appreciated outside the U.S.S.R., for though the Communist party is a relatively small core of persons guiding the destinies of the entire country and thus attracts people who enjoy the perquisites of power, there are here, as among any group of leaders, not only those who enjoy a sense of power but also those who have a sense of mission. It is upon those individuals who seek admission to, and continue within, the party because they have a sense of mission that persuasion especially acts as a means of enforcing discipline. These have joined voluntarily, and they remain voluntary. To be sure, if they resigned they would be considered "quitters" and would lose favor both with those whom they left behind in the party and also with millions more who have not desired or could not gain membership but who accept party values. But while such social opprobrium is to be reckoned with before resigning, there is a still stronger force for those who feel a sense of mission—the force created by a consuming interest, without which life would not be worth living.

To those who have entered the Communist party with a sense of mission, the party leaders who seek to win them to a point of view have only to explain policy in terms of improving conditions within the U.S.S.R. and even, eventually, throughout the world—the declared mission of the party. If the explanation is well phrased and convincing, it will be seized upon and incorporated as a design for living without serious question. For such persons, persuasion is a mighty instrument of control, and the training of Communist party secretaries, on whom the primary burden of persuasion rests, includes a very extensive portion of the art of effective public speaking.

Punishment awaits those party members who feel less or no sense of mission and are not persuaded by argument to accept the orders of their superiors within the party. It takes several forms. There are the moderate forms of admonition, reprimand, and censure, which are entered on the registration card. There is also the harsher form of reduction to candidate status for one year. The most severe form consists of expulsion from the party: for the disillusioned party member who has compelling personal reasons for remaining within the party while disliking official policy, the threat of expulsion is a strong incentive to conform. Each of these forms of punishment is designed to attach to the culprit a measure of social stigma in the eyes of fellow party members.

Members of the Central Committee of the party, and of the executive committees at each lower level within the party hierarchy, are protected against disciplinary action by the primary party organization to which they belong. Under the rules, penalties may be exacted of such persons only if approved at a full meeting of the Central Committee or of the executive committee concerned, and then only when a two-thirds majority consents. The leadership has thus assured itself of no surprises from below.

Statistics for 1966 indicate that disciplining to the extent of expulsion remains an important feature of party life, although it occurs less frequently than in earlier years. During the year 62,868 persons were expelled and 17,244 dropped out. The latter figure suggests that withdrawals, for which there is no provision in the party rules and which were not feasible during Stalin's time because they would have been interpreted as evidence of hostility, have become increasingly possible under cloak of expulsion for non-payment of dues. Expulsions between 1956 and 1962 approximated 200,000, while withdrawals in each of the four years preceding 1966 increased by about 1,000 each year.

Further expulsions were announced in 1976, it being reported that "around 347,000" persons were denied party cards during the exchange conducted between 1973 and 1975 because they had deviated from the norms of party life, infringed discipline, or lost contact with the party organization.

Internationalism within the Party

Group organization on the basis of ethnic origin has been opposed within the Communist party from the outset. Lenin insisted, even against serious opposition from fellow members belonging to ethnic minorities within the Russian Empire, that the party was not to be a federation of ethnically organized groups. He opposed any suggestion that Jews have a party organization that would bring together Jews wherever they might live and that would co-operate with a Russian or Ukrainian or Lithuanian organization similarly constituted. He demanded that the party structure be centralized without regard to the ethnic origin of its members.

Due to historical migrations, the population of the U.S.S.R. contains many ethnic groups living in relatively compact communities in various parts of the U.S.S.R. Thus, the Ukrainian minority lives in one corner, the Georgian and Armenian minorities in another, the Finnish minority in another, the Latvian, Estonian, and Lithuanian minorities in still others. Under the system of organization based upon broad geographic areas, in which all party members within a republic are represented through their provincial delegates in the party congress of that republic, it may appear to an outsider as if there were separate Ukrainian and Armenian and Latvian party units. Communist party leaders have always emphasized, however, that there is no basis for ethnic representation within the party. Consequently, the unit named the "Ukrainian Communist party" is not conceived as an ethnic unit comprising all Ukrainians wherever they may live but rather comprises Communist party members of whatever ethnic group who happen to be living at the time within the borders established for the Ukrainian Republic. It includes Russians and Jews and Armenians and Georgians who live within the Ukrainian Republic's borders. Even its head, bearing the title of "Secretary of the Central Committee of the Ukrainian Communist Party," may be, and has been, a man of Russian rather than Ukrainian ethnic origin. Usually the party secretaries are chosen from the ethnic unit that has the largest representation within a given area, but this need not be so. In consequence, the way is open to substitute a secretary of another ethnic group if there should appear among the Communist party members within any republic a sense of conflict of interest between the ethnic unit from which most of them come and the whole party.

This concept of "internationalism" of party structure, as contrasted with "nationalism" or structure based upon ethnic groups, aided Stalin, a member of the Georgian ethnic minority, to maintain his position among the very much more numerous Russian ethnic element within the Communist party. He could claim to represent the Russian element as well as all other ethnic elements because he was to be thought of not as a Georgian but as an internationalist—as a member of the working class, which is supposed, in Communist theory, to have no ethnic loyalties cutting across its class line.

In spite of the theory of internationalism within the party, it was common gossip in the U.S.S.R. before Stalin's death that to please the people his successor would have to be a Russian. Lip-service was given to internationalism, but political wisdom suggested that attention be paid to the sentiments of the majority ethnic group in selecting the party boss.

Funds to maintain the Communist party are obtained through a system of party dues levied upon each party member. There is collected from each candidate member a small initiation fee of 2 per cent of one month's wages. Thereafter all candidates and full members pay monthly dues graduated on the basis of monthly wages. The tax begins at 10 kopecks on 50 rubles of wages and advances from ½ of 1 per cent of wages under 100 rubles to 3 per cent of wages exceeding 300 rubles a month.

It is remarkable that the Communist party, with its control over the finances of the entire Soviet state, has chosen to continue a system of party dues. One might expect the party to dip into the state treasury for its maintenance and to abandon the payment of dues as an outmoded heritage from prerevolutionary days when its political campaign against the government of the Russian Empire could be financed in no other way. Nevertheless, the dues are still collected and are supplemented by receipts from the publications of the vast party press. Perhaps expenses beyond those covered by admitted receipts are hidden in some item of the state budget. Such subsidization by the state treasury, if any exists, is not, however, reported specifically in any line of the state budget devoted to Communist party administration expenses. Presumably the Communist party's leaders have concluded that there is an additional emotional bond established between a member and his party if he is made to feel that he is sacrificing the satisfaction of some personal need to maintain his party, or it may be that relations with the non-party public are facilitated if there is no published support for an argument that the public is taxed to fatten the Communist party apparatus.

In spite of the various control features built into the Communist party's system of democratic centralism, party bosses have often found it expedient to go beyond even them. The most notable violation of the Communist party's own rules is the infrequency with which meetings of the representative party groups at the various levels of the party structure have occurred, and local party secretaries are occasionally criticized openly in the Communist party press for failing to call the required meetings of their county or city conference. But these local party leaders have not been set a good example, for The All-Union Communist Party congresses were called during Stalin's lifetime only at rare intervals, in spite of the requirement of the rules. The Congress held in 1952 should have been held in 1942, had the then existing requirement of a congress every three years been fulfilled. The Congress of 1939 took place at an interval of five years after the preceding Congress of 1934. To be sure, the Second World War intervened between the 1939 and the 1952 congresses, and few party members could have been expected to resent postponement in the light of war conditions. Yet the war ended, and still no congress was held for six years after its end. Only since Stalin's death have the leaders seemed to be prepared to follow the rules. The twentieth party congress was held within the prescribed four-year period after the nineteenth party congress. Since then the practice has varied. A five-year interval between congresses was set by amendment to party rules in 1971, and it was observed in the call for the twenty-fifth congress in 1976.

The Focus of Party Power

Stalin focused power in his person so completely and for so long that the Soviet system of government came to be associated with one-man dictatorship, differing if at all from other dictatorships only because this man exercised his power not only with the help of a strong security police but also through the instrumentality of the Communist party. Events since his death suggest that the characterization is no longer apt. Power is being shared, the question being with how many.

Analysis of the structure of the party has shown it to be a hierarchy, leading up formally to a pinnacle which is the party congress, but no one supposes that power lies there. Over four thousand delegates meeting once in five years for a few days at a time cannot wield power. They can but formalize what has been prepared for them by others—but which others? The organization chart shows the existence of three smaller bodies at the top: the Central Committee, the Political Buro and the Secretariat. Of these three, the Central Committee has the place of honor because it names the members of the other two. Stalin reduced the functioning of the Central Committee to a formality, calling meetings on rare occasions and paying little attention to it. In this he provided a contrast to Lenin, who had found the body useful as a place in which to try out ideas but who never permitted discussions without structure. This was provided by members of the Political Buro, in which Lenin concentrated the wise men of his party. But even the Political Buro as Lenin used it was not binding upon him, for he never accepted opinions with which he could not agree. At moments of crisis he exercised his great persuasive powers and organizing ability to gain his way over what was sometimes strong dissent, so that the Political Buro had little real power; Stalin reduced its influence even further.

The Secretariat was originally conceived by the founders of the party in 1903 as a service instrument, not an instrument of power. Stalin changed that, for he used the Secretariat of which he was put in charge to make appointments of men loyal to him. During Stalin's tenure the Secretariat was often identified as the mechanism of greatest importance within the power structure: an instrument of rule to be coveted by any who wished to succeed Stalin in power on his death.

Nikita Khrushchev utilized the Secretariat to further his own ascendance to a position of prominence, but with less success than Stalin. His career showed that he was never able to overcome his opponents as Stalin had done, but he was not without skill in political maneuvering. This he demonstrated in 1957 when, after a trip to Finland on a diplomatic mission, he returned to Moscow to find that three of Stalin's erstwhile closest collaborators, Molotov, Kaganovich, and Malenkov, had utilized his absence to organize a faction against him within the Presidium, and had the majority of votes. Playing for time, Khrushchev postponed the formal session at which he would have been outvoted on his plan to decentralize industrial command, and through his son-in-law he called into Moscow the far-flung members of the Central Committee, among whom he had a majority of admirers. He also sought and won to his side the army leaders. This combined force turned the tables on the Presidium majority, and the Central Committee voted to support Khrushchev and his plan. Then the three who had led the revolt were ousted from their high positions, suggesting for the first time in party history that the Central Committee, at least when supported by the army leaders, was strong enough to discipline its own Presidium.

Again in 1964, when Khrushchev was on vacation at his Black Sea home, his opponents organized to oust him because of his position on a wide variety of issues, including party structure and decentralization of industrial command. On this occasion the Central Committee failed him when he returned in haste to make his defense. He was dismissed and a new collective leadership was created, headed by Leonid I. Brezhnev as party Secretary and Aleksei A. Kosygin as President of the Council of Ministers. The question put forward by foreign analysts of the Soviet power structure is whether the Central Committee has arrogated power to itself, in reflection of the changes occurring in party membership, making centralization of power not only in a single man but even in a small Political Buro unacceptable to the greatly increased number of intellectuals comprising the party's membership. To answer this question a glance is necessary at what has been happening within the party during the period of the war and notably since Stalin's death.

A Challenge to Party Centralism

The urbanization and intellectualization of the Soviet Union have been prominent features of its development, as with all countries advancing from an agrarian economy to one focused on industrialization. Peasants are fewer, having dropped in percentage from about one half of the population in 1939 to one sixth in 1976. Schooling is widespread: there were more than 46 million pupils in the general schools in 1977, 5 million in the universities, and about 3.5 million in technical institutions. This situation has compelled a new approach to admission to the leadership group. Lenin had been reluctant to admit peasants and the educated, whom he called, in accordance with Russian tradition, "intellectuals," into this key body. No longer can his views prevail, but since those views still have some influence, they bear recapitulation in brief.

Lenin declared that the workmen required the support of the peasants to win a revolution, but he felt that peasants were inclined toward individual exploitation of the land rather than toward community exploitation. The peasant's attitude seemed to Lenin to be in contrast with that forced upon the factory workman by the circumstances of his job. The factory workman could see in his daily toil that co-operation was necessary to achieve results, for no machine in a factory was of any use unless it was operated in concert with the other machines in the factory. The workmen seemed to Lenin certain to accept the socialist form of production that he had in mind, with its heavy emphasis on state operation of production rather than on the individualism of private enterprise. The peasant could not be counted upon to accept the discipline of socialism, and so Lenin assigned him a subordinate place in the power structure.

The intellectuals were the most doubtful people, in Lenin's opinion. He declared that they had no rooting in a production process, as did the workmen or the peasants. They had skills required by the party leadership, but they took positions based upon intellectual reasoning, and one could not anticipate which way they would turn as ideas crossed their minds. They made poor followers, for each thought his mind as good as the next man's. In short, intellectuals in the aggregate could be useful and were to be tolerated so long as they accepted leadership from Lenin and his small group of colleagues, but they were to be watched lest they turn against the party leaders.

Stalin inherited Lenin's distrust of the intellectuals. Like Lenin, he had to use the skilled men and women of the old regime to develop the country and, in particular, to perform the technical operations of government offices, but he let very few of them into the ranks of the Communist party. He established a hierarchy of categories of persons seeking admission to the party, according to a descending order of prospective loyalty, and required persons in the successively lower categories to produce correspondingly more recommendations for admission to membership and to serve longer in the period of candidacy. The intellectuals were at the bottom of the list, in the least-favored position.

Under the system of selection of party members, which left unchallenged within the party the few men who had education and experience in leadership, the Communist party was molded by degrees into the disciplined group that it had become by the late 1930's. Those of the small circle of intellectuals who had been members of the party in its early years were purged when they questioned Stalin's position as party boss.

Time has wrought change within the party, in reflection of the changes in structure within the Soviet population. Educated men have come to the fore, but not to the complete exclusion of workmen and collective farmers. It is on this point that Lenin's policies still have influence, for continued representation of the workers in large numbers has become a rule of practice. The desirability of maintaining this grass-roots element is constantly restated, and the principle is applied. In consequence, on January 1, 1977, 40.7% of the party's members were bench workmen and 14.7% were collective farmers, making a total of over half.

While the intellectuals are, therefore, a minority, they have great influence in the higher agencies of the party, and the number of members with advanced education is constantly increasing. In 1976 party members with college educations had become 24% of the total of educated men and women, in comparison with their status in 1922 of less than 1%. Those with high school educations have increased even faster to reach almost 39% in 1976 in comparison with 6% in 1922. With these increases in representation of educated men and women in the party, the party's influence among educated citizens generally has been advanced until by 1977 party members or candidates accounted for a total of 25.5% of all Soviet citizens with a college education.

The educated men and women are about evenly split between those concerned directly with the technique of production as engineers and technicians and those engaged in administration of state, party, and trade union agencies or in professional activity as scientists, teachers, doctors, nurses, writers, and artists.

Aging of party membership was evident up to the early 1970's when heavy admissions of youth (70% of the 1975 intake) reversed the aging trend to bring the under-30 age group to 16.6% of all Communists. One-third of all members had joined during the preceding decade. Women members also increased to total 24.7% by 1977.

The Influence of Intellectuals

With the increasing percentage of educated men and women within the party, the top posts have fallen to those with university degrees. Nikita Khrushchev was the last of the men who could make the traditional prestigious boast of a pipe fitter's training. Brezhnev and Kosygin are engineers who might be called elsewhere "university men." Their style is not that of the flamboyant revolutionary leader who moves multitudes from a balcony. They are men of the statistical table, of the unimpassioned analysis of facts; they are respecters of orderly processes and are supported at lower levels by engineers, scientists, lawyers, professional soldiers, professional public administrators, and professional educators.

The influx of educated men into positions of power dissipated the suspicion previously attached to intellectuals as men of uncertain loyalty requiring observation by Communists who knew by what used to be called a "visceral reaction" what was right for the revolution. From a position of a suspected specialist the educated man moved to the position of a model Communist to be emulated by all. They were quietly but perceptibly inheriting from the older men their positions of leadership. When a problem needed solution, the proposals were prepared not by specialists outside the party to be presented for review and reformulation by the trusted generalists within, but by Communist specialists who went to the few remaining generalists only when they could not agree about which of two approaches might assure the speediest advancement of the Communist way of life.

Increasing reliance upon specialists is not peculiar to the U.S.S.R. It is part of a trend that industrialization has made both inevitable and irreversible. Educated men cannot longer be kept in any country in a pool to be called forward for advice and then sent back to their laboratories and studies while generalists decide policy on the basis of visceral reactions. Automation's problems can no more be met in the U.S.S.R. than elsewhere by men whose only education has been the factory lathe, nor can court procedures be prescribed successfully by men who know nothing of the problem of determining truth.

In the face of this advance of the educated men to party membership and even leadership, an advance which was facilitated by elimination of the provisions in the party rules, which prior to 1939 discriminated against the admission of intellectuals to party membership, the generalists who remain have sensed some element of danger. In the U.S.S.R., as elsewhere in developing societies, newly educated specialists have sought to prove their new status by demonstrating their aloofness from the workbench and the cow barn. There has been a tendency to sit in clean front offices behind desks and to make pronouncements as if from on high without entering the machine shop or riding the tractor.

Khrushchev as a generalist resented the development of a leadership composed of engineers. He stressed preservation of Lenin's policy of recruitment from among the workers and peasants, and he tried to acquaint the intellectuals of the youthful generation with the life he loved. To do so, he required students training for careers needing no long period of preliminary technical preparation to serve an internship in a factory or farm before proceeding to higher education. His hope was that potential leaders would acquire in this way some practical knowledge of the work to be performed and the attitude of citizens in whose name the revolution was fought. Then they might rule with more sympathy when they assumed high positions as specialists.

Khrushchev's internship program failed in practice. The intellectuals rose almost to a man to condemn it. They thought it out of keeping with technical needs of the industrial age, which were so demanding as to permit no time out in the educational process. Generalists within the party now rub shoulders with the rank and file, but they have had the training of specialists at an early age and their thought is of abundance and the future good life which abundance makes possible. Consequently, the twenty-fifth congress in 1976 focussed on the need to center policy on developing a "scientific and cultural revolution."

The expansion of the educated group within party ranks has had another influence, also hard to measure but obvious nevertheless. This has been exerted on Stalin's practice of demanding unreasoning discipline. Educated men, even when the educational system is designed to create skills rather than facility in political innovation, have begun to demonstrate their desire to participate in the selection of leaders and in the determination of policy. Emphasis at the lower levels of the party is now on popular choice of officials and upon consultation rather than upon command. At higher levels, consensus has been restored as a feature of meetings of the Central Committee. While the Politburo still prepares the drafts of proposals taken before the Central Committee, its influence has waned. It strikes no terror into the hearts of the men on the way up, and in this fact lie the seeds of change. It is not unlikely that the Politburo will become something like a "cabinet" for the General Secretary, who can be expected to try to convince his colleagues but can no longer command them as Stalin used to do.

Finally, there is the matter of the party purge. Stalin's epoch was characterized in many minds by this technique of ridding the party of his enemies. Provision still remains in the party rules for use of the technique, but it is today of a different character. Party intellectuals seem confident that never again will there be purges like those of Stalin, when leaders were not only expelled, but sometimes accused of treason, brought before a court established for the occasion, and killed. Khrushchev may be able to take credit in history for this change in attitude toward dissenters, although he could not have denounced Stalin's methods without the support of his colleagues. When he ousted Molotov, Kaganovich, and Malenkov in 1957, the world press awaited a purge of the Stalin type, but there were no criminal trials and no executions. These men were demoted, dropped from their party offices, sent for a time to insignificant posts in the provinces, and in Molotov's case permitted finally to return to dignified retirement in the capital.

When Khrushchev was ousted from his party and state offices in 1964, he suffered no public humiliation, no trial. He was relagated to retirement at a country home until the excitement of his ouster had abated, and then he reappeared on occasion at his Moscow apartment to vote and conduct interviews until his natural death in 1971.

While expulsion and eclipse of political opponents in the Soviet manner is shocking to Westerners accustomed to parliamentary procedures created to assure respect for dissident views, the analyst who fails to draw comparisons with Stalin's procedures will miss what is happening in the Soviet Union. There is a growing sense of moderation, still far short of what is expected in a stable government in the West, but one which has reached a point of qualitative difference in the politics of the Communist party. It is the intellectuals who are forcing the change, and it is their influence within the party to which moderates look to prevent a slipping back into old techniques for which there are still partisans.

CHAPTER 3

RADIATING INFLUENCE

Communist party leaders have heralded as the role of the Communist party official the guidance of others in their performance of the many functions required in a complex modern society. Officials have been called upon to step into operating positions in times of crisis, but generally they are expected to attend to party affairs. A party secretary at any level is not supposed to manage a factory or preside over a collective farm or head a ministry. Until the war crisis of 1939 the General Secretary of the Party, Stalin, was kept aloof from administrative tasks relating to the economy of the country as a whole. At that time Stalin stepped into the chairmanship of the Council of Ministers, where he remained until his death.

When Stalin's many functions were divided among his heirs, the role of party secretary was again separated from that of chief administrator of the country, but within five years the two functions had been merged again in Khrushchev's hands. On his ouster in 1964, there was another attempt to return to the pattern preferred in party theory, and this lasted for 12 years. Then, in 1977, Brezhnev, while still party Secretary General, assumed the role of Chief of State, but he did not become chief administrator. That task remained separate, presumably because the administrative task in a state owning and operating all industrial, construction, transport, and sales institutions as well as housing and state farms is so great that a single man cannot do justice to both policy making and its execution.

The rank and file of the party is in a different position. An individual's election to party membership has not meant alteration in his employment: a steel worker admitted into the party remains in the steel mills, a government clerk in a ministry remains at his ministerial desk, a brigade leader on a collective farm continues to be responsible for the operations of the dairy or of the chicken house. A distinction is made between the role of the party professional, who is paid for full-time work as a party secretary or as a member of an executive committee of a county or city party conference, on the one hand, and that of the rank-and-file party member, on the other.

While the professionals within the party are relatively few, the rank-and-file members are many and are scattered throughout every branch of activity within the U.S.S.R. The reason for this scatter lies in the party leaders' desire to facilitate the radiation of party influence throughout all the nation's activities. Party members are located nearly everywhere, and they know personally what is happening so that they do not have to ask for reports. They provide a skilled network of observers to collect the information that the party leaders need to formulate policy.

The rank-and-file party members in industry, on the farm, and in the office perform an additional function. They are at the right and left hands of the non-party millions, situated to propagate party policy in a thousand subtle ways under instructions from the party secretary of the primary party organization to which they belong. They are given every two weeks little printed pocket books for "agitators," containing themes to put forward not only in the general shop meetings but in daily conversation in the factory canteen. Their task is to win by intelligent argument unanimous approval of all party policies.

Whenever there is a meeting of persons interested in any specialized activity, such as the improvement of the courts or the writing of poetry or the feeding of pigs, the Communist party members who are present because of personal expertness in the matter under discussion are required by party rules to gather in caucus to determine what should be the decisions of the entire interested group, and to work for the general adoption of those decisions by skilful use of the opportunities available. If the meeting is of very great national importance, as when it brings together all the principal writers of the country in a writers' congress, the party members present will receive instruction from the Presidium of the party itself regarding the policy to develop. In less important meetings, decisions of the party caucus at the affair are sufficient, perhaps excepting the assistance of the secretary of the nearest big city or county party conference. It is presumed that party members read the daily party newspaper, *Pravda,* and the bimonthly party journals, *Kommunist* and *Partiinaya Zhizn,* as well as the journal specializing on the subject matter of their professional training, whether it be agriculture, or industry, or the writing of belles-lettres, for these journals provide an idea of the positions which the top party leaders, and the top party experts in the subject under discussion, expect to have taken.

A Communist Organization for Youth

The Communist party increases its influence by enlisting young age groups under its banner through the *Komsomols* and the *Pioneers.* These two organizations interlock with one another and with the Communist party itself to provide a core of Communist-indoctrinated youth down to the age of ten. They bring close to the Communist party millions of the young boys and girls on whom the party relies for its future.

It is the task of the Komsomols to organize the most politically minded and active of the country's youth into a centralized disciplined community second only to the Communist party itself. Membership is open, since 1958, to individuals between the ages of fourteen and twenty-eight, but those who are elected to high office within the organization may continue to be members so long as they hold that office. Until 1954 any member was permitted to continue his membership beyond the then existing age of twenty-six for as long as he liked, with the result that the supposedly "youth" organization became heavily weighted with older brothers and sisters. This was probably not without the intent of the party leadership, for the older heads assured conformity within the youth group to the policies of the party. From the early years of the Komsomols up to the late 1920's, the young members had often protested against policies forced upon them by the party—especially against the tightening of discipline and the restraints on the choice of leaders and determination of policy, which were eventually made the same as for the party itself—but this vocal insubordination had been silenced, and the Komsomols in their public meetings had for twenty-five years followed without question the policy established for them by the party.

However, at The All-Union Congress of the Komsomols in 1954, it was proposed that the custom of continuing membership in the organization beyond the age of twenty-six be modified. It was suggested that ordinary members, on reaching the age of twenty-six, have the option of filing with their Komsomol primary organization their wish to continue as members until the age of twenty-eight, after which time they would have to withdraw unless elected to official position within the organization. In this move, which must be regarded as a concession to growing discontent on the part of the youth with the domination of their elders, there was evidenced the readiness of Stalin's heirs to relax some measure of the strict control that the party had been exercising through these elders. Yet the relaxation of control was not complete. There was no proposal to exclude the older members from positions as officers in the organization, and thus the party retained a means of direct influence upon the youth at the control point.

This opening has been utilized, for leadership positions still fall to older men and women, several of whom exceed the normal maximum age. Thus, in the 1968 Congress, 371 delegates were over 30, and 589 ranged from 29 to 30, accounting for one quarter of those attending. The Communist party influence was evidenced by the presence of 2,306 members or candidate members among the 3,821 delegates, and of these 666 held the responsible posts of members of party elective bodies. To counteract the impression given by these statistics of age and party domination the First Secretary claimed that during the seven years preceding the Congress the accent had been on youth. Admissions from the lower age groups had been at such a pace that those between 18 and 25 increased by 23 per cent. In spite of this campaign to restore youth to the front of the Komsomols, leadership remained with mature members.

The structure of the Komsomols parallels that of the Communist party. Individuals apply to primary organizations for admission, and these are located in places of employment. Each primary organization elects its secretary and its delegates to a higher level in the structure until The All-Union Congress of the Komsomols is reached. This, like its counterpart within the Communist party, chooses its Central Committee. The congress itself meets only once every four years. The Central Committee meets only semiannually, leaving the conduct of daily affairs to its "bureau."

At each level of the structure the Komsomol unit must, according to the rules, accept direction and control from the Communist party organization at the same level, whether it be of the republic, the province, the county, or the big city. Since Komsomols work in the same places as Communist party members, there is constant interchange of ideas in personal relationships between them at the factory, in the school, or on the farm. When Communist party members are too few to provide the basis for a primary party organization in any such unit, they join the Komsomol organization to carry out programs. This makes for broader Communist party influence in organizations in which youth predominates, such as the professional schools and the universities.

Membership in the Komsomols is achieved more easily than in the Communist party—for example, there is no period of candidacy—but it is still granted on an individual basis. There are no blanket admissions of an entire school class. An application must be supported by recommendations from two members of at least one year's standing or from one Communist party member, and those who recommend are held accountable with their own membership just as in the party. Dues are exacted of members.

In contrast to the analogous policy governing the Communist party, there is no restriction placed upon the number of Komsomol members. While the Communist party had permitted 16,203,446 persons to join its ranks by mid-1978, the Komsomols had in 1978 at their 18th congress 38,807,399 members, said to be more than half the country's younger generation. Fifty-eight per cent were reported to be working in the national economy, state administrative agencies, or the cultural sphere, having presumably completed full time schooling. The party's policy is, evidently, to open membership to many so as to provide a large pool of tested men and women from which to select the most effective people for party membership. This practice also provides a committed group of persons to disseminate party policy throughout groups which, because of generational differences in attitudes, are beyond the reach of the older party members. Youth's morality is shaped by youths.

The party's General Secretary feels strongly the need to build for the future. At the Komsomol's Congress of 1974 he told the delegates, "By every day of one's working life one must build and affirm the future, bringing it closer and make it a reality." In 1978 he emphasized the need for production in industry and on the farm, but he touched a moral theme as well, saying, "Indifference, parasitism, cynicism, the claim that one is entitled to receive more from society than one gives to it—these moral flaws should not escape the vision of the Komsomols." He also stressed internationalism: youth must work for Communist solidarity worldwide.

Experience has shown that for Soviet youth the slogans of the party are less meaningful than the exciting tasks they have been called upon collectively to perform. In the 1920's they were charged with building a great city in the Far East, named Komsomolsk in their honor. In the late 1930's they turned to the Moscow subway, the show piece of the nation. In the late 1950's they were opening the frontier in Asia by plowing up the virgin grass lands. In the mid-1970's they were building the Baikal-Amur railroad, linking North-central Siberia to the Pacific. At the fiftieth anniversary they were told to take on a still larger task: fraternizing with the youth of the world by becoming ambassadors of the Soviet land, and also by stimulating to greater activity the relatively dormant children's organization of the Soviet Union, for which the Komsomol is responsible to the party, namely, the Pioneers.

A Communist Organization for Children

Almost every school child is a member of the Pioneers. Statistics for 1978 show 20,000,000 members. It can be presumed that membership corresponds almost exactly to city populations between the ages of ten and fourteen and probably includes as well a high percentage of the children on the farms. This is the only age group that has a distinctive uniform for, unlike the Nazis, the Communists have adopted no uniform or arm band for party or Komsomol members. The Pioneers are the exception probably because boys and girls of the age enlisted in this organization find a uniform appealing. Simple, and much like that of the boy and girl scout organizations of the Western countries and of the United States, it had consisted of a white blouse and blue skirt or trousers, and a red kerchief held around the neck by a metal ring on which is stamped the Pioneer motto *Vsegda Gotov*, "Always Ready"—or even "Be Prepared," in emulation of the motto of our Boy Scouts. In 1967 it was replaced by a more distinctive costume.

The Pioneers have no hierarchy of national organizations. They exist only in "brigades," to each of which a Komsomol is assigned as leader. There are no requirements for admission and no recommendations expected, although a child must serve as a candidate for two months to show his capabilities and to impress upon him or her the seriousness of membership. Programs include camping, bird watching, and all the many activities for which youth groups in other lands give badges, but they also include extensive political education and military sports training suitable to young people of this age. In contrast to the thoroughly mature official journal of the Komsomols, *Molodoi Kommunist*, and to the Komsomol daily newspaper, *Komsomolskaya Pravda*, the Pioneers have a journal, *Pioner*, profusely illustrated in color and containing many simple children's stories and poems, and a daily newspaper, *Pionerskaya Pravda*, written in easy fashion so that the children themselves can read it.

The Communist party seems to hope that this group of young children will radiate influence not only among the youngsters of the country but also in the parents' circles and into the family itself. In the early years following the Revolution, Pioneers were encouraged to report political deviation in their parents' attitudes, and a statue was erected in honor of one young Pioneer, Pavel Morozov, who was alleged to have been persecuted by an enraged parent for political reporting of this nature.

For small children below the age of ten there was re-created in 1957 the organization called the Little Octobrists to provide politically directed recreation, under Komsomol supervision, for children prior to entry into the Pioneers. This organization had been abolished during World War II when preschool education was disrupted. Its functions were then absorbed by reducing the entering age of Pioneers by one year and by intensifying political work among preschool teachers. Since 1967 its membership coincides with school attendance.

While the interlocking Komsomol and Pioneer organizations would seem to be effective instruments for spreading Communist party influence throughout the land, they are often criticized in the Soviet press for their lack of vitality. For example, Komsomols have been accused of failing to take on leadership of Pioneer brigades. It is evident that in spite of the efforts that have been made to excite youth to join these organizations because of the stimulating programs which they offer, there is some apathy among the members. Soviet youth is much more indoctrinated and disciplined than that of Western countries, but it is still human. Homework is drudgery in many cases, even though it is sugar-coated with promises of political preferment and accompanied by the explanation that it must be performed in loyalty to the regime. The system of enlisting youth to spread Communist doctrine is effective, but not completely so.

The Soviets as the State Apparatus

The Communist party's greatest sphere of activity lies in policy-making for the state. Here it has performed its major function, and here it is that the organization called the Communist party has established a position that, in its view, permits it to lay claim to being a political party.

The mechanism called the "state" has been adopted from one inherited from the period of revolutionary opposition to the Tsarist government of the Russian Empire. This was created in the year 1905, when a first attempt was made to conduct a general strike and even to seize power in local municipalities, with the result that the Tsar established a limited form of parliament called the "Duma." It was utilized again to organize the radical left of the revolutionary movement that forced the abdication of the Tsar in March, 1917. Upon the Tsar's abdication, the Duma created a provisional government representative of all elements in the Russian populace and, simultaneously, the parties of the left in the Duma re-created the mechanism with which they had promoted the revolutionary riots of 1905. The left-wing parties called this apparatus a "soviet," because it was based upon the concept of committee organization rather than upon one-man responsibility.

During the spring of 1917 this "soviet" type of organization spread throughout the countryside as a rallying point and coordinating mechanism for the parties of the left, until by June it was sufficiently widely organized to permit creation of a national organization. To establish such an organization there was called in Moscow what became known as the "First Congress of Soviets." At that time the political group that was eventually to take the name "Communist," but was still using the title of "bolshevik wing of the Russian Social Democratic Labor party," claimed the loyalty of only a small minority of the delegates. Control over the majority of delegates to the First Congress of Soviets was in the hands of the more moderate elements of the left, of which the Socialist Revolutionary party represented the most people.

When in the autumn of 1917 the provisional government established by the Duma, and presided over by Alexander Kerensky as prime minister, split sharply with General Kornilov, its commander-in-chief, the various soviets were ready to exploit the dissension. The bolsheviks had utilized the summer to strengthen their apparatus and, establishing a "military-revolutionary committee" in Petrograd, which was then the capital of the country, they were able to bring to a final stage the movement of the left-wing parties for the overthrow of the provisional government. The weakening of the Kerensky regime had thrown Kerensky himself into the arms of the Petrograd soviet to maintain his power, and the military-revolutionary committee saw that a coup was now possible. The Congress of Soviets was convened for a second meeting, and troops and armed workers were put into the streets to capture the city's key spots, including the Winter Palace in which the provisional government was maintaining its existence. The coup was crowned with success, and the leader of the bolsheviks, Lenin, chose to use the Congress of Soviets to succeed the provisional government.

Lenin may have had no other choice, for the ranks of his bolshevik party were still very small. The revolutionary peoples of Russia, and particularly the peasants, were inclined toward a program less radical than that of the bolsheviks. The peasants supported the Socialist Revolutionary party, and many of the moderate intellectuals and some of the trade unions supported the "menshevik" wing of the Social Democratic party. To bring unity into this variegated revolutionary mass, the Congress of Soviets provided the only possible effective instrument for action. Certainly the bolsheviks could not have governed alone. As it was, the mensheviks, except for a small group calling themselves the "internationalists," and the main part of the Socialist Revolutionary party withdrew from the Second Congress of Soviets after the provisional government was seized. There was left as ally to Lenin's bolsheviks only the left wing of the Socialist Revolutionary party.

The Congress of Soviets provided Lenin with a valuable instrument for maintaining the power which had been seized, and he turned to it immediately. He asked it to "legislate" a program implementing the principal slogans with which the revolutionaries had won popularity, namely, peace with Germany and socialization of the land. Lenin used the congress also as a convenient and relatively representative body from which to obtain some mandate of authority for a small group of his henchmen. To clarify the mandate, the congress called this group a "Council of Peoples' Commissars" and divided among the members of it the portfolios of the former Council of Ministers of the provisional government. Having achieved his aim, Lenin sent the Second Congress of Soviets home. It was not to be reconvened until the end of January, 1918, when power had been more firmly established in the hands of the bolsheviks. By that time Lenin had eliminated competition from the constituent assembly. This body, which had been promised at the time of the Tsar's abdication as a means of choosing the form of the new government of Russia and to which many people still looked for salvation, was prevented in mid-January from making a decision by the armed intervention of guards loyal to the bolsheviks.

Having his working committee in the form of a provisional Council of Peoples' Commissars, Lenin next convened the Third Congress of Soviets and obtained from it complete approval of the provisional system as the permanent government. To solidify their gains, the bolsheviks prepared for the drafting of a constitution.

The history of the origin of the soviets has had much to do with their character and with the relation of the Communist party to them. The left-wing Socialist Revolutionaries attempted to moderate the actions of the Council of Peoples' Commissars and of the Congress of Soviets but met with very little success, and the Socialist Revolutionary commissars finally withdrew from the government in protest, in the spring of 1918, leaving the bolsheviks in control of the soviet system. In effect, the bolsheviks, who adopted the name "Communist" in 1919, became the sole effective political party in the new Russia. Jealous of this position, the leaders kept alert to potential opposition, and any indication of a rise in strength of the remnants of either the mensheviks or the Socialist Revolutionaries precipitated violent suppression. In 1936 the factual monopoly of the Communist party was incorporated into the Constitution as a principle of law.

With a hindsight of many years, it is thought-provoking to ask why Lenin and his colleagues did not abolish the soviets after victory in the Revolution and establish a system of public administration through the executive committees of the various levels in the hierarchy of the Communist party. The party might have become the state apparatus, and its Political Buro might have been today the Council of Ministers of the U.S.S.R. The question is all the more intriguing at the present time, when the party's Secretary General has become the Chief of State; when members of the party's Political Buro hold key portfolios of the Council of Ministers; and when in the public discussion of a draft constitution in 1977, some citizens proposed that the state apparatus be abolished and the party assume directly the legislative and administrative functions.

To answer the thought-provoking question as to why there has been no amalgamation of the Communist party and state but rather a development of interlocking directorates in two separate instrumentalities, an examination of the apparatus which still uses the name "soviet" is necessary.

Structure of the State Apparatus

Under the third Constitution of the U.S.S.R., adopted in 1977 and presently in effect, the soviets have both policy-making and administrative functions. At levels above the local one, they are structured in the same way as is the Communist party. There is, therefore, a Supreme Soviet of the U.S.S.R. which corresponds to The All-Union Congress of the Communist Party. The Supreme Soviet is authorized to choose a presidium as its alter ego to make policy decisions in the form of legislation during intervals between its meetings, these intervals being usually six to eight months. Each sitting of the Supreme Soviet lasts only from four to six days under normal circumstances. The Supreme Soviet also chooses formally a council of ministers to be the executive branch of government.

Below the level of the Supreme Soviet of the U.S.S.R., there are supreme soviets in each of the fifteen republics which are federated in the U.S.S.R. Each such supreme soviet has its own presidium and its own council of ministers. Below the republic level there is a soviet in each province. At the level below the province there are soviets in cities and in rural counties. Each has its executive committee. The various soviets in the republics are elected, formally and directly by the people, every 5 years, while deputies to the lesser soviets are named in direct election for 2½-year terms. In these elections, all adult citizens of the geographical area defined as under the jurisdiction of the soviet may vote and be represented, regardless of their place of work. There is no system of indirect elections, such as in the Communist party conferences functioning at the level of the county, the big city, the province, the republic, and the union, according to which delegates to higher levels of the party system come from the party conference immediately below.

At the local level there is a marked difference between the soviet apparatus and the party apparatus. While the party apparatus comprises all party members of the local employment group at a given level of the organizational hierarchy, the soviet apparatus is composed of only a selected group of persons, nominally elected every 2½ years, and thus bears some formal structural resemblance to the town or city council, or board of selectmen, of many an American village or city. In substance, however, it is very different, as will be indicated below.

The soviet at each level of the hierarchy is not in permanent session, but is called by its executive committee at intervals, as specified in the Constitution. In practice, prior to adoption of the 1977 Constitution, the intervals were longer than those specified by law. The Moscow press noted that some local assemblies rarely met, permitting executive committees to rule as they pleased. This situation changed progressively after Stalin's death as local soviets created "standing committees" composed of deputies with special knowledge and outside experts which focussed on topics of local concern. By 1977, 80.6% of local soviet deputies were members of standing committees. Standing committees concern themselves with budget, industry, construction, agriculture, public education, youth, health, labor and family, and deputies' credentials. Executive departments report to them and follow their policy directives.

The importance of standing committees as institutions of public participation is marked, for Soviet general assemblies are large, except in villages, where the maximum membership is 35. Thus, provincial soviet assemblies exceed 200, and city soviet assemblies usually number from 700 to over 1,000 deputies. Most cities are subdivided into boroughs, each having its own soviet assembly and standing committees. Soviet authors declare that these institutions of participation have realized the 1977

Constitution's Article 1, and proclaim the Soviet state to be a "state of the whole people."

Party Influence on the Soviets

By no means are all deputies in the various soviets members of the Communist party, although party members are strategically placed throughout the system. The higher the soviet, the higher the percentage of party members. Thus, the Supreme Soviet with 1,500 deputies elected in 1979 has 71.7% party members in the chambers and 28.3% non-party spots. The Supreme Soviets of Republics have varying percentages, but less than the federal Supreme Soviet—usually around 65%. In provincial soviets the average was 55.3% after the 1977 elections; the county soviets had 49.1, the city soviets 46.6, the borough soviets 47.4, the industrial settlement soviets 41.6, and the village soviets 41%. In all soviets the Komsomol members who are deputies provide additional support within the group of non-party members, for they number about one-quarter of the non-party deputies in the provincial soviets and one-fifth in the village soviets.

Executive committees of local soviets with their greater power have attracted closer attention from the Communist party. Only 12.1% of the 2,229,785 deputies seated in soviets at the province level and below sit on executive committees. Of these 71.6% are Communists. Fewer Komsomols sit on executive committees, but they add some weight, for they constitute 7.8% of the non-party members. Executive committees at the province level have 93% Communists, while those in villages have only 68%.

Variations in percentages of party members in local soviets is unexplained. No longer is there a correlation with the time the republic has been in the U.S.S.R. Formerly, soviets of new arrivals had fewer Communists. In 1977, however, Latvian local soviets had 46.6% Communists while Kazakh soviets had 40.2%. Executive committees were no different, Latvian having 77.2 and Kazakh 66.4% Communists.

These statistics suggest that the Communist party is able, through the soviets, to spread the influence of its limited membership among a large number of people. More important, it is thus able to bring many of the most active non-party people into an apparatus which makes some policy decisions, even though these decisions are limited in character, and, in so doing, develop in them a sense of participation and, presumably, a corollary sense of loyalty to the regime.

Reports from the soviets indicate the subjects of their policy debates. A school milk program is one such subject. The manner of distribution of schoolbooks, whether to be through kiosks in the schools or through regular bookstores throughout the city, is another. The distribution of natural gas to consumers for their cooking stoves is studied and a policy established. Those few party members who are deputies can, through their caucus, prevent an undesirable conclusion to the debate, and meanwhile they may learn from an irate mother or from an angry housewife what needs to be done to improve the distribution of schoolbooks or milk or cooking gas. The end result is that the party need not spend the time of all its members on such details.

In the Supreme Soviet of the U.S.S.R., to which matters of greater national concern are presented, the pattern of Communist party membership is, as we have seen, different. Every election prior to that of 1954 named to the office of deputy to the Supreme Soviet of the U.S.S.R. a higher percentage of party members than to the preceding Supreme Soviet. One can conclude either that the matters presented were of such great concern that the party felt increasingly that its members had to be present in mass or that almost all politically active citizens had already been made members of the party.

Such crowding of the Supreme Soviet of the U.S.S.R. with party members may have defeated the purpose for which it was established as the peak of the state apparatus, for it brought very few people in touch with policy matters who would not ordinarily be close to them anyway by virtue of their Communist party membership. Such an approach may have been that of the Communist party leadership for two years after Stalin's death. A suggestion that party thinking was along these lines is to be found in the manner in which important changes in the national economic plan were made. A decision to introduce a greater quantity of consumers' goods into production was made by the Central Committee of the party and issued over the signatures of the Central Committee, together with the signatures of the officers of the Presidium of the Supreme Soviet and the Council of Ministers. The same was done with a program of agricultural expansion into virgin lands that was adopted in 1953. Both these very important matters would in earlier years have been brought before the Supreme Soviet or discussed at a meeting of the Supreme Soviet following adoption by the Supreme Soviet's Presidium. Yet neither program was brought before the Supreme Soviet for discussion in any form, except in so far as the programs were reflected in the annual budget approved by the Supreme Soviet at its annual sessions of 1954 and 1955. Perhaps the Supreme Soviet was being permitted to lose even the limited importance it had had in the past in bringing a group of the most active of the non-party citizens into close relationship with the economic policies of the government.

If the tendency of Communist party leaders was to ignore the Supreme Soviet on important economic issues immediately after Stalin's death, that policy began to change in 1955. Sessions of the soviets were held on schedule, and the work of each was enlivened by activity of the standing committees, which during Stalin's time had met in secret if at all.

It is these committees which have provided the measure of change in attitude toward the work of the Soviets. Under arrangements made for organization of the Supreme Soviet after the 1937 elections these committees functioned to discuss the budget, new legislation, foreign affairs, and credentials of the deputies, and they were established in both chambers. The first of these to become active publicly after 1955 was the committee on the budget of each chamber. Hearings were held prior to the plenary sessions of the Supreme Soviet, and ministers were questioned on the justification for requested appropriations. With the major reforms in the codes of law initiated after Stalin's death, the legislative committees also came to life, and reviewed over long periods drafts submitted by the Council of Ministers. Witnesses were heard, issues debated, and some drafts returned to the Council of Ministers for revision. Still, the committees did not participate in all cases, for from 1961 to 1965 its preliminary consideration was limited to 53 of the 241 laws enacted.

Foreign policy was not debated in the same way, even when the Supreme Soviet was asked to ratify treaties signed by the government. Khrushchev and his ministers merely stated the positions they had taken and asked for confirmation. The committee made a report supporting what had been done, and the report was then adopted by a show of hands in the assembly without debate or dissent.

The work of the Soviets was a major item of concern of the

twenty-third congress of the party, held in 1966. The party's General Secretary stated that in the soviets was to be found the place to manifest a new emphasis upon democracy. Practice since that time has pointed the finger at the committees of the soviets as the focus of the attempt at democratization of what used to be moribund bodies. The committees have proliferated. Thus, for example, the Supreme Soviet at its 1966 organizational meeting added six new committees in each chamber to those already existing, these being to consider matters of transportation and communication, construction and the building materials industry, agriculture, public health and social security, public education, science and culture, trade and services. The budget committees' duties were expanded to include review of the national economic plans, which had formerly issued from the party alone. Since the budget concerned economic matters, the Economic Committee, formerly existing only in the Council of Nationalities, was discontinued as no longer necessary.

The movement reached into the Republic Supreme Soviets in 1967, when they were organized after new elections. The Russian Republic followed the federal soviet's pattern to create seven new committees to add to the traditional ones. These corresponded in the main to those in the federal soviet, but concerned some matters reserved by the Constitution to the republics alone, such as sports, which were added to the new committee on public education and culture, and public catering, which was added to the committee on trade. Committees for which nothing comparable existed at the federal level were created in the republic for activities conducted by the local soviets in providing communal services, as well as for civic improvements and nature conservation. The committees were small, numbering from 30 to 40 persons, while that for foreign affairs had but 13.

From these events, it is evident that the role of the soviets is being reassessed. From bodies which served Stalin to ratify his proposals and publicize them among the people of the deputies' homelands, they are becoming forums for discussion and perfection of plans and performance in economic and cultural fields, and for discussion of legislative proposals affecting the personal life of large numbers of citizens. They are not, however, places for voting contests, as the decisions are based on consensus and are always unanimous.

The conclusion seems justified that the state apparatus, which Lenin created out of necessity when his party had to share with others in the formulation of policy and which was continued by Stalin to serve the useful purpose of radiation of party influence throughout the whole population, has been reformed. Its functions are now dual: radiation of influence as before, but also the gathering of experts in administration and with specialized knowledge to consult on detail necessary to the formulation of policy. The Communist party members among these relatively popular bodies are always present to provide guidance, but the new vitality of the soviets permits party members to hear witnesses from outside the ruling circles in meetings which could not easily be organized inside the party where the tradition has been one of secrecy of meetings.

CHAPTER 4

CONTROLLED MASS PARTICIPATION

A strengthened socialist democracy has been the theme since the fiftieth anniversary, but it presents problems to the Communist party leaders. Even with a tradition of firm leadership by the party of the political life of the country, Soviet citizens have become restless. Increasing numbers travel abroad to represent the state or to study or to tour. Ideas from abroad in a form sympathetic to Western democracies are still withheld from the masses by limitation of foreign newspapers except those published by foreign Communist parties, but foreign radio broadcasts can be heard. Soviet citizens know that modernized mankind now measures democracy in terms of opportunity to choose leaders and to influence policy formulation. The Communist party leaders cannot escape consideration of the reflection of these world-wide aspirations upon their own people. They are trying to meet the demand, but without sacrificing what they believe essential to progress at the U.S.S.R.'s current stage of economic and social development, namely strong leadership by the party.

The Soviet state apparatus provides the means through which democratic aspirations are balanced with the desire to retain strong leadership. Fortunately for the Communist party leadership, the state apparatus was never merged by Stalin with the party, so that there is ready for use in execution of the new policy a form preserved by Stalin. Still, that form is not to be developed as Western Jeffersonian democrats would expect. Communists cannot bring themselves to open wide the gates to unrestricted selection of leaders and determination of policy. They insist on creation of a pattern of action designed to balance freedom of choice with control over what they believe to be its irresponsible use. The theme is to be controlled mass participation, differing from Stalin's concept in that emphasis is to be on participation rather than on control.

Elections and the One-party System

The key to mass participation in the eyes of the world is the electoral process, and since 1936 the Communist party has opened elections to all when deputies are to be chosen for the bodies comprising the representative agencies of the Soviet state apparatus. The restrictions existing until 1936 denying the vote to those who hired labor, served as priests or monks, or had been former members of the Imperial Police or the royal family were revoked at that time. Elections were simultaneously opened to every person of eighteen years of age and over, regardless of social origin, occupation, race, or creed.

Elections were also made direct for all levels of soviets. Since 1936 the indirect system of election, still maintained within the Communist party, under which delegates to all higher levels within the party are chosen not by the rank and file of party members but by the next lower party body, has been abandoned. Further, since 1936 all elections to the various soviets have been secret. Printed ballots are used, and curtained booths are provided for the voter to scrutinize and mark the ballot. Herewith, the U.S.S.R. is able to offer to its citizens and to the world a picture of general, direct, and secret elections, and to claim that it has established institutions that are the cornerstones of democracy.

To understand how little risk is really being taken by the Communist party in reforming the electoral procedure, the Westerner must note the counterweights that have been set up to prevent popular selection of state functionaries who might be unwilling to accept the guidance of the party. The most important of these counterweights is the constitutional provision establishing the Communist party as the sole political party within the U.S.S.R. No other political party may be organized in competition for votes.

While Western peoples do not consider one-party systems compatible with the processes of democracy, it must be admitted that there are parts of the world that are accepted as democratically governed and in which there is only one effective party because the competing party is traditionally too weak to make the slightest challenge to its rule. It is possible, therefore, for a system to merit attribution of the democratic label if there be only one effective party, but, in such cases, there must be a choice of candidates within that party. In many places this choice is provided through a party primary, in which the citizen can select the candidate he prefers. If he belongs to the traditional minority party, he may even declare membership in the perpetual majority party, so as to have an opportunity to vote in its primary and thus share in the selection of candidates.

Opportunity for such choice of candidates is denied in the U.S.S.R. The Communist party holds no primaries, nor does it permit the placing of more than one name per office on a ballot. Nothing in the law prevents a multiple-candidate election. On the contrary, the new constitutional provisions applied in elections for the Supreme Soviet in 1937 provided for a ballot on which was printed the instruction to the voter to cross out all but one name. This same form of ballot is still in use. There is nothing in the regulations to show that there is no choice.

The nominating procedure provided by law appears to make possible the naming of more than one candidate for each office of deputy. Under this procedure, public organizations, such as sports clubs, trade unions, and co-operative associations, may propose candidates in addition to those named by the Communist party. However, none of these organizations may be a political party or conceal the mechanism of a political party under a mask, so it is clear that its basic program must conform to that of the party. It can be imagined that one organization would propose a candidate who would emphasize local school improvement, another might enter a candidate who favored building branch libraries or sports fields. All would have to favor basic party policies such as progression toward communism. None could seek to retrace steps from state-owned enterprise to private enterprise, but candidates could differ in emphasis and, easily, in ability.

In spite of the legal possibility of a choice of candidates in the elections of 1937, the first held under the new rules, there was no choice. On the day the ballots were printed, there appeared on each ballot only one name for each position. The individuals who had been nominated by different organizations within each district had been reduced to one, presumably after the executive committee of the party conference at the county or big-city level had made its selection from among the nominees. To this day, there has appeared on the ballot only one name for each place.

Soviet specialists argue that there is popular choice in select-ing the single candidate. This is because names are sent to dis-trict electoral commissions by nominating groups in factories, universities, trade unions, sports organizations, and farms, and representatives of these groups extol their nominees before the commissions where final choice is made. Admittedly this is a method of choosing, but not by the general public, even though electoral commissions for the 1977 elections for local soviets comprised 9,223,355 citizens. These were thought representa-tive in that 61.5% were workmen and collective farmers, 47.6% were women, 26.6% were under 30. Still, the party dominates the choice, for 35.7% of the commission members were party mem-bers and 17.1% were Komsomols. This permits selection of individual candidates to form part of a composite slate believed by party authorities to be desirable, since it includes nationally prominent figures as well as a balance between ages, sexes, pro-fessions, and party members.

Soviet defenders of the claim that the soviet system of govern-ment is democratic often point to the fact that citizens may cross out the name of the sole candidate appearing upon the ballot. The voter may even write in a name, so the defenders say. Soon after each election the electoral commission in each voting dis-trict publishes statistics on the number of scratches, and on each occasion a considerable number are reported. For example, in the 1975 elections for the Supreme Soviet, the scratches were said to have totaled 332,664 for deputies to one chamber of the Supreme Soviet and 245,750 for deputies of the other chamber. Reports on scratches show constant reduction, for in 1979 they dropped to 175,600 for one chamber and 185,422 for the other. In spite of these scratches all candidates were elected, for in no instance did the scratches exceed the number of affirmative bal-lots for a candidate.

In the local elections of 1977 there were reported 61 cases in which the single candidate for the position of deputy to a village, city, or county soviet failed of election because the total number of scratches constituted a majority of the votes cast. These fail-ures were not many, however, for over two million deputies were successful in the elections at these local levels. Clearly, the pub-lic opposition was to individuals and not to basic party positions.

The desire to express opposition to individuals led to propos-als in the press in 1965 to give the voters a choice of candidates. No one needed to explain that the choice would not concern party programs, but only personalities and their concern for local issues. No change in electoral procedures has resulted, nor has there even been public discussion of the matter by high party officials. Still, the fact that they were published at all in a controlled press indicates some desire to extend the concept of socialist democracy to include a choice of candidates in an election, even when all have to adhere to the fundamental strategy of the party.

Controls over Voting Procedure

Foreign correspondents who have visited U.S.S.R. polling booths since World War II report that there has developed another practice which yet further reduces the possibility of dissent. Although curtained booths are always provided for the marking of ballots, voters are not required on pain of punishment to enter the booths whether or not they wish to mark the ballot, and zealous citizens are permitted to stand ostentatiously in the open room, fold their ballot without marking it, and then move to the urn and deposit it. Such a practice illustrates the possibilities open to leaders who want to control the vote: folding the ballot unmarked, in plain view of the poll watchers, can and probably has become a sign of loyalty to the regime, which timorous persons dare not fail to give.

It is clear that even though the elections for soviets at all levels are now open to all and are also secret and direct, they are subject to various strict controls so that they cannot result in a serious surprise to the Communist party leaders who guide them. The laws provide the formal framework of democratic institutions, but the counterweights prevent their operation toward an unhindered expression of opinion.

Notwithstanding this, Soviet leaders make much of full participation in elections. It is impossible for foreigners to verify the attendance, but it is currently reported to be in the neighborhood of 99.9 per cent of the eligible voters. It may be that the attendance indeed approaches this percentage, for by all accounts nearly everyone votes, if need be in the ballot boxes that are carried into the hospitals and the homes of the sick, onto Soviet ships at sea, or to Soviet troops abroad. Communist party pressure to vote is so great that it results in an even higher percentage of participation than is found in those democratic countries were the law itself requires a citizen to vote and provides a penalty if he does not.

Voting by deputies within the soviets is controlled by the simple procedural expedient of voting by show of hands. It may be that a deputy would always choose to vote for the party's program out of gratitude for the prestige brought him by election to the soviets, for prestige obviously accrues to being a deputy. Yet, even if he wished to vote against some measure, he would probably think twice lest he lose the confidence of the party and the seat he holds. He might even fall under the observation of the repressive agencies, of which more will be said later. That there are no such public dissenters—at least in the Supreme Soviet, to which foreign diplomats and correspondents are invited as observers—is proved by the fact that there has never yet been a vote, on any subject, which has not been unanimous. This was so even on the dramatic occasion when in 1955 Malenkov was replaced as Prime Minister by Bulganin. Although the move came as an obvious surprise to some of those in the room, not a voice was raised against it. Everyone must have assumed that the change had been arranged by the Presidium of the Central Committee of the Communist party, and, with such sponsorship, there was no likelihood of opposition from the floor.

Given the system that evolved during Stalin's time for the election of deputies to soviets and their participation in meetings, the representative function was that of a rubber stamp on a program prepared by the Communist party. Still the drama of deputy participation in budget-making was presented in realistic form. After the Minister of Finance had read the budget proposals, the two chambers of the Supreme Soviet met separately to hear the reports of their respective budget committees. These reports made detailed suggestions for changes in the government's proposals, recommending items to be added to the revenue and expense sides of the budget. When the draft was resubmitted for action by the deputies, the committees' proposals were always incorporated.

The drama was too well acted in Stalin's time to have substance, particularly for those with knowledge of the planning of the Communist party for each Supreme Soviet meeting. For the Communist party there could be no surprises, and it seemed obvious that the drama had been planned in advance.

Since 1955 the emergence of committee hearings well before the Supreme Soviet sessions to which reference has been made in the preceding chapter may be preparing the way for a change. The Communist party, notably since 1966, gives evidence of having decided that it is to its advantage to utilize the committee structure to seek to improve efficiency through consultation with the republic and provincial experts who sit on committees. Such consultation would, of course, be possible within party circles alone, but it is being sought through Supreme Soviet committees as well.

Explanation of the increasing importance of budget committees suggests that the drama of committee consideration without the substance of real participation may have seemed undignified to those who participated in it, especially in light of the exposure of its lack of substance by critics abroad. The value the drama may have had in winning friends for the U.S.S.R. among peoples who really did not know that it was being staged may have been reduced as explanations of competent observers of the Soviet scene reached their ears through advanced media of mass information.

Whatever the explanation, a report on activity within the Supreme Soviet cannot omit consideration of increasing committee activity. Yet, the conclusion is still justified that the forum provided by the Supreme Soviet is still a highly controlled forum. It provides nothing like the place provided by parliaments in Western lands for the introduction of ideas unexpected by a party in power and for the possible rejection in totality of a scheme introduced by that party.

Limitations on Freedom of Expression

Democracy is measured in the public mind by more than parliamentary representation. Before the Russian Revolution, Communist party leaders claimed for their adherents the right to speak their minds, and the first Soviet Constitution included this as a right to a free press and to free speech, but a qualification was added. In this qualification the policy-makers of the new state showed their concern with a counterweight to complete freedom of expression. They provided that the constitutional freedoms be extended to the general public for a limited purpose. They might be exercised solely in the interest of the socialist revolution, and, if exercised contrary to that interest, the responsible person might be deprived of them.

Limitations upon freedom of the press and of speech were stated less precisely in the 1936 Constitution, but the 1977 Constitution is clear. Its Article 37 declares, "Enjoyment by citizens of their rights and freedoms must not be to the detriment of the interests of society or the state or infringe the right of citizens." Article 50 adds that freedom of expression exists to strengthen and develop the socialist system. The Criminal Code states that it is for the courts to determine whether speech is contrary to the interests of the toilers and whether it is exercised with the intention of harming the Soviet state.

Probably few among those who supported the Soviet regime in the early years thought that the limitations on the right to free speech and press would prevent a significant part of the citizens from expressing their views. None of the revolutionaries felt sorry about constitutional limitations on their enemies. The opponents of the regime were thought to be relatively few and all to be members of classes that had supported Tsarism or the provisional government that followed it. These classes were accused of having failed to provide the masses with economic benefits, and Marxist supporters of the new regime felt them to be outright traitors to the Russian people in opposing a development that was an outgrowth of a scientific analysis of the course of history. As political failures or even as traitors who would prey with their ideas upon the uninformed millions who had not yet come to understand the program of the revolutionaries, these opposition elements had to be silenced, at least until the new regime had established its own power. Writers of the time indicated that the restraints which they espoused were to be operative solely upon the enemies of the regime. They did not anticipate that any but the obviously capitalist elements would be denied the exercise of democratic rights, and they cared nothing for these elements. They trusted the new state apparatus to preserve the rights inviolate for their own purpose.

History has proved the peril of thinking that democracy can be preserved if any group is deprived of the right to a free press and to freedom of speech unless it is established beyond reasonable doubt that a clear and present danger to the state is threatened by persons attempting to exercise the constitutional freedom of speech and press. The Soviet authorities began with a limitation which seemed to them to be beyond question a reasonable measure for preserving power over their enemies. They have since turned it, again and again, against citizens who have no desire to upset the regime but who have wanted to grumble against some detail immensely important to them.

Early judicial decisions interpreting the constitutional guarantees in the course of application of the criminal code's ban on speech designed to overthrow the regime exemplify the type of extreme action that was taken by local officials to silence the opposition. A man was convicted for opposing the plan for spring sowing in his village by speaking up in the meeting of the village soviet in which he was a deputy. His opposition was in no sense an effort to overthrow the regime; he simply wanted to discuss a very concrete problem, since it affected his personal life, and was doing no more than many an American farmer who opposes his government's plan for agricultural subsidies. Yet the local soviet judge, on motion of the local prosecutor, found the soviet peasant guilty of violating the criminal law. Only on appeal to the Supreme Court of the Russian Republic was the peasant successful in having his conviction quashed, and then it was not because his words were not deemed seditious. It was concluded that he could not have intended to overthrow the regime since he "was a workman, he had been at the front in the civil war, he was an invalid, and he was not a class enemy." In short, the Supreme Court felt that the speaker had been one of those who were presumed to support the regime, and his criticism of the sowing plan must therefore have been intended by him to be a proper, rather than an improper, exercise of the constitutional guarantee of free speech.

A class enemy in the form of a well-to-do peasant also was convicted of counterrevolutionary speech, in opposing a plan of self-taxation introduced for approval of the village soviet. His conviction was appealed, and the Supreme Court of the Republic freed him because it found that no harm had come from his opposition to the plan since it had been adopted by an overwhelming majority. The peasant was, however, convicted of criiminal defamation because he had cursed the officials of the soviet in "unprintable words" while registering his opposition to the proposal.

The Supreme Court of the Russian Republic reveals in these two decisions of the early 1930's that it was trying to establish some yardstick which would remove from the ban against seditious speech grumbling against proposals introduced into soviets, even when those proposals were deemed necessary by local party bosses to the success of a program. The court, in establishing its yardstick, examined the class origin of the speaker to see if he could be presumed to be a class enemy and also looked to the result of the speech. The court seems to have felt that the local authorities needed correction for reading revolutionary intent into speech of a limited critical character.

Examination of class origin to determine the real intent of a critic continued into the 1940's. For example, a Soviet army sergeant training recruits on the drill field during World War II was heard to make derogatory remarks about the rights granted by the Soviet Constitution. In a trial for counterrevolutionary speech in violation of the criminal code, he was acquitted because the court could not believe that he meant to harm the regime. He was found to have served most of his life in exemplary fashion in the army, had been a member of the Communist party for twenty-three years, and had always conducted himself in a manner which suggested that he was devoted to the motherland.

By these court decisions top Soviet authorities are obviously trying to make a good impression upon the public. They are hoping to put a popular meaning into their Constitution's guarantee of free speech. They have built an official record designed to show that while the guarantee is not unlimited, it will be held to be meaningful in circumstances when no real harm is caused, or when the speaker can be presumed loyal because of his record of loyalty or class origin. Testimony of *émigrés* indicates that lower Soviet officials are not so careful and that here the guarantee provides very little restraint on repressive action against the vocal dissenter, even when his dissent is expressed on a subject of local concern having no connection with the stability of the regime.

Practical Restrictions on Printing and Meetings

Limitation upon the constitutional guarantee of freedom of the press is even more clearly defined by Soviet law and regulation. Because of a constitutional ban on the employment of labor by a private individual for any commercial purpose, no private individual may own a printing establishment in which labor is employed. In consequence, operation of a mass-circulation daily paper or even of a less frequent periodical is impossible, unless it were to be by a co-operative association of printers. But even this is forbidden, because the licensing instructions under which private enterprise without employed labor may be conducted, within limits, excludes specifically the operation of any reproductive apparatus. A citizen may not, therefore, so much as operate a mimeograph or duplicating machine for the publication of hand-bills. He may not use the printed word to spread his ideas, except through channels provided by the state.

Even state-operated printshops have been censored under a law requiring submission to a central censorship office prior to publication of all matter prepared for reproduction. During Sta-lin's time this office on occasion licensed a book or drama only to have the license revoked when Stalin saw the play or read the book and demanded that the play end and the books be de-stroyed. Private citizens at that time even hesitated to keep a questionable book in an apartment lest it be taken as indication of lack of support for Stalin and subject the owner to suspicion and surveillance. Khrushchev claimed to have abolished centralized censorship, and to have left the decision to publish to the edito-rial committee of each state publishing house, but there have been indications that a central office still exists for the difficult decisions. Soviet authors even protested publicly against central censorship in 1967.

The right of assembly as a popular democratic right is also guaranteed by the Soviet Constitution, but a statute requires that all public meetings be licensed, whether to be held indoors or out of doors. No meeting to which representatives from all parts of the country are to be invited may be licensed without the consent of the Council of Ministers of the U.S.S.R. If the meeting is to bring together only people from within a single republic, the consent of the council of ministers of that republic is required. If the gathering is to include only members of a single ministry, the minister must consent. When the people to be invited are only from within a single province or smaller unit, the Provincial Soviet's Executive Committee has discretion to determine what shall be permitted.

The right of association is also guaranteed by the Constitution, but, again, is subject to limitation. Any association must be licensed, regardless of the purpose for which it is to be formed, and each republic is authorized to establish a procedure under which such associations may receive a charter.

By virtue of these licensing provisions, public opinion can be effectively expressed only through a licensed agency. This is not to say that the Communist party wants to hear no public opinion.

The contrary is true. The party has always been attentive to rest-lessness among the masses, for such restlessness can spell difficulties for the leadership. If there were no way short of violent revolution for dissent to find expression, the Communist party would not only have little chance of convincing anyone at home, much less abroad, that a democratic system existed within the U.S.S.R., but would find out about the unrest so late that it would have to apply expensive measures of repression, causing perhaps even greater unrest.

The state-owned and -licensed press is therefore thrown open to letters to the editor. Analysis of great numbers of these letters has indicated that their subject matter is far different from that which might be found in any American newspaper. For one thing it is limited to complaints about public administration, and never refers to a basic matter of policy. Further, criticism of administrators is limited to those only slightly higher in the administrative hierarchy than the writer. Thus no bench operator would write in criticism of the minister under whose supervision his factory might be but rather of his foreman or, at most, of his factory manager. No one has ever had published a criticism of the leadership of the Central Committee of the Communist party, or even of the Presidium of the Supreme Soviet. The highest position to be criticized seems to be that of minister, and such criticism is usually made by a deputy to the Supreme Soviet either in a letter to the editor of the local newspaper or in a speech from the floor of the Supreme Soviet.

All letters to the editor are obviously subject to clearance in the editorial office of the party-controlled newspaper, just as any proposed speeches in the Supreme Soviet must clear the office of those who plan the agenda. It can be presumed that censorship, or anticipation of censorship, causes the exclusion of those letters and speeches which touch upon matters too sensitive to air. Still, many criticisms are aired, and a letter to the editor is usually followed some days later by an article in which the editor reports on action taken to set right the administrative shortcoming in question. It is quite possible that many Soviet citizens interpret such action as proof that the public can influence administration and that the Soviet system is democratic.

Soviet citizens with little knowledge of the extent of public criticism in Western countries and of the influence brought to bear upon major policies by associations of irate citizens cannot measure their success against anything but the experience of their own limited past. Although Soviet youths sometimes think out for themselves the political shortcomings of the Soviet system, it has been more usual to find the defectors from the Soviet system among those who are sufficiently old to remember accounts of the freedoms of Western democracies read in their childhood or who have been brought into touch with Western practices through capture during the war, visits outside the U.S.S.R., or Western broadcasts.

Limitations on Trade-Union Organization

Trade unions represent the largest non-governmental system of organizations in the U.S.S.R. and, as such, have probably presented Soviet leaders with their most difficult problem in controlling freedom of association. During Tsarist times the workmen had come to associate trade unionism with the democratic goals for which they were struggling, and after victory the bolsheviks had to permit trade unions to function if they wished to retain the loyalty of these working masses in the factories. Moreover, since these were the people to whom the leaders turned for maintenance of their leadership, trade unions were given wide powers. At the outset they could do no harm to the Soviet leadership, and indeed, since they helped to eliminate the remaining private owners of industry, in accordance with the bolshevik policy of nationalization of resources, they were not only a necessary evil to humor the laboring masses but also a useful tool.

With the progress of events following the turbulent revolutionary years, private industry became extinct in all but its artisan form. Of this category of industry, only the self-employed artisan, or the closely controlled co-operative of artisans, was allowed to produce goods. Since the great factories and mines were state owned, producing in accordance with a national economic plan, the question was raised, in the Communist party's Central Committee in 1928, as to whether trade unions still had a place.

The issue was made quite clear, because the leader of the trade-union movement, who had been placed in his position by the Communist party, had been won over to the cause of his charges, the workmen. He saw in state-owned industry very little less opportunity for arbitrary direction by management than the Communist party as a whole saw in a private enterprise system. He thought that the workmen would now have to be protected against overly ambitious state managers seeking to enhance their own reputations within the administrative hierarchy by cutting costs of wages, lengthening hours, and being inattentive to workers' grievances. The Central Committee concluded that it could not support the position of the man it had placed in charge of the trade unions, and it ousted him. It declared that there could be no antagonism between state managers and the workmen because the manager was representative of the state, and the state was the creature of the workmen. This was clearly not the case, as the state was the creature of the Communist party which ruled in the name of the workmen, and the workmen were by no means admitted to the Communist party in such numbers that it could be said to be directly responsive to their demands. Nevertheless, the party had to find a solution to its problem of keeping the trade unions as the most important institution through which the democratic right of association could be exercised and, at the same time, holding these multimillion-member organizations in check.

To be sure, party members had permeated the trade-union organization as they had permeated all organizations within the U.S.S.R., and these members had tried in their caucuses to influence all its decisions. But this seems to have been an inadequate form of control for such a body. One of the strong men of the inner party circle, Lazar Kaganovich, was therefore put in the position of the ousted trade-union chief, and the task of the trade unions was finally defined clearly. It was not to combat management but to assist management in increasing production.

New Functions for Trade Unions

To popularize the trade unions in their new role, the Communist party leaders sought a dramatic function for them. They achieved their aim by abolishing the Ministry of Labor in 1933—then called a Peoples' Commissariat—and transferring its labor-inspection service to the trade unions. This meant that the trade unions were placed in control over safety devices and could require management to meet the safety rules established by law. Further, the trade unions were given the task of administering those provisions of the social insurance system requiring payment of workmen incapacitated on the job and believed by the doctors to be able to return to work after a temporary absence.

With these new functions, the trade unions could again appeal to the masses. This appeal was enhanced by a provision in the social-insurance law which doubled for trade-union members the payments made to non-members. Finally, the trade unions were provided with supervision over a grievance procedure under which workmen who tangled with foremen or with managers over details relating to the performance of their job might express their grievance and obtain a decision as to its merits.

No mass pressure was to be brought upon management through strikes, nor was the trade-union system to be permitted to influence, through collective bargaining with management, the level of wages or the number of working hours. These came to be set by statute, and for a time collective bargaining ceased. It was resumed only after World War II, when it seems to have been found useful in providing an occasion for arousing enthusiasm among workmen for greater production, and in providing a dramatic *quid pro quo* in allocation, to projects chosen by the trade-union members, of funds set aside by law from the receipts of the enterprise.

To preserve the popularity of the trade unions in the face of legal restrictions and narrowly defined functions, the trade-union chief was given honors. In 1946, on the death of the long-time chairman of the Presidium of the Supreme Soviet, Mikhail Kalinin, the trade-union chief, Nikolai M. Shvernik, was placed in the post. His successor as trade-union chief, V. V. Kuznetsov, was made a member of the Soviet delegation to the first General Assembly of the United Nations, to argue for inclusion of the World Federation of Trade Unions within the framework of the United Nations. By this act the Soviet leadership sought to win friends among the trade-union membership of the world.

Following a period of apparent reduction in prestige after Stalin's death, the trade unions have been given a more important place than at any time since 1937, when Stalin forbade trade-union interference with management at the plant level by abolishing the formal structure of the "triangle" of management, trade union, and Communist party representative, through which major plant decisions had passed.

While the "triangle" has not been restored in name, the role of the trade-union shop committee has been enlarged by the Central Committee of the Communist party in its decision of December, 1957, instituting "permanent production meetings" to consult with management on matters of output and efficiency.

Although this institution, which was strengthened in 1962 by the creation of a permanently sitting committee to serve as its executive, is not to be permitted to upset the principle of managerial responsibility for conduct of factory affairs, its existence serves as more of a check on managerial predominance than has been evident since before the war. It is far from the "workers' council" lauded by Marshal Tito in Yugoslavia and demanded by Hungarian workers during their short-lived revolt of 1956, but it appears to be the Soviet answer to an ill-formulated desire of Soviet workmen to obtain some measure of participation in the operating decisions in the plants in which they work, particularly those decisions regarding dismissals for incompetence and unfitness, as well as holiday arrangements and pay. It may also be a means favored by the Communist party to restrain arrogant plant managers. That this is not unimportant is suggested by the fact that in 1959 the party's Central Committee ordered the creation in primary party organizations of a commission of control of enterprise administration, with the right to make proposals which must be examined immediately by management.

The trade unions in 1958 were also enhanced in prestige when the Council of Ministers of the Russian Republic ordered that matters of planning and organization of production, labor, and wages, together with the safety and culture of workmen be investigated by the ministries and other administrations with representatives of the central committees of labor unions. The 1977 Constitution reasserts this policy.

Trade-Union Structure

Trade unions in the U.S.S.R. are structurally organized so that control by top state agencies is relatively easy. They do not take the form of craft unions, such as has been traditional in the United States, and thus there are no unions of bricklayers, carpenters, or longshoremen. Instead, employees in all the agencies falling within a given branch of economic activity are brought together into one union comprising the craftsmen and the charwomen of the industry. Under such a system there can be no coming together in defense of a common professional or craft interest. Management has to deal with only one union, instead of with several as is still frequent in the United States. In the plant there is a factory trade-union committee, which works with the factory management. At the county level there is a trade-union committee, for each union, to co-ordinate the work of the various factory committees of that union within the county. There is a similar co-ordinating committee for each union at the provincial and republic levels and an all-Union committee for each trade union in Moscow.

Prior to 1957 when industry was directed by a large number of ministries, trade unions were organized to parallel each ministry, and they were numerous, numbering 43 in 1954. Co-ordination of the activities of the many trade unions functioning within a city, a county, a province, or a republic was achieved through an inter-union council to which each union sent delegates. When the ministries operating in the industrial sphere were largely abolished in 1957 and regional economic councils were created to direct industry, the total number of trade unions dropped to 23. The interunion councils were given new prestige since they provided at the regional level trade-union representation in the economic councils.

The 1962 reforms in industrial and agricultural direction brought changes also in trade-union structure. The interunion councils were reconstructed. At the provincial level two inter-union councils were established in place of one. Each was concerned with the unions operating in one sector of the economy. One co-ordinated the trade unions functioning in industry, construction, transportaion, and municipal services; the other co-ordinated the trade unions functioning on state farms and serving the rural population, including state wholesale and retail outlets, consumers' co-operatives, schools, cultural institutions, scientific institutes, the rural building industry, and industries producing building materials. Below these at the county level, interunion councils co-ordinated the work of trade unions in the industrial zones or in large cities, or in the state farm–collective farm administrative regions of the agricultural sections of the country.

With Khrushchev's ouster in 1964 and restoration within a few months of the single line of soviets from top to bottom without division into agricultural and industrial zones, the trade unions reverted to their original structure, but with a small difference. The interunion regional councils, which had been strengthened under Khrushchev's system of economic management to co-ordinate the trade union activities in the provinces, counties and cities were told not to revert to the relative inactivity of the pre-Khrushchev period. The trade union chief demanded that they become strong agencies exerting direct influence upon the work of all trade unions in the regions in which they sat. They did not have to go through channels in each union to its top to influence local policy.

When the decentralized system of economic administration which Khrushchev had introduced was abolished in 1965 with restoration of the centralized ministries, outsiders expected the unions again to be split into organizations paralleling management in each ministry, but this did not occur. Their number remained almost what it had been under Khrushchev's system, in which there had been 23 unions. Subsequently the number was increased to 25 through splits.

Co-ordination of the trade unions is provided at the all-Union level by a congress of delegates from the governing body of each union. In 1977 this Congress brought together 5,033 delegates from the 25 unions, and these elected a large Presidium and a small Central Council of 25. It is through this Council that the Council of Ministers exercises its influence over the entire trade union hierarchy and the 113.5 million trade union members. The Congress meets only once in five years, and the Presidium only twice a year, while the Council is in permanent session. Its chairman represents trade unions in Soviet policy-making circles and also in international associations of trade unions.

The trade unions have regained some of the prestige lost during Stalin's declining years. The chairman of the Central Council of the all-Union congress of trade-union delegates was named an alternate member of the Presidium of the Central Committee of the Communist party immediately after Stalin's death and a full member in 1957. His successor became an alternate member in 1961 and remained so after the twenty-third party congress in 1966, but a surprise occurred in July, 1967, following a reassignment of the chairman to the Moscow Communist party committee. As his successor a full member of the Political Buro of the party was named. Foreign analysts tended to explain the move not as an upgrading of the political standing of trade unions, but rather as a first step in downgrading a high official beginning to lose favor, an analysis supported in 1975 when he was dismissed from the Political Buro and from his trade union post. His successor, A. I. Shebaiev, was not elevated to Political Buro membership, although trade unions continued to receive close party attention.

Creation of the "permanent production committees" to co-ordinate employment matters with the managers of the factories has increased trade-union prestige at that level, but the presence of the Communist party's commission of control of enterprise administration in every economic unit keeps the trade unions in their customary secondary place.

Trade unions in a socialist democracy do not perform the function normally associated with the right to trade unionism in a traditional democracy. They are an instrument of state policy, rather than a pressure group through which interested citizens may formulate a program beneficial to their special interests and press for its adoption over programs presented by similarly organized associations of citizens with other interests. Their role as an instrument of state policy was somewhat broadened by the 1977 Constitution of the U.S.S.R. Its Article 7 empowered trade unions to participate in deciding political, economic, social, and cultural matters, and its Article 113 extended this right to the initiation of legislation. Much was made of the fact that for some time before adoption of the 1977 Constitution legislation concerning labor had in practice been submitted to the trade union's Central Council for comment. Through this procedure specialists on labor among Communist party members were given a formal role in lawmaking, but their role was far different from that of labor leaders in the traditional democracies. Without the right to strike and with officers subject to Communist party discipline as members of the party, trade unions could not act as an independent force in society.

CHAPTER 5

THE HERITAGE OF TERROR

Terror became synonymous with the Soviet system of government during Lenin's and Stalin's time. Even after Stalin's death the threat of its return provided a measure of restraint on the reformers within the ranks of the Communist party and among citizens generally. While Stalin's heirs have denied that they will ever revert to his ways, the history of terror as an instrument of policy is so long that it is an uncautious Soviet innovator who refuses to give it a second thought, especially since some elements of Stalin's terrorizing apparatus still exist. An examination of history will show what the innovators still fear. From the earliest days of 1917, members of classes that owned productive property, as well as priests, monks, policemen of the Tsarist government, and members of the royal family, were considered to be enemies of the government and were terrorized accordingly. In a sense they were outlaws, although no formal law declared them subject to arrest and execution if apprehended. Punishment was to be meted out to citizens only when there was crime, yet in practice the "class enemy" could expect no leniency if he aroused the hostility of anyone in authority.

The exclusion of a part of the population from participation in government was formally accomplished by the Third Congress of Soviets in a resolution of January, 1918. The first Constitution of the Russian Republic, adopted in July, 1918, made the rule specific by listing in detail the classes of people who could not vote or hold office. They were, in effect, second-class citizens, subject to all the obligations of citizenship but denied any share in the determination of policy or in the administration of the state.

The first law establishing a Soviet court system to replace the courts of the Tsar created a special bench called a "revolutionary tribunal" to try allegations of opposition to the bolshevik regime. Contemporary accounts indicate that although these tribunals were supposed to act with some semblance of legal procedure, they reached quick decisions on limited evidence whenever they had before them a member of the enemy classes. There appeared two yardsticks of criminality, one for the worker and peasant, and another for the property owner and the priest.

As if this double standard of justice were not enough to protect the regime, there was created an "Extraordinary Committee" called the *Cheka,* with power to ferret out conspiracies against the state and with authorization to take immediate action, even to the point of execution, to prevent a new revolution. During the winter of 1917–18 the Minister of Justice opposed the extensive powers granted to the *Cheka,* because he, as a member of the Socialist Revolutionary party, anticipated that the apparatus would turn eventually against the leaders of the state itself. But his voice went unheeded. Ardent supporters of the new regime seemed to feel that the *Cheka* could be kept within bounds and directed solely against the class enemy. The records of the time show no signs that any definable group within the government except the Socialist Revolutionaries anticipated what was eventually to come. Only the Socialist Revolutionaries feared that the *Cheka* would turn upon some of its masters.

As the day loomed, the *Cheka* agents infiltrated into the activities of workers and peasants, and finally into the ranks of the Communist party itself, the bolshevik commissar of justice who had succeeded the Socialist Revolutionary incumbent began to appreciate the danger and to struggle for the supremacy of his own commissariat in maintaining order. By December, 1921, hostility to the lawlessness of the *Cheka* even in dealing with supporters of the regime had gone so far that the Ninth Congress of Soviets voted its abolition and the assumption of most of its duties by the revolutionary tribunals and the regular courts. Only its investigatory functions were to be left, and these were given in February, 1922, to a newly created State Political Administration known as the G.P.U.

When federation was accomplished in 1923, a new federal office known as the O.G.P.U. was created by the Constitution to attend to security problems. It arrogated to itself greater authority than had been given to it, for its tribunals were soon trying citizens in secret without benefit of counsel. Its lash became so hated, especially during the campaign for complete collectivization in the early 1930's that Stalin found it necessary to make a change. In 1934, he transferred its functions in limited form to a People's Commissariat of Internal Affairs, but this ministry also expanded its powers. Its initials, first as the N.K.V.D. and later as the M.V.D., caused as much terror as had the former O.G.P.U.

The Terrorizing Apparatus

From an examination of evidence brought to light by those who have escaped from the U.S.S.R., the pattern of terrorizing and its part in the system of government have become clear. The instruments were the Ministry of Internal Affairs and a companion agency that has sometimes been within the Ministry and sometimes outside it as a Ministry of State Security. The Ministry of State Security has had the task of ferreting out potential threats to the stability of the regime and investigating them. These investigations have been exposed by the Soviet authorities themselves, since Stalin's death, as characterized by the practice of physical and psychological torture to obtain confessions of guilt. With such confessions, or even without them, the Ministry of State Security has made a report, and a decision has then been made, presumably by the Prosecutor General of the U.S.S.R. or his representative, either to prosecute before a court or to permit the case to be handled by a special board of the Ministry of Internal Affairs.

The special boards in the Ministry of Internal Affairs were created by statute. They were not required to hold their proceedings in public, nor to provide any of the procedural guarantees of the Constitution such as right to counsel, nor to follow the procedural provisions of the criminal code. According to the testimony of some whose fate has been settled by one or another of them, they often heard cases in the absence of the accused. Under a 1934 statute, they were permitted to sentence persons found to be "socially dangerous" to five-year terms in remote places in the U.S.S.R. or in concentration camps. No definition of social danger was set in the statute, and, from what is known from refugees, the provisions and definitions of the criminal code did not bind the special boards to prove a charge. On the contrary, their primary task was to apply terrorizing methods when there was no specific crime involved. They had no function if crime could be proved, for in such circumstances the case was tried by a criminal court in accordance with the code of criminal procedure and the constitutional guarantee of counsel.

Documents stolen from files of the Ministry of Internal Affairs in the Baltic states indicate that the terrorizing process has been applied to frighten into submission communities in which opposition to the regime was of serious proportion. To arrive at this effect, local representatives of the Ministry were instructed to arrest and deport to camps in the Russian Republic specified numbers of persons of given categories, but no specific individuals were named. The categories were those of prospective enemies, such as army officers of the former Latvian army, estate owners, factory owners, and merchants. The local official determined which persons within the given categories were the most likely enemies and proceeded to arrest them under conditions as mysterious and dramatic as possible. The entire operation was designed to strike fear into the hearts of those who remained and thus to silence them, lest they be next. Some of the effectiveness of the system would be lost if it were not arbitrary, that is, if one could predict where its hand would fall. Apparently, it is in popular insecurity that the regime's security has been thought to lie.

The Ministry of Internal Affairs and its security police, sometimes organized as a separate security agency, were given a privileged position under Stalin. Although the central office operated through ministries in each of the republics, its chain of command was completely centralized below that level in that the on-the-spot officials were free from any influence of local soviets. These officials were appointed or dismissed by the Ministry in Moscow, and they were beyond the reach even of local Communist politicians. Only the Prosecutor General of the U.S.S.R. had administrative authority over the Ministry of Internal Affairs and its security agents.

Immediately after Stalin's death the Communist party's surviving leaders indicated a desire to redesign the political arsenal to eliminate terror as Stalin had used it. In September, 1953, the special boards of the Ministry of Internal Affairs were abolished. Jurisdiction over all security cases was transferred to military tribunals, responsible to the Supreme Court of the U.S.S.R. and obligated to adhere to the same code of criminal procedure as regular courts.

Somewhat later the Ministry of Internal Affairs in the federal government was abolished for a time, leaving only the ministries of like name in the republics to administer the prisons and the regular police. These local ministries operated under a new name as Ministries of Public Order. The experiment was short-lived, for the traditional name was eventually restored, as was the federal Ministry to supervise the republic ministries. Since the reform excluded reconstitution of Special Boards, reversion to the traditional name looked more like a concession to traditionally minded bureaucrats than a signal that Stalin's methods of control were being reinstituted.

Even while the federal Ministry of Internal Affairs was eliminated and its republic counterparts transformed, the Ministry of State Security survived. It took on a new form as a Committee of State Security, entitled the K.G.B. It was subordinated to the Council of Ministers of the U.S.S.R., and its republic agencies were subordinated to the Councils of Ministers of each republic. Administratively this committee obtained a preferred position over other governmental agencies functioning in both the U.S.S.R. government's and the republics' apparatus, in that its agents in the provinces were made independent of the executive committees of the provincial soviets. This freed them in their investigative function from any local influence. In the 1958 reform of criminal procedure their authority was limited to the investigation of state crimes, but in subsequent years this authority was extended to include economic crimes as well. The K.G.B. was not, however, freed by the decrees from the obligation to deliver its prisoners after investigation to the courts for trial.

To facilitate its work, the Ministry of Internal Affairs during Stalin's era had found it desirable to enlist large numbers of informers from the rank and file of the population. Through them, much information was obtained about unwary neighbors. It came to be expected that police informers would be present in every group, and this enhanced the terror of those who had reason to fear the hand of the state. Since Stalin's death this network of informers is reputedly greatly reduced in size, but there is ample evidence that informing is still an important feature of the Soviet security system, especially with regard to the activity of foreigners living or traveling under circumstances of suspicion within the U.S.S.R.

Terrorizing was a weapon designed by Stalin to maintain his power, not only within society generally but within his own Communist party. Events since his death suggest that terror has lost much of its former political value in the eyes of his heirs. Not only have the instruments of terror been reduced in number and those that remain brought under various controls, but gestures have been made to indicate a change in policy. Large numbers of individuals sent to hard-labor camps by Stalin's Ministry of Internal Affairs have been amnestied and returned to their families. Those that were executed or died in the camps have been publicly rehabilitated politically with announcements that they were not traitors. The epithet "enemy of the people" with which Stalin branded those he purged has been dropped from the vocabulary of politics. Torture has been denounced officially, although *émigrés* report it continues in sophisticated psychological forms.

The Rationalization of Terror

With the wave of revulsions against the methods of the past, evidenced to the world through speeches in the congresses of the Communist party and by legislative action amending codes and abolishing some of the instruments of the terrorizing process, the foreigner is justified in asking how Stalin's system was tolerated for so long. Why was there no seething revolt, or at least an attitude of distrust that would have caused Russians to welcome the armies of Hitler as liberators from the Stalin yoke?

The answer to these questions lies, of course, in the notoriously brutal manner in which Hitler's S.S. troops conducted their pacifying operations in Soviet villages. This viciousness proved to many that Hitler's dictatorship would be worse than Stalin's, but there are other deeper reasons. Many of those who experienced the harsh treatment of Stalin's officials have lived to recount their experiences, and they declare that millions did not seethe on the verge of revolt even during the worst of the epoch of purges from 1935 to 1937.

To understand this apparent paradox, one must consider the unusual phenomenon of a people, who appear in the main to have accepted terror during Stalin's time as a necessary evil. In short, one must understand that terrorizing as a technique of government was rationalized by Stalin for most of the rank and file of Soviet citizens. The popular acceptance of his methods was confirmed when Khrushchev denounced him in 1956 and removed his body from the Lenin mausoleum in 1961. Voices were raised in Red Square to ask whether Stalin did not deserve respect as the man who had made the U.S.S.R. a socialist country of great political, military, and economic power and had saved her from Hitler's invaders. Opposition to Stalin's terrorizing technique came not from the masses but from an inner circle that had, in Khrushchev's words, feared at each personal consultation that they might be imprisoned or executed for incurring his displeasure. These incidents the rank and file did not know, nor could they have known them unless they happened to be parties to specific instances of injustice within their own families.

The rationalization of terror and the instruments that disseminated this rationalization must be understood if the outsider is to grasp the reason why Stalin was able to rule so long. The situation is unfamiliar to those with a knowledge only of Western democracies.

In a Western democracy, where there is no "official" philosophy of government and no monopoly of the press and the public platform, it is incredible that any governmental propaganda line would have universal or nearly universal acceptance. There is always a powerful opposition newspaper to act as critic of the government and of its propaganda. As has been seen, the Soviet system has eliminated the possibility of an opposition party, and the media of information and propaganda remain completely subject to the Communist party's control. These media, augmented by compulsory study groups for all members of the population, are employed to convince the people of the correctness of certain propositions. These propositions bear examination, because it is through their acceptance that the Soviet leaders expect to reduce and in some quarters even eliminate opposition to the policies of the regime, including terrorizing.

The foundation of the Soviet government's propaganda line is that its program rests upon scientifically proved fact. To twentieth-century man in any land an aura attaches to a thesis said to rest upon scientifically proved fact, and Soviet leaders can exploit this situation by quoting Marx and Engels, who claimed to be always scientific in evolving their doctrine of revolution and the dictatorship of the proletariat. The strongest card played by these nineteenth-century writers, on whom Lenin based his own thinking, was the claim that the process of historical development had finally been analyzed correctly and the key to the process found. It could then be argued that it was now possible for man to control the future course of history.

In strengthening his thesis, Marx argued that there was no God, no inscrutable divine being who intervened in the development of human history. Only the interplay of discernible factors caused man to develop the structure of his society at any given period. The primary discernible factor was said to be the instruments of production, the tools with which man worked to obtain his food, his clothing, and his shelter. So long as the tools were primitive, man could produce no surplus. He had to share with others, each of whom did his part to keep the family alive. The structure of society was centered in the family.

By degrees man learned to domesticate animals and to improve agricultural implements, and this permitted production of a modest surplus. Engels argued that some families specialized in animal husbandry and traded their surplus for the surplus grain of a neighboring family, and with trade Engels found developing the concept of ownership, which he believed to be essential to trade. With constant improvement in tools of production, families grew in size until they became clan groupings with an increased quantity of property. At this point Engels distinguishes a very important step. He says that those who were leaders of the family by virtue of birth and age developed a lust for property, appropriated family property to themselves as individuals, and built around themselves an apparatus of force in the form of clansmen with whom they shared a portion of the property as the purchase price of support. Thus, according to Engels, there was created the first state apparatus.

Marx and Engels concluded that the first state apparatus rested upon a need to protect private ownership with brute force, and that those who owned the most productive form of property at the time became the rulers. They argued that the state was born as an instrument to be used by a rich ruling class to exploit less wealthy classes, and that in this fact lay the key to subsequent social development. As new tools were developed, new and more valuable types of property came into being, and the class which came to own the most valuable property seized the state apparatus, by revolution if need be. In this way Marx and Engels attempted to explain the fall of Roman ownership of slaves and the growth of feudalism with its ownership of land. They moved on to explain

been designed in part to prevent the foreign view, and even the facts of Western economic life, from reaching the ears of the masses of Soviet workmen and peasants.

The success of Soviet propagandists in preaching their line at the height of Stalin's power can now be measured by means of interviews with those who escaped. These interviews, conducted by teams organized by Harvard University, indicated marked success in certain fields, which is the more remarkable because they were held with people who had come to dislike the Soviet system so much that they were willing to flee, often at risks to themselves and to the families they left behind.

It is generally true of all those interviewed that they were convinced by Soviet schooling, press, and radio that production for maximum public benefit was possible only when factories, natural resources, and means of transportation and distribution were state owned. In short, private enterprise as a way of life was rejected even by those who hated the Stalin regime. The key to long-range prosperity came to be for most Soviet citizens, whatever their political persuasion, state ownership of the means of production.

This acceptance of state ownership as the key to prosperity extended even to the peasants, although among these there was divided opinion. Among the older farmers in the displaced-persons camps of Europe in which most of the interviews occurred, there was found strong opposition to state ownership and to its hand-maiden, collective-farm operation of the land, on the ground that such communal use of the land was not right. The younger farmers, on the other hand, as reported by Alice C. Rossi, seemed to have accepted their Soviet education. While these younger people thought that the collective farms had been bad, their criticism was of management rather than of the system. All, both young and old, were agreed that there must never be a return to the system of estates under which large landowners owned the land and employed peasants to work it.

With mass acceptance of the basic tenet of Marxism—that there is no room in modern society for private ownership of productive resources—the Soviet leaders scored their major victory. They did not have to worry about any serious opposition to the fundamental principle of their society. No large group of persons was likely to try to restore private enterprise in relation to the primary sources of wealth. There might be individuals who would want to make a profit on the sale of homemade products or of home-grown vegetables or meat, and there might even be individuals who would want to steal state property and sell it on the open market, particularly during periods of short supply when the price was high. But there was not to be expected a demand for a basic change from the policy of state ownership of the means of production. The basic principle behind the implementation of this tenet—the principle that workmen require leadership to reach the goal of abundance—was also generally accepted. Respect for education was high, and leadership based upon superior skills, whether in operating a factory or in conducting the affairs of the state, was revered.

Here Marxist doctrine has helped the Communists especially, for it relates political parties to class interests. It teaches that in Western democracies one party will normally represent the landowners, another the peasants, a third the wealthy industrialists and their associates, a fourth the shopkeepers and small producers, and a fifth the working class; then, that class lines are clearly drawn in the differences between political parties, whence it can be argued logically that multiple political parties develop to represent the different economic interests existent in a given society. Conversely, where instead of multiple economic interests there is but a single economic interest, there need be only a single party. Soviet society is said by the Communists to have reached the stage where there is only one economic interest, that of the "toilers," whether these be workmen, clerks, or farmers. In consequence, there need be only a single political party to provide the leadership which all agree to be necessary. Since both refugees from, and recent American travelers in, the U.S.S.R. say that belief in a necessity for multiple parties has lessened there with the years, it is probable that most Soviet citizens accept this tenet of Communist doctrine.

It is probable that most accept also the idea that they can have a democratic system under conditions of state ownership when there is only one political party. What doubt there has been within the U.S.S.R. has centered on the desirability of permitting factions or organized voting blocs to exist within the single party. Stalin thought it necessary to preservation of his own power to stamp out with violence those of his colleagues who wanted to retain factions within the Communist party, but it is uncertain how successful he was in eradicating the lingering desire to form them.

Since Stalin's death factions have emerged within the party, and there is ample proof that although members are denied the right to organize voting groups before entering party meetings, they are doing so. Several of those who opposed Khrushchev's policies in 1957 organized a vote against him in the "Presidium" of the party while he was on a state visit to Finland. By his maneuvers with the Central Committee and the Army he succeeded in overcoming the negative vote and in ousting from the "Presidium" the ringleaders of his opposition. Again in 1964 his opponents prepared a negative vote prior to a meeting of the Central Committee, and when Khrushchev arrived to make a speech in his own defence, he lost the vote and was forced to withdraw from his position as First Secretary and from his government post. Whenever strong opposition develops it now seems likely that factions will be formed in spite of the rule against them. The difference from Stalin's time lies in the fact that terror is no longer being used to discourage them.

This does not mean that factional grouping will be encouraged. On the contrary, the Communist leadership seems still to fear the effect of factional disputes. This may explain why there has been no move to accept the recurring proposals that a choice of candidates be offered on a ballot for a seat in any of the various soviets, as has been permitted in some of the other Communist-led countries of Eastern Europe. The multi-candidate system might invite the formation of factions to support candidates, even though such bloc struggles are forbidden. Such a democratic development, if organized on a party-wide scale, still seems perilous to men and women who think in terms of monolithic leadership.

The Beginning of Disbelief

With an understanding of this background to support a policy of terrorizing in the interests of preserving power, the outsider will ask why there has been the change of attitude toward terror since Stalin's death. One answer was given by Khrushchev when he indicated that the inner circle of Stalin's colleagues had come to fear for their lives. This may be explanation enough, but any lasting reform must rest on a wider acceptance of a policy of institutional and legal restraints on the exercise of power and on disbelief in the infallibility of leadership. Has there been evidence that such a trend is emerging in the thinking of large numbers of Soviet citizens?

The role of the new intellectuals has already been considered in the analysis of trends within the Communist party. It is evident that these men and women consider themselves good Communists beyond suspicion of disloyalty. Further, they want to share in policy making with the expert knowledge which they have acquired and which no generalist can master in sufficient detail to understand the problems of a complex industrial society. While they probably accept wholeheartedly the necessity of preservation of the economic system of state ownership and the idea of one-party government, it may well be that they now oppose terrorizing because it threatens predictability of tenure of office, for themselves and their colleagues in whom they have confidence and on whom they rely.

The managers and bureaucrats of today witnessed or have read about the purge of the late 1930's when their superiors were blacklisted, declared enemies of the people, imprisoned, and often executed. They are determined to avoid a return to such a situation. They are sophisticated, educated people who reject Stalin's application of the label "capitalist" to all opponents of his scheme of things. For them the rationalization of terror as an instrument to achieve what they are prepared to accept as the good and inevitable life has worn thin. They have found spokesmen in the writers both of the Stalin era who are now speaking out and in the new generation. These writers may seem to some Communist traditionalists to have exceeded safe bounds in challenging the base of Soviet authoritarian leadership. There is evidence that this is so in the criticism leveled at them in 1963 by the Central Committee, and again in the trial and sentencing of two authors in 1966 to terms at hard labor for anti-Soviet agitation. Severe as this punishment was, it was not like Stalin's purge, for it was not a trumped-up charge, nor was the punishment death. They had smuggled abroad through a foreign diplomatic pouch highly critical manuscripts already rejected for publication at home, and they had used pseudonyms. Authors were executed or imprisoned by Stalin for much less, even after making abject public apology for their deviation from Stalin's criteria of suitable literary and artistic production. While the toleration shown dissent bears no resemblance to that exhibited in Western democracies, its discouragement by the criminal process rather than by terrorization bears noting by those assaying the measure of development in the U.S.S.R. of a stable society.

Some astute students of Stalin's regime, such as the former

Communist Wolfgang Leonhard, have gone so far as to suggest that Stalin's terrorizing methods proved uneconomical and politically ineffective in promoting the growth of Soviet society. To Leonhard the U.S.S.R. had reached toward the end of Stalin's era a level of industrial and social development that required sophisticated methods of government as well as men and women capable of initiative and personally motivated to cope with complex new problems. The party and state bureaucracy, the army officers, the educated men, and even the workers and collective farmers had to be freed from fear in order to produce. This argument corresponds to that used by the advisers of Tsar Alexander II in 1861 when he freed Russia's serfs. It rings true in historical perspective, and if it is not overcome by a resurgence of Stalin's rationalizations, perhaps in a paroxysm of fear among leaders who see their entire system endangered by some international development or by such internal collapse of discipline as to threaten complete loss of control, it will determine the future.

To this conclusion there appeared one challenge during the decade from 1957 to 1966 in the form of a "social assembly," which looked to some outsiders and even to Soviet law-trained Communists to be a potential source of terror. Its rationalization was the necessity to discourage "parasites," who were defined as persons living with no evident source of income, namely, as blackmarketeers exploiting the situation of shortages in consumers' goods to establish often quite extensive illegal economic activities.

These social assemblies were established outside the regular court system and even the administration, although there was a measure of restraint exercised by the latter. Under the 1957 legislation, which emerged first in the border republics, they were conceived as gatherings of citizens in factories, administrative institutions, apartment houses, and on the state and collective farms. They were convened on call of a community public order committee, composed of Communist party members and other community leaders.

Charges were brought by the Communist youth league, a trade union, or other public organizations against a citizen whose conduct revealed "an anti-social, parasitic way of life." No definition was provided, and reports indicated that it covered not only cases of speculation, but even of listening to foreign broadcasts. Clearly the bodies served a political function.

Penalties authorized to the social assemblies were banishment from the community of residence to a remote area for periods up to five years, during which the citizen was to reform himself through work to which he would be guided by the local authorities at the place of banishment. Procedure was of the simplest variety at the trial. Vote was by a show of hands. There was no appeal, but the sentence had to be approved by the executive committee of the county soviet so as to avoid injustice on the basis of personal grudges. The accused had to be present unless he refused to attend.

Soviet lawyers in the Russian Republic criticized these institutions as likely to violate the new legality established by the procedural reforms of 1958, and it was presumed by many that they would cease to function. On the contrary, they spread to all of the republics, but in a form indicating some restraint. In the statute of 1961 adopted by the Russian Republic and subsequently copied by all other republics to replace their previous legislation, the social assemblies were given jurisdiction only over parasites who already had some regular job and performed their speculative activities in their spare time. Further, it was for the prosecutor to decide whether the person against whom charges were brought should be tried before such an assembly or by a regular court. Practice indicated that the prosecutor in the preponderant majority of such cases sent the charge to a regular court, although the latter did not follow the rules of criminal procedure but acted in less formal fashion.

When the individual accused of parasitism had no regular job at all, only a regular court was given jurisdiction by the 1961 statute. This further emphasized the court's role in the punishment of anti-social conduct. Previous requirements that the executive committee of a county soviet approve a sentence of banishment by a social assembly were retained in the new legislation. Press reports tell of such referrals to the executive committees and of approvals of the social assembly's sentence.

Some outsiders saw in these social assemblies, when they were inaugurated in 1957, a substitute for the recently abolished special boards of the Ministry of Internal Affairs. They appeared to permit the same feature of banishment that was the competence of the former special boards but with one difference. The individual sentenced to banishment was not confined in a hard-labor camp but remained at liberty, subject to the obligation to report to the local officials of the region of banishment and also to work during the term of sentence. The social assemblies under this view became a modified form of terrorization in that individuals, as in the past, could not anticipate the circumstances that would incur the wrath of the social assembly, so they would feel the urge to establish for themselves forms of self-restraint in the exercise of freedom of criticism and action that they might otherwise have thought enjoyable under the post-Stalin reforms.

In response to criticism leveled at the social assemblies from forces within the Communist party and abroad, they were abolished in September, 1965. In their place the courts in the great cities of Moscow and Leningrad were to be given the task of determining the offense, and elsewhere the executive committees of the county soviets were to make the decision without prior review by a social assembly. In form, this left open to the party a means of terrorizing speculators and those who might be assimilated to speculators as undesirable elements of the community, but it was an administrative mechanism far different from the special boards of Stalin's time. Hearings were no longer secret, the accused was present, and the penalty was not confinement at hard labor, but banishment without confinement to another community where a reformed life was to be lived.

While the changes in policy relating to terrorizing are beginning to be impressive, the end is not yet. Stalin's excesses have been denounced, but there are still some within the Soviet leadership who are reputed to be "Stalinist" in their sympathies. This evaluation comes from men who know them well, namely citizens of some of the People's Democracies of Eastern Europe on the fringe of the U.S.S.R., who have occasion to visit the U.S.S.R. on business. Whether these potential Soviet Stalinists are isolated figures who could, if they wished, oppose the trend established by the bulk of the educated men and women of the post-Stalin epoch who dream of a communism bereft of terror has yet to be determined. Treatment of dissidents suggests that Stalinism is not dead, but muted. Some who have protested have simply been tried and imprisoned, like Alexander Ginsburg in 1978. Others who enjoy an international reputation and seemingly some immunity from confinement have for that reason been expelled, like the Nobel Laureate author Alexander Solzhenitsyn. Some have been deprived of Soviet citizenship while abroad, like Valery Chalidze. The noted physicist Andrei Sakharov remains in his homeland at liberty but is deprived of work suited to his qualifications. Dissidents argue differently about terror's role in the system. Solzhenitsyn thinks it so ingrained that only democratization in traditional form and humanization could make the quality of life tolerable. Chalidze says that the Constitution, if observed, could provide a framework for society without terror, since the problem is not the law, but ingrained bureaucratic attitudes which need to be eradicated. Sakharov argues that the system is generally acceptable, but by terrorizing citizens to avoid Western contacts, it cuts communications and becomes obsolete and inefficient.

For Western democrats the danger of reversion to terror in its Stalinist model can be avoided only if a political opposition, whether as a party or as factions within the Communist party, becomes permitted. This form of political pluralism seems unlikely so long as the Constitution forbids it and Marxist philosophy is interpreted as requiring leadership by a structure such as that of the current Communist party.

CHAPTER 6

THE FEDERAL SYSTEM

Democratic institutions have sometimes been said to depend upon a federal system of government. The experience of the United States has made its impress upon the world, and federations have appeared in countries such as Brazil, Mexico, Argentina, Venezuela, Canada, Australia, India, Indonesia, Burma, and Yugoslavia. The reorganized German Federal Republic was consciously shaped in the form of a federation so as to improve its chances for the development of firm democratic institutions. It was thought that its *länder* might provide grass-roots democracy that would restrain any trend toward authoritarianism at the center. To many people who shared in the planning for Germany, a centralized government spelled potential dictatorship, even though the history of France, with her great centralization, had indicated that a centralized state could also be democratic.

The Soviet leaders have made much of the fact that the U.S.S.R. is also a federation. They have claimed that through the federal form the various peoples of the U.S.S.R. have obtained control over their own affairs, and that they have more privileges than states in other federations. The status of the various Soviet republics that make up the U.S.S.R. is said to be further proof of the democratic base upon which the Soviet system rests.

In spite of the familiar terminology used to describe the relationship among the various peoples of the U.S.S.R., the Soviet federation has some special characteristics. It is not as loose a federation as that of the United States, and by no means as decentralized as Canada or Australia. The Soviet leaders have characterized their system as being a federation that is "national in form but socialist in substance." An examination of its details will indicate what is meant.

The federal structure of the U.S.S.R. grew out of the efforts of the bolsheviks to win friends to their revolutionary plans. The Tsarist empire, unlike the United States, had been a territory in which large numbers of persons of different races, religions, languages, and cultures lived in self-contained pockets rather than diffused throughout the empire. In addition to the Great Russians, representing the most numerous of the Slavic branch of mankind, there were large numbers of Ukrainians and Byelorussians, who were also within the Slavic group but had cultures and languages differing from the Russian. There were the Latvians, Lithuanians, Estonians, and Finns, who had quite different cultures and religions from those of the Slavs. In the areas south of the Caucasus there were the ancient Armenians and Georgians, and in Central Asia and Siberia the numerous Turkic peoples and some Mongol peoples.

Tsarist practice had been to give the underdeveloped peoples of the non-Slavic groups in Central Asia and Siberia considerable cultural autonomy, but for all peoples the official language of the empire had been Russian, the positions of prestige were given primarily to Russians, and the empire had been administered in a completely centralized manner, except for the Grand Duchy of Finland. Even Finland had been closer to union with the Russians than the Finns had been willing to admit. Because of the policy of centralized government and what seemed to the minority peoples to be a policy of "Russification" of culture as well, considerable hostility toward Russian domination had developed by the turn of the twentieth century. Lenin decided to play upon this hostility in winning friends for his program. In 1912 he set Stalin to work to write a program for the national minorities that would enlist them in bolshevik ranks on the basis of the subject of their dreams, namely, independence. Stalin, being himself a Georgian, was well fitted to dramatize the willingness of the Russian Lenin to accede to the wish for independence expressed by the national minority groups.

Stalin's Concept of Self-determination

In Stalin's book, which subsequently became the bolshevik propaganda manual for dealing with the minority peoples, the position is taken that ethnic groups have the right to self-determination, that is, they have the right to determine their own political future. Stalin knew that all of them had but one desire, and that was to be independent. He knew that in taking his position he was inciting revolution against the Tsar and dismemberment of the empire.

Stalin anticipated the trouble which might befall his bolshevik party in the event of ultimate victory in the revolution. The newly independent national minority peoples might go their own ways and become splinter groups so weak as to be absorbed by another empire. He argued, therefore, that while each people had the indubitable right of self-determination, the party for which he was writing would oppose the exercise of self-determination if it did not represent a step toward what the Marxists called "progress," namely, communism. Stalin warned that his party would not agree to the passing over of the minority peoples, once they were free from the bonds of the Russian Empire, to a capitalist camp hostile to what was to be the new Russia.

When the Revolution had been won in the capital of the Russian Empire, Petrograd, the bolsheviks found themselves tested in their policy toward the peoples who had been the national minorities of the old empire. The right of self-determination had been promised, and it had to be offered, at least to the peoples who were sufficiently numerous to present a problem in control if it were denied. In some cases, as with the Finns, it meant losing them for the Soviet system, yet they, and the Ukrainians, the Byelorussians, the Armenians, Azerbaidjanians, Georgians, and Baltic peoples, were permitted to break away. The Central Asian principalities that had been in close union with, but not a part of, the empire were likewise permitted to establish their own states. Yet, for the peoples of Buryat Mongol, Yakut, Bashkir, and Tatar stock, no such privileges were granted. They were kept within the new Russian state, although it was called a "federation" to indicate that they were to have at least token autonomy.

Lenin could not afford to fail to fulfil his party's promises of self-determination to the really vocal minorities. He probably thought that in fulfilling these promises he was gaining more in good will than he was risking in ultimate loss of these peoples and of the territories they controlled. Lenin had two reasons to expect that the newly emancipated peoples would eventually return to his fold. One reason was the Communist party, and the other was force of circumstances.

The Communist party had been organized as a unitary body soon after its permanent creation in 1903. The minority peoples who had asked that they be permitted to create their own party organizations and to federate them with the Russian organization had been denied that privilege. In consequence, the members of the Communist party who lived in the territories of what had become the new Ukrainian and Byelorussian and other republics were under orders from the highly centralized headquarters of the Communist party. Their task was to bring back into close association with Lenin's new Russian Republic the peoples with whom they lived. Their ideal was "internationalism" of the working class, and not nationalism. They knew full well that their party had bowed to the demands for self-determination in order to win friends and that it was their task to bring back the various new republics into the fold as soon as possible. In most cases they proved themselves competent to the task.

Force of circumstances greatly aided the Communists in their effort to reunify the republics. The Revolution had taken place in November, 1917, a year before the Germans, Austro-Hungarians, Bulgarians, and Turks were finally defeated by the allied and associated powers in the First World War. The German army was still a very powerful force on the Russian front, and it continued to press its advantage as the Russian troops disintegrated. The republics on the fringes of what had been the Russian Empire were being overrun. The peace of Brest Litovsk in the spring of 1918 brought only a respite, for there soon began a merciless civil war in which those who remained loyal to the past sought to unseat the bolsheviks. This civil war raged most prominently in the Ukraine, and the forces hostile to the bolsheviks finally captured all but a small part of it in mid-1919. Various foreign powers participated in the civil war, the most effective being the Poles, who marched into the Ukraine and captured its capital in 1920. It was a time when the Ukraine and the other fringe areas could conclude with reason that their future as independent states depended upon military and economic support from the Russians.

The lesson that unity was necessary for survival in war was reinforced by the lesson that unity was necessary for economic development in peace. The empire, quite naturally, had developed its economy without thought of ethnic boundaries. Railroads ran where the terrain was best, crossing and recrossing what had now become the new ethnic frontiers. Raw materials from one province had been used to supply industry in another. After the Revolution, these provinces were often separated by what was in law an "international" boundary. It was clear that if the boundaries were not to be eradicated, a very difficult economic readjustment would become necessary, and in this readjustment productive capacity would be reduced. Unification within one state was the obvious solution to the problem.

Creating a Soviet Federation

Playing upon the growing realization of most of the minority peoples, fanned by the Communist party in each republic, that there must be a new unity within what had been the Russian Empire, Lenin and Stalin planned a federation. Communist party delegates from the various republics that had adopted the Soviet system of government, frequently under the pressure of military operations, met during the late summer of 1922 and evolved a draft constitution that called for a federation of four republics. Three of these already existed as the Russian, Byelorussian, and Ukrainian republics. The fourth was created by bringing together in a new Transcaucasian Republic the three existing republics of Azerbaidjan, Armenia, and Georgia.

While each of the latter was to retain its own republic structure, it was to be within a federation which, in turn, would join the larger federation of the U.S.S.R. The reason given later for the subfederation of the Transcaucasian Republic was that the peoples south of the Caucasus had to be forced into a mold of co-operation because of their long history of conflict with one another. Presumably it was easier to do so with them than with the more numerous Ukrainians and the Byelorussians. One can speculate that if the Ukrainians had been more pliable and less nationalistic in outlook, they also might have been brought closer to the Russians than was done in 1922.

Having secured agreement among the Communist party members living in the various republics, the Russian party leaders had to take only a step to obtain formal agreement among representatives of the four republics that were to join in federation. A constitutional congress was held in Moscow at the end of December, 1922, and the delegates from the four republics accepted the treaty of union that had been drafted. They then declared themselves the new All-Union Congress of Soviets, which was to be the body bringing together delegates from the whole territory of the new U.S.S.R. A constitution was ordered prepared; it was completed and adopted provisionally in July, 1923, and when the Congress of Soviets of the U.S.S.R. met in a second session in January, 1924, the Constitution was ratified.

Where was the federal principle to be found in the governmental structure of the new Union? As in all federal constitutions, there were clauses allocating powers to the federal government and clauses reserving powers to the states that had come together to form the federation. Those who know the history of the Constitutional Convention in the United States know of the struggles between those who wished to reserve to the states significant powers and those who urged greater federal powers. There is no indication that such a struggle occurred in the Communist party group that formulated the first draft of the Constitution, nor in the drafting committee of the Congress of Soviets which prepared the formal document for adoption. The Communist party seems already to have become sufficiently sure of its power and of the acceptance of its leadership by the minority peoples to plan for much more centralism than was acceptable to the Founding Fathers in Philadelphia.

The federal government in the U.S.S.R. was granted by the Constitution some powers familiar to the system in the United States. The federal government alone could coin money, maintain a postal service, establish standards of weights and measures, regulate citizenship in the Union, and settle disputes among republics. The federal government also had sole power to declare war, conclude treaties, and conduct diplomatic relations. At this point similarity ends for the Soviet Constitution gave additional powers to the federal government, of which the Founding Fathers in the United States had not even heard.

This grant of additional powers stems from the Marxist doctrine of what is necessary to achieve maximum production. As has been seen, the Marxists deny that private enterprise can produce as much as state-owned enterprise. One of their professed reasons for such a belief is that the workman will labor harder when he anticipates payment in full for his work rather than payment of only that part which is left from the value he produces after the private enterpriser's profit has been siphoned off. Another reason, one which has been elaborated by the Soviet leadership on the basis of limited implication by Marx, is that economic planning will save waste and duplication. In a planned economy there should be no surpluses seeking customers.

For both these reasons, economic planning has become one of

the major tenets of present-day Soviet leadership, and the reflection of this view is to be found in the first federal Constitution of 1923. The first Constitution empowered the federal government to develop a general plan for the entire national economy; to establish general principles for the development and use of the soil, mineral deposits, forests, and waters; to direct transport and telegraph services; and to conduct trade.

Special Features of the Soviet Federation

While the Soviet federal Constitution transferred far more economic power to the federal government than did the United States Constitutional Convention in 1787, there were some notable omissions in other areas. The Soviet federal Constitution included no bill of rights, such as did the United States Constitution in its first group of amendments. The Soviet bills of rights, such as they were, existed in the constitutions of the republics that had formed the Union, and it was decided, apparently, to leave them in these constitutions alone. It was also left to the republics to develop their own electoral law. No federal provisions declared who might vote and who might not vote. Finally, the federal Constitution left unmolested the civil, criminal, family, land, and labor codes, and the codes of criminal and civil procedure, as these had developed in the republics before federation. While some of these codes might be affected by such general principles for the use of the soil, mineral deposits, forests, and waters as the federal government might adopt, the Communist party seems to have preferred to rely upon the unifying influence of its members in the various republic legislatures rather than to require the republics to accept a system of federal codes.

The concept of federation found reflection in the structure of the Central Executive Committee of the U.S.S.R., which, under constitutional provision, was to be elected by the Congress of Soviets to legislate and generally to supervise the administrative and judicial arms of government during the year-long intervals between meetings of the Congress of Soviets. The Central Executive Committee was made bicameral: one chamber was to be chosen on the basis of population representation alone, while the other chamber was to be chosen on the basis of representation from each national minority group within the U.S.S.R.

The chamber in which each national minority group was to be represented seems to have been the major concession made to the minority peoples in the federation. It may also have been introduced into the Soviet system of government to appeal to other peoples outside the U.S.S.R. In 1922 it was still anticipated that revolution of the Soviet type would occur in Europe and in Asia in the foreseeable future. It was equally anticipated that German and other Western European Communists, who were by this time sending delegations to a Communist International with its seat in Moscow and having as its goal world revolution, might be sufficiently proud to want a share, in any future union, equal to that of the very numerous Russians. The bicameral Central Executive Committee could serve as proof to national groups outside the U.S.S.R. that they would not be submerged in a sea of Slavs.

The second chamber of the Central Executive Committee was to contain representatives not only from the constituent republics that had formed the Union in December, 1922, but also from other national minority groups as well. The Communists had to think of the sensibilities of the Azerbaidjanians, the Armenians, and the Georgians, who had started as independent states after the revolutions organized in each and thus had been of equal status with the Russians, Ukrainians, and Byelorussians. While these three peoples south of the Caucasus had been brought into the federation as a sub-federation, they were proud, and each was therefore given the same number of seats in the chamber of nationalities as each of the three larger republics, rather than only a one-third share of the seats which might have been given to their subfederation. Then there were the Buryat Mongolians, the Yakuts, the Tatars, the Bashkirs, and the Volga Germans, as well as some less numerous peoples who had been, since the Revolution, given the title of republics within the Russian Republic. These peoples had, apparently, expressed through party channels in 1922 the feeling that if the Byelorussians and Ukrainians were to be brought into the Union on an equal basis with the Russians, there was no reason why they should be one step removed from the top level and required to channel their relations with the federal government through the Russian Republic.

A Place for Small Minorities

Stalin reported at the constitutional convention of 1922 that some thought had been given to the status of the small ethnic groups within the Russian Republic. He said that he believed that their relationship with the Russian Republic had been established on a satisfactory basis and that to put them on the level of a constituent republic would be to take a step backward and to loosen a bond which had been tightened. In making this remark, Stalin indicated the direction in which he intended to move and clarified the reason why the federal rather than the unitary form of state was being adopted. The reason was simply that no closer bond than that provided by the federation was politically possible at the time.

As a concession to the pride of the Tatars and of the other peoples within the Russian Republic who had cultural minority status as "Autonomous Republics" but not the higher political status of a constituent republic, the Communists offered them a number of seats equal to that of the Russians and of the constituent republics in the chamber of nationalities of the Central Executive Committee. With this provision there appeared the curious form of representation that has become a peculiarity of the Soviet federal system: subordinate parts of the republics that comprise the Union send representatives to the highest body of the federation, somewhat as if the Pennsylvania Dutch had a representative in the United States Senate alongside the senators from the Commonwealth of Pennsylvania. Even the Eskimos and other very small national minority groups were given seats in the chamber of nationalities, though not in the same number as the larger groups. In consequence, the chamber of nationalities contained a large number of representatives of non-Russian peoples. To the minority groups, and to the world at large, it looked as if the Russians were prepared to share power with their small neighbors in the U.S.S.R.

Yet, in assessing this situation, the role of the Communist party must be kept in mind. Throughout each national group there were Communists, required to think of themselves as internationalists and subject to strict discipline originating at the center. These might even be nationals of groups other than the one in which they were ordered to make their home. Further, they had been trained in the party to propose only those programs which central party officials favored. Under their influence, the representatives of the national minority groups have never expressed a special interest in any but very limited local policy matters, such as the allocation of funds for irrigation in

Central Asia or for housing in Georgia. The minority representatives have always voted unanimously for any program presented by the party, and it has never been necessary to reconcile through reconciliation procedure any contrary views of the chamber of nationalities and the chamber composed of representatives selected on the basis of population alone, although the Constitution provides for such an eventuality. The very real contrast between the Soviet legislature and those of Western democracies is indicated by the fact that there has never been a public difference of opinion between the chambers.

The Influence of the Years

With the passage of time, the local nationalism of the minorities seems to have been reduced, although events in Georgia in 1978 suggest that it may still be aroused by signs of discrimination against a minority people. Soviet text writers declare that a lessening of local patriotism is inevitable, since these minority groups have found that no "Russification" of their cultures is occurring. However, such a declaration does not accord with the facts. It is true that Soviet law does not require that Russian be the sole language spoken in schools, government offices, and courts. On the contrary, the law guarantees that both schools and government business will be conducted in the language of the local ethnic community. Nevertheless, Russian is compulsory as a second language, and any young man or woman who wants to achieve a position of prominence in the U.S.S.R. learns Russian to the best of his or her ability because it is a key to social and geographic mobility. Knowledge of Russian opens doors to the highest professional schools, where it is the language of instruction. Knowledge of Russian enables a man to communicate both in any part of the country to which the party orders him and also on the international scene. The Russian language has become a political and social asset, and the ambitious Ukrainian, Georgian, or other minority representative cultivates the use of it. Nevertheless, in 1978, when republic constitutions were being redrafted, Georgians, Armenians, and Azerbaidjanis protested successfully against elimination of previously existing clauses granting their languages official status in their respective republics.

While minority cultures are fostered, if need be through Russian subsidization of their opera, drama, and literature, local authors are admonished not to be "chauvinistic" in their art. Some of them have even been criticized and disgraced within the Communist party for alleged preaching of national pride and of hostility toward the Russian culture.

The Communist party criticism has not, however, silenced cultural dissent. Indeed, it became intensified during the 1970's as theorists fostered a rapprochement of cultures to create a new homogeneous culture of "Soviet man." Their enthusiasm alarmed critics in minority areas who feared for the future of their cultures, and the party Secretary General sought to calm their fears by denying that there was any desire on the part of the party to merge national cultures into a single culture of the U.S.S.R.

The 1977 Constitution and Federation

While presenting the final draft of the 1977 Constitution to the Supreme Soviet, the party's Secretary General revealed that a group had proposed abolishing the federation to create a unitary state. The proposal revived a position taken originally in 1928 by the State Planning Committee, which had asked whether part of the Ukraine and all of Byelorussia should not be attached to the Russian Republic in the interests of economic integration and effective planning. The issue was taken to the party's Political Buro, where the answer was in the negative on the ground that the proposal was untimely. Presumably the Political Buro sensed that ethnic rivalries and fear of Russification were not yet dead among minority peoples. While no one in 1977 stated reasons for rejecting the proposal out-of-hand, it is likely that the Political Buro held to the same view and for the same reasons. At least no provision was made for transition to a unitary state, and the republics were carried into the new constitutional era as they stood on the eve of the document's adoption, although a few innovations were made in detail.

One has to refer to the "eve" of the 1977 Constitution's adoption, for the original 1936 pattern no longer existed: it had been altered in the intervening years, and the alterations suggested that forces had been tugging policy makers in opposite directions. Some amendments had expanded the republics' jurisdiction, and some had narrowed it.

Expansion had occurred in 1944 through two amendments: one authorizing union republics to conduct foreign relations, and the other establishing a military force. Both were limited in that the federal authorities retained supervisory powers. A third amendment in 1957 had authorized union republics to enact their own codes of law, a power they had lost in 1936 when the Constitution passed to the federal parliament the right to enact legal codes. Again, the new legislative power was limited, for republic draftsmen had to adhere to federal fundamental principles established by the federal Supreme Soviet.

Narrowing occurred when in 1958 the Karelian union republic was deprived of its constituent status established in 1936 and was incorporated within the Russian Republic as an Autonomous Republic. This caused it to lose its full representation in the chamber of the Supreme Soviet representing republics, since Autonomous Republics had been given by the 1936 Constitution fewer seats than their higher-level colleagues in that chamber. Also the Karelian administrative agencies became subordinate to those of the Russian Republic instead of reporting directly to the federal Ministries.

Interpretation of trends indicated by these divergent moves requires consideration of their individual circumstances. The 1944 amendments were made at a time when Stalin was maneuvering with President Franklin D. Roosevelt to obtain greater weight in the United Nations, which was then being formed. He altered his Constitution to give his union republics some of the attributes of sovereignty, and then demanded seats for them in the General Assembly of the United Nations. Roosevelt resisted the move, but finally, in compromise, allowed the Ukraine and Byelorussia to have seats. Thus, the 1944 amendments were understood by the world to be preparation for political maneuvers rather than a concession to internal pressures from minorities. This became even clearer when it was discovered that no republic established a military force, although two republics minted medallions to pin on the lapels of native recruits. Further, except for the Ukraine and Byelorussia, the conduct of foreign relations was limited in the other republics to ceremonies pertaining to relations with neighboring states.

The 1957 amendment authorizing union republics to enact their own codes of law seems no more important. Since no federal codes had been enacted under the 1936 authorization, republics had continued in the period since 1936 to apply their old codes, most of which dated from the years prior to federation. Thus, the 1957 amendment represented no more than recognition of the facts and abandonment of the 1936 move to centralize lawmaking, even with regard to minor matters. It was emphasized that in a country of many cultures, climates, and geographical conditions, some variation in law was desirable. The federal authorities showed themselves content with the influence they maintained by claiming the right to require that republican draftsmen adhere to the federal fundamentals, and most especially to the constitutionally required fundamentals of state ownership of the means of production and the one-party political system.

The interpretation of the demotion of Karelia needs some knowledge of Soviet history. It had been created as a union republic when hopes ran high that Finland might some day be brought into the Soviet federation, just as it had been part of the Russian Empire when a Grand Duchy. It was seen as a desirable buffer against what was seen as a hostile Europe. The Finns showed no willingness to make the change, and even resisted military pressures during the Russo-Finnish war of 1940. Preservation of union republic status must, therefore, have seemed unjustified in light of the need for more rational economic planning for the rump group of Finns on the Soviet side of the frontier. The Russian Republic was the logical center for the economic life of the frontier territory.

This interpretation gains support from well-explained moves by Secretary General Nikita Khrushchev in other regions, as when in the early 1960's he moved to unite economically the Central Asian republics in a Central Asian Regional Economic Council. He even spoke of uniting republics in other regions in similar economic groupings, notably the Baltic republics and those south of the Caucasus. His plans were terminated when the party dismissed him from power in 1964, and the Central Asian experiment was ended.

The standing of union republics as administrative units was enhanced soon after Khrushchev's ouster. As will be shown in chapter 7, some industries previously operated directly by federal ministries, such as steel and non-ferrous metallurgy, were placed in 1965 within the category of a type of ministry split between federal and republic governments, so that the federal government planned and the republics operated the industries. The move looked like a victory for the republic-oriented forces, but it seems not to have been based on ethnic considerations, but rather on administrative convenience.

In view of this experience, disclosure in 1977 that voices had called for abolition of the federation and restructuring of the U.S.S.R. as a unitary state came as a surprise to outsiders, even though demands for ethnic recognition were known to have weakened over the years. This points out a contrast between 1977 and 1957, when a Soviet professor of administrative law told visiting foreign scholars that the Supreme Soviet's chamber of nationalities had resisted amendment of the Constitution because they thought the amendment would lessen republic influence on government. The issue was raised by a proposal to remove from the 1936 Constitution the articles establishing lists of ministries in the federal and republic governments, whose enactment would have made it easier to shift authority away from republics to the federal Council of Ministers. By 1977 the ethnic opposition to such a move had faded, as is evident by the fact that the 1977 Constitution took the very step that had been opposed twenty years earlier and eliminated all lists of ministries. The result is a separate law which may be changed without constitutional amendment, thus making it unnecessary to obtain consent of two-thirds of the deputies from the republics each time that administrative change is desired.

Preservation of the dignity of the republics is another matter. Dignity impinges neither on economic planning nor on maintenance of political power. It is enhanced by a new provision of the 1977 Constitution, namely, the provision requiring that the two chambers of the Supreme Soviet be equal in number of deputies. Under the 1936 formula, the chamber based on population grew in size as population grew, and overshadowed the chamber representing republics, because a fixed ratio of representation had been established, namely, one deputy to 300,000 citizens. The new formula is to require that both chambers have an equal number of deputies, so that the ratio will be changed with each census to prevent increase in the number of deputies.

The Right to Secede

Dignity is also enhanced by the constitutional guarantee to union republics of the right to secede. No Soviet citizen who reads, much less a member of the Communist party, can think this right realizable in light of the historical record. While it was inserted in the first Federal Constitution of 1923, presumably to calm fears of Russification, the Communist party was on record as opposing secession if it meant retrogression to capitalism. As early as Stalin's 1912 pamphlet on the national question, it had been clear that "self-determination" was a formula designed to split empires, not to hamper the development of socialism and communism. After the Russian revolution, Stalin repeated his position, making it clear that self-determination was to be opposed if it meant abandonment of the Soviet system. Under this thinking, if leaders of a soviet republic opted for secession, they would have been seen as violating their party's discipline, and they could expect merciless opposition from those who remained loyal to the center. To have been effective, secession would have had to become a mass revolt against the center, and civil war would probably have ensued.

Not only republican leaders, but ordinary individuals as well have had their way blocked when they have wanted to exercise their right of free speech, guaranteed by the Constitution, to urge secession. This has been the conclusion of specialists on Soviet criminal law who note that the definition of "treason" includes "an act intentionally committed by a citizen of the U.S.S.R. to the detriment of state independence, the territorial inviolability or the military might of the U.S.S.R." Arrest and prosecution of dissenters urging secession have indicated that the code has indeed been implemented.

In view of this record, the right to secession must be only symbolic, designed to enhance the dignity of the union republics and to implement formally the declaration in Article 76 of the 1977 Constitution that union republics are "sovereign." Perhaps draftsmen thought that sovereignty without the right of secession would be limited, although theorists have not suggested as much. On the contrary, they have argued that mere membership in the U.S.S.R. enhances a republic's sovereignty, presumably on the assumption that it is better to hang together than to hang separately. In short, federation is thought to contribute to wealth, prestige, power, prosperity, and protection, all of which are goals of sovereignty. If this argument is correct, the right to secession seems in no need of constitutional sanction. Consequently, its continuing inclusion must stem from the shock, both at home and throughout a world unlikely to support the U.S.S.R. in such an irreversible step, that might follow if the right were excised.

Budgets and Sovereignty

Many federations accord their members the right to levy taxes and dispose of revenues as they wish. The Soviet system denies to its republics the right to tax and to dispose of revenues, except in accordance with terms established by the federal authorities. This means that the federal Supreme Soviet annually adopts a budget for the entire federation. Although the republics are consulted, the final decision is the federation's. Revenues are computed by republics, based primarily on a "turnover tax" on production of state enterprises, but also there are revenues from taxes on personal incomes and collective farm income. Needs of republics are reviewed and revenues allocated by the federal Council of Ministers, on advice of the state planners.

With few exceptions, the share of the revenues made available to each union republic and its geographical subdivisions is limited to the taxes collected within it, but if revenue is inadequate to meet planned tasks, the desired activity is subsidized by transfer from collections in other republics not requiring all that their industries and citizens pay as taxes. The final budget of each union republic is established in detail by the Supreme Soviet of the republic, within the general limits established for that republic by the federal budget.

If a union republic's authorities believe it possible to increase production beyond the plan, they are encouraged to do so, and they may then keep extra revenue resulting from expansion. This system, like others in the Soviet incentive program, encourages increase in production, but it cannot be said to make for economic independence within the federation. The position of the republics is far different from that of the provinces of Canada or the states of the United States. Budget procedures may contribute to a sense of participation in governing and to a sense of dignity, but they are surely a limitation on a republic's power to plan its own future.

Criteria for Status within the Federation

The fact that there are varying types or levels of republics within the federation often provokes outsiders' curiosity as to the criteria for status. In 1936 several Autonomous Republics were elevated to union republic status when the constitution of that year was enacted; Bashkir and Tatar, however, were not. In 1977, when the third constitution was introduced, no elevations occurred, even though some republics seemed to outsiders to be likely candidates.

In his explanation to the constitutional congress in 1936 why the Bashkirs and Tatars had to remain Autonomous Republics while their colleagues were promoted, Stalin set forth three criteria: sufficient population, compactness of population, and location on a frontier of the U.S.S.R. The Bashkirs and Tatars fulfilled the first two criteria, for they were compact ethnic groups, and their populations numbered over a million; but neither was on a frontier. To Stalin, the frontier location was important, for if an internally located republic were to secede, it would become a foreign island within the U.S.S.R., and Stalin felt that such a situation was intolerable, probably because he expected a seceding republic to revert to capitalism. At that time the U.S.S.R. was surrounded by capitalist states, and Stalin gave frequent evidence of his fear that the "encirclement" was a major threat.

To outsiders, the Bashkirs and Tatars had reason to want union republic status because, under the 1936 Constitution's provisions, such status carried with it a higher rate of representation in the Supreme Soviet than did Autonomous Republic status. Also, it probably enhanced the prestige of the peoples who were granted it. Nevertheless, Stalin seemed to associate the higher status solely with the union republic's right to secede, and since he could not countenance that, he held down these two aspiring peoples.

There may have been, however, another unspoken reason for refusing elevation to Bashkirs and Tatars, namely, a historical one. Historically the Bashkirs and Tatars had been brought successfully within the Russian Republic during the early years of Soviet history, before the U.S.S.R. was formed. This incorporation was achieved without the fierce resistence offered by the peoples of Central Asia. Once incorporated, the Bashkirs and Tatars presented no political problem requiring solution by compromise. Consequently, none was made. The Central Asians, who had resisted sovietization, had to be treated differently, and their elevation to union republic status, with its heightened dignity and right to secede, represented an effort to pacify them.

From a doctrinal point of view, there was added reason to refuse elevation. Communist party doctrine, in application of the principle set forth in the 1848 Communist Manifesto written by Marx and Engels, anticipated that as socialism became a reality, workers would relate to their class and not to ethnic origins. Consequently, elevation to union republic status when no political pressures required it would have been doctrinally retrogressive.

Thus, on several grounds, elevation of Bashkirs and Tatars to union republic status would have been undesirable, although Stalin chose to speak of the geographical problem of location within the heart of the country. Because he favored this explanation in 1936, the place of the Bashkirs and the Tatars became of interest to outsiders in 1977. The question was raised, Why were they not elevated to union republic status, since by this time the frontier test seemed unrealistic? Events following World War II had changed notably the political complexion of the U.S.S.R. No longer was there what Stalin had called "capitalist encirclement," at least in the geographical sense, for two neighbors, Poland and Romania, had been brought into the socialist system by their Communist parties with the help of the Soviet army.

In view of the changed situation, had the Ukrainian and Byelorussian republics chosen to exercise their right of secession, they would have become islands in a socialist commonwealth, which although looser than the Soviet Union's federation, was, nevertheless, a close association. Islands, even within the commonwealth, would have been likely sources of trouble, especially if their leaders had chosen to adopt patterns of government unacceptable to commonwealth leaders. It seemed evident that Stalin's border test had become irrelevant to status within the Soviet federation, and outsiders wondered why Bashkirs and Tatars could not be elevated to a position of dignity equal to that of Ukrainians, Latvians, Armenians and the other peoples of union republics.

No published explanation has been given for failure to seize the opportunity, provided by the 1977 Constitution's adoption, to elevate those minorities who could meet Stalin's other two tests. Private conversations with Soviet constitutional specialists, however, have suggested an answer based upon assessment of the strength of the ethnic pressure coming from Autonomous Republics for elevation in status: since pressures seem to be manageable among the Bashkirs and Tatars, there is no thought of changing their status to that of union republics.

In view of this assessment of pressures, outsiders are asking why the republics continue to exist, why the proposal of the group favoring a unitary state which would meet the needs of economic planners was rejected. Evidently, the Political Buro sensed that some of the ethnic groups now governed as union republics were still restive, as evidenced in part by demonstrations in 1978 when the party proposed to demote Georgian,

Armenian, and Azerbaidjanian from their "official" status as republic languages. The federal structure appears still to be politically necessary to give ethnic minorities a sense that their cultural autonomy will be preserved, even though economic and political direction are becoming increasingly centralized.

There may be an additional audience to which Soviet politicians want to appeal by maintaining the federation, namely, the Third World of Africa, Asia, and Latin America. Peoples on these continents still suffer the trauma of dependence upon metropoles in the developed world. If the Communist party were to create a unitary state, the step might seem to potential converts to the Soviet system to be a move against the world trend toward independence of peoples. It might give rise to suspicion that from the ruins of the former Russian Empire there is emerging a new Soviet Empire, and this could hamper Soviet efforts to make friends among the developing nations.

CHAPTER 7

POPULARIZING ADMINISTRATION

"Bring the housewife into administration!" This was one of the slogans by which Lenin hoped to dramatize a popularization of public administration. He declared that the new Russia was to depart from the system of the past under which a highly skilled and conservative group of professional employees manned the offices of the state. His plan was to simplify management procedures and to discard the red tape that is characteristic of all large-scale administrative machines. This he expected to be able to do if he could put the housewife and her husband into the local soviets, which were the administrative bureaus of the new regime, for short periods of time. To effect his plan, he provided in the first Constitution of the Russian Republic that the term of deputies to the local soviets should be but three months.

While espousing the popularization of administration at the local level, Lenin held no brief for the decentralization of policy-making. He wanted citizens to take turns at local offices performing the tasks of the state, but he wanted the principles on which the tasks rested to be established by the central government. He and his party opposed vigorously a January, 1918, attempt by the left wing of the Socialist Revolutionary party, with which the bolsheviks were still in coalition government, to place policy-making as well as operating functions in the local soviets. Just as he had opposed any decentralization of policy-making within the Communist party, Lenin opposed decentralization of authority in the state apparatus.

Lenin had his way. The left-wing Socialist Revolutionaries finally withdrew from the coalition government in the spring of 1918, and with them went the last effective challenge to Lenin's favored principle of centralization of policy-making. Lenin adhered for some years, however, to his program for the popularization of administration. It was not until December, 1921, that the terms of deputies to local soviets were extended from the original three months to one year. The change coincided with the abandonment of many other early policies, in order to establish a mechanism capable of administering the modified system of capitalist economy introduced in late 1921 to restore the economy after the devastation of the civil-war period. Lenin found it necessary at the time to sacrifice some of his precious principles to the needs of the people for food, clothes, housing, and industrial goods. Among the sacrifices was the concept of a non-professional civil service.

The principle of popularization of the administration not only was applied at the local government level but was set as an ideal for the central government of the Russian Republic as well. Yet here there was less opportunity to place the housewife in government. Administration of a central government in a huge state could not be simplified, and it was necessary to maintain an apparatus at headquarters composed of professionals. Many of these had to be held over from the offices of the old regime, for few of the bolsheviks could cope with the details of complex operations such as those of the Ministry of Finance or of the Ministry of Communications. Thus the old ministries were bound to influence the structure of the new commissariats, even though Lenin hoped to avoid such influence by eliminating the Tsarist bureaucrats as fast as new personnel could be trained to replace them. Meanwhile he could do nothing more than place his own supporters at the head of each commissariat and sprinkle throughout the ranks a few "commissars" who would have the task of watching the professionals and stopping sabotage on their part. The policy of utilizing such political commissars was even extended to the new army, in which the old officers had to be retained because they alone knew the skills of war.

Mass Psychology Requires Attention

Public opinion was always a matter of grave concern to Lenin. He had gained the mass support necessary for his revolution from workmen and peasants, to whom much had been promised. Lenin knew that these largely uneducated people would lose interest in his regime, and even become hostile, unless he carried out his promises of democratization of the state administrative apparatus. He had to be careful lest the masses conclude that they had supported no real revolution but had only changed one authoritarian state for another. Lenin discussed the council of heads of administrative departments with his colleague Trotsky, who recorded their conversation. Lenin asked Trotsky what might be done to indicate to the public that the new Council of Ministers would differ from the old. Trotsky said that he recommended a new name for the body, "commissar," because this term had become popular in its application to the watchdogs of the new regime scattered throughout the old apparatus. Trotsky further proposed that, to indicate superior rank, the men who would perform the function of ministers be called "Peoples' Commissars," and their government or "cabinet" the "Council of People's Commissars." Lenin is reported to have been delighted with the suggestion. He said, "That is splendid. That smells of revolution."

The title "Council of Peoples' Commissars" was retained until 1946, when the name was restored to the traditional "Council of Ministers." The government gave little explanation for the reversion, except to say that the old name was more conventional and that there was no longer need to emphasize the new character of the council in this way since its special character had been established by the practice of the preceding twenty-nine years.

The scheme of administration established in the Russian Republic in 1917, and subsequently in the other soviet-type republics that emerged within what had been the Russian Empire, accorded with Lenin's concept of centralized policy-making and localized operations. The new "Peoples' Commissariats" in the capital were to establish policy, while the executive committees of the provincial, county, village, or city soviets were to execute policy. Thus, the Peoples' Commissariat of Justice enunciated the policy to be followed in establishing the courts, but the actual establishment was the work of the county bureaus of justice within the executive committees of the county soviets, and these were co-ordinated within each province by the department of justice within the executive committee of each provincial soviet.

The local soviets were so sure of themselves in the early months that they often determined their own policy instead of waiting for the decisions of the Peoples' Commissariats in Moscow. In the early days, local policemen were recruited and put to work by local soviets, and it was some months before the

Peoples' Commissariat of Internal Affairs was able to establish its policy direction over the police function of the local soviets. It was a time when the men and women who had fought the Revolution were drinking the heady wine of power, and they were slow to relinquish any part of it, even to a central government to which they had pledged allegiance and in which they were supposed to have confidence.

Only in a few matters, such as the conduct of foreign affairs, did the local soviets play no part. In such realms the central government both determined policy and conducted operations. In the great bulk of administrative matters touching the people, the conduct of affairs was otherwise. The people were given the authority to decide questions of local concern subject only to the policy set by headquarters. In fact, they often usurped even the policy-making function. It was not until 1919 that the Moscow commissariats began to pull the reins into their own hands and not until late in 1920 that a strong centralized policy-making authority was clearly apparent. It is hard to tell whether the men around Lenin during this period were being forced to centralize because of the inefficiencies caused by decentralization of policy-making or whether their political philosophy dictated centralization while mass resistance against it compelled them to compromise. Most students of the period incline toward the latter view that Lenin and his colleagues were in favor of centralization from the start but had to move slowly lest they unseat themselves.

The Effect of Federation on Administration

Federation of the republics in the U.S.S.R., at the very end of 1922, raised again the question of administrative structure. As has been seen, the federal rather than the unitary form of government had been thought necessary by Lenin and Stalin to win the confidence of the national minority peoples, who were suspicious of highly centralized government after their experience with the unitary system of the Russian Empire. This concession to the sensibilities of the minority peoples found further practical reflection in the structure of the new federal administrative apparatus. It was impossible, under the circumstances of the time, to give policy-making authority in all fields exclusively to the federal government while leaving only operating authority in the hands of the republics.

The division of powers between the federal government and the governments of the republics had given the federal government certain monopolies, such as the conduct of foreign affairs and foreign trade, the conduct of defense, and the preparation of economic plans and basic rules for the use of the land, but nothing had been said on such a vital matter as education. Education was obviously closely linked to the preservation of culture, and culture was a touchy subject. The fear of "Russification" had been one of the primary reasons why the minority peoples had wanted to separate from the Russian Republic immediately after the Revolution. Culture was a field into which the federal government could not intrude without stirring up old hatreds and losing mass support from the minorities whom it was trying to woo.

Those who drafted the first federal Constitution prescribed an administrative structure suited to their purposes. In the economic areas whose development seemed essential to the materialist Marxist, the emphasis was upon centralization. Most of the state factories were placed under an agency like a commissariat but called "the All-Union Council of National Economy," which was charged with centralization of policy and sometimes of operations as well. For the cultural areas such as education and judicial administration, no commissariat was established in the federal government. Both policy-making and operations in the form of the conduct of schools and courts were left solely to the republics comprising the federation.

Because of the policy of nationalization of factories and of other instruments of production, the U.S.S.R. had at its inception in late 1922 an unusual administrative problem. Although very few cabinet members in countries such as the United States devote even part of their time to the administration of natural resources and of industry, this had become the U.S.S.R.'s principal administrative burden. This weighting on the industrial side was evident in the first federal Council of Peoples' Commissars, of which The All-Union Council of National Economy was one major member. Within the offices of this specialized agency sat the men who supervised and sometimes operated the nationalized industries. The All-Union Council was still a relatively small body at the time, but it was destined to grow in importance until its administrators became so numerous that it was split into many parts, each given the rank of a Peoples'

Commissariat dealing with a specific and limited branch of industry, such as steel, chemicals, textiles, machine-building, coal-mining, petroleum, or copper.

For the industrial plant there was thought to be no problem of hostility on the part of the national minorities toward centralization. The sole consideration for those who established Soviet administrative policy in this sphere of industry was, therefore, efficiency. The question asked at headquarters was whether the operation of a given industry would be better if it were turned over to the republics or if it were retained by the commissariat in the federal government. In some fields, such as textiles, the Russian Empire had achieved a reputation for production, and there were already numerous textile mills that had been nationalized by early decrees following the Revolution. In other areas, such as metallurgy, the Russian Empire had been less developed, and the new regime, with its desire for self-sufficiency in the field of heavy industry, called for rapid metallurgical development as a matter of defensive necessity.

New Forms of Ministries To Aid Efficiency

As events have proved, the policy decision taken at the time of federation or soon after seems to have been to retain in the federal government's hands complete authority to plan and operate the various heavy industries of the land, while passing on to the republic governments the authority to operate the consumers' goods industries within a framework of policy established by the federal government. Two distinctive types of commissariats were designed to administer these two kinds of industry: the type that planned and operated heavy industry was called the "All-Union type" while the type that did the planning but left operations to the republics was called the "Union-Republic type."

Although these two types of ministry, with roots in the federal government, seemed peculiarly fitted to administer industry, they were expanded to other fields as well. Foreign trade is still planned and conducted by a ministry of All-Union type. Until 1944, foreign affairs and defense were planned and conducted by ministries of All-Union type. Until 1955, communications (telephone and telegraph) were planned and operated by the federal government through a ministry of All-Union type.

The All-Union type of ministry is to be found only in the federal government at the federal capital. Thus, a Ministry of Railways exists only at Moscow, and its chief sits in the Council of Ministers of the U.S.S.R. To operate the trains in faraway Siberia, the minister in Moscow acts through agents responsible directly to him. Although such agents are supposed to be considerate of local sensibilities in performing their functions, they often are not. For example, Soviet newspapers once complained that men from the Ministry of Communications cut down the prized boulevard trees in a provincial town to make room for the wires they were stringing. Although the local state officials could complain in the newspaper or by telegram, they had no administrative channel through which they could require consideration of their views, for the Ministry of Communications was at the time and until 1955 an All-Union type of ministry, responsible to Moscow alone.

The Union-Republic type of ministry is different. In the federal capital there is a Ministry of Communications, and there is a ministry of the same name also in the capital of all but one of the republics. If Ukrainian officials and citizens with authoritative voices have a complaint against the local employees of such a ministry, they have more than an opportunity to write letters to Moscow. The Minister of the Ukrainian Ministry of Communications sits in the Council of Ministers of the Ukrainian Republic in Kiev. He is responsible to the ministry of the same name in the federal government in Moscow, but he is responsible also to the government of the Ukrainian Republic. He is not remote and unapproachable for the Ukrainians he serves.

As the trend toward centralization of authority, to which reference was made in the last chapter, extended, the effectiveness of complaints from enraged citizens to nearby ministers of the Union-Republic type probably diminished. Nevertheless, although, under Stalin, the republics lost political power, the fact remains that the Union-Republic type of ministerial structure provided a direct channel through which the influence of local officials could be brought to bear upon operations. There was no such channel in a ministry of the All-Union type. This difference may have been of some importance under Stalin and is probably more important since his death.

The possibility of local influence upon operations is enhanced by the manner in which ministries of the Union-Republic type usually conduct their affairs locally. Unlike the linesmen of the Ministry of Communications, who were responsible only to the head office in the federal government at the time of the tree-cutting episode, the managers of public health clinics in a given province or city are not responsible solely to a distant ministry. This ministry decentralizes its operating functions by channeling them through the executive committees of the provincial, county, and city soviets. Within each executive committee at these levels, there is a "department" charged with the duty of serving as the administrative arm of the ministry of Union-Republic type in connection with operations in the province, county, or city of the kind controlled by that ministry. It is these departments that employ the civil servants who coordinate relevant activities in the territory over which the soviet has jurisdiction.

Facts and figures on public health in a given locality are gathered by these departments of local soviets. Also, administrative orders containing policy directives pass through the hands of these departments for distribution within the territory over which they have jurisdiction. Thus, the Ministry of Public Health in the Ukraine will not transmit its orders directly to the heads of public health clinics throughout the Ukraine but will channel them through the department of public health in each province of the Ukrainian Republic, whence they are fanned out to the many counties within each province and, finally, may be sent to various small city soviets for execution.

There are exceptions to systematic procedures in any administrative system, and the U.S.S.R. had a large share of them under Stalin. Thus the efficient operation of some units of industry subject to the control of a ministry of the Union-Republic type was deemed to be so critical for the nation as a whole that administrative authority for the unit was given directly to the ministry in the federal government. For example, a particular textile mill or shoe factory was sometimes subordinated to the then existing Ministry of Light Industry in the federal government rather than to the Ministry of Light Industry in the Latvian Republic in which it was physically situated and to which it would normally have been subordinated in accordance with the principles established generally for units of the textile or shoe industries. Shortly after World War II, when the Soviet economy was barely able to put itself on its feet, a considerable number of such key units were transferred from the administrative supervision of ministries of the Union-Republic type in the various republics to the ministry in the federal government. In mid-1956, many of these plants were returned to the operating control of the ministries in the republics, as a first step in recognition of the advantages of local direction of operations.

The transfers to centralized operation after the war and back to local operation in 1956 have suggested to foreign students that loss of skilled personnel in the war reduced the number of able administrators in the provinces and counties so greatly that the central authorities dared not trust the judgment of local men. In spite of the increased red tape to be expected from centralization, these authorities seem to have decided to risk loss of efficiency through overloading central planners with operating functions rather than to lose production because of lack of skills at the local level.

Reorganization of industrial administration in 1957 marked recognition of the failure of the policy of centralization of operations to solve managerial inadequacies. Soviet public administration was set on a new course. The character of the change and its durability will be examined after discussion of republic monopolies.

Administrative Concessions to Minority Cultures

The cultural affairs of a republic have been classed, for the reasons indicated, in a category different from that of industry. As has been indicated, there is more involved in cultural relations between the federal government and the government of each republic than efficiency of operation. There is the whole matter of "Russification" with its overtones of Tsarist days. To meet the problem raised by the sensitivities of the national minorities, the first federal Constitution left education solely to the republics. The Ukraine and the other republics were to plan for their own schools and to operate them. The same was true of the judicial system; there was no ministry of justice established in the federal government by the first federal Constitution.

Certain other activities also were left exclusively to the republic governments by the first federal Constitution. Since the first Constitution established categories, some ministries have been removed from the exclusively republic group and others have been added. Some have moved back and forth. Some have been abolished entirely. In April, 1963, the Russian Republic's newly constituted Council of Ministers contained republic ministries dealing, respectively, with automobile transport and highways, municipal housing and services, protection of public order, grammar school education, social security, trade, and water transport. Trade became Union-Republic soon after.

Transfer of ministries from one category to another has reflected philosophies of administration. During Stalin's time when the emphasis was upon increasing centralization the federal government assumed planning and policy control over various vital matters. One such was agriculture, and the ministry was moved into the Union-Republic category. After Stalin's death his heirs reversed his pattern, in part, because of their preference for placing at the republic level as much decision making as possible. Justice has been moved about. In 1966 the federal ministry was abolished, and later some republics also abolished their ministries, distributing their functions among non-ministerial agencies and republic supreme courts. The experiment was abandoned in 1970, and the original structure re-created, although with somewhat less supervisory control over courts. Education, which was originally subject to the sole control of the republics has progressed through various stages which illustrate not only the fluid attitudes of Stalin's declining years and the decade after his death but also the extent to which current leadership is willing to relinquish centralized controls.

A committee on higher education was established as an appendage to the federal government's Council of Ministers during World War II. This committee was given broad co-ordinating and planning authority. The authority seems to have proved inadequate, for in 1946 the committee was transformed into a Union-Republic type of ministry, but of a special character. It was authorized not only to plan for higher education but to operate directly a group of key institutions of higher learning and to guide the republics in operating the rest. Through this action the republics lost the last vestige of control over education at the higher level, although they still retained nominally sole control over the grammar schools. Yet even these schools were brought closer to conformity with a uniform policy; the federal government set minimum limits on compulsory education, and its decrees established standards for teaching and model textbooks.

The trend toward centralization of what little monopoly administrative authority had been left to the republics by federation in 1922 reached its zenith after Stalin's death, for in March, 1954, a Ministry of Higher Education of All-Union type assumed the duties of operating the universities and higher schools. The central authorities seem to have overstepped the bounds of national minority sentiment by this latter decree, for in December, 1954, a cautious step was taken in reversal of policy: higher education was restored to the jurisdiction of a ministry of Union-Republic type. But it was not to be a ministry of the usual kind, for there was to be a republic Ministry of Higher Education only in the Ukrainian Republic. In all other republics the higher schools and universities were to be operated by the federal government. The trend toward restoration of republic authority was advanced in 1959 with transfer of all institutions of higher and specialized secondary education to ministries newly created in all republics. The ministry in the federal government, however, retained important powers: control over certification of faculty members, approval of textbooks, and the giving of assistance in the organization of teaching, methodology, and research. The reservation of these powers was clear evidence of the limits within which the republics might operate.

Experiments with Widened Local Autonomy

The year 1957 marked a sharp reversal of the trend toward ever increasing centralization of industrial management to cope with the failure of industry to achieve the levels set in the economic plans. The reversal had not come entirely without warning. There had been the cautious step with education, but that was linked with cultural sensibilities. More important had been a partial return to republic operation of two heavy industries, coal and petroleum. In 1954 both were assigned to new ministries of the Union-Republic type, and their ministries of the All-Union type abolished. The standard pattern of the Union-Republic type of ministry was not duplicated, however, for in each instance only one republic of the federation was authorized to establish a ministry subordinate to the ministry in the federal government. Those mines and refineries located in other republics were still to be operated from the federal capital.

Khrushchev took personal charge of the implementation of the policy of decentralization of operations. The Central Committee of the Communist party accepted his proposals in February, 1957. He announced that while the centralized direction of industry had been necessary for the quick development of heavy industry in the early days, it was unsuited to postwar conditions, especially since there were being operated more than 200,000 state industrial enterprises and 100,000 construction projects. To continue the former policy of attempting to reduce burdens upon ministers in the federal government by subdividing their responsibilities and creating new ministries would, in Khrushchev's view, reduce co-operation between branches of industry, increase administrative costs by duplicating ministerial services, and separate more and more plants from the local communities in which they functioned.

The national interest had to be served, in Khrushchev's opinion, by a radically new approach: by developing local decision-making. To make his proposals concrete Khrushchev published theses in March suggesting the creation of councils of national economy, to be called *Sovnarkhozy*. Each was to be placed in a region established with regard to ease of communication with plant managers and co-operation between related industries. The All-Union ministries were to be abolished, except for a few activities transcending republic boundary lines. The planning advantages provided by the former ministries in co-operation with the co-ordinating functions of the State Planning Committee of the U.S.S.R. were to come in the future only from that Committee and the State Planning Commissions in each republic. To meet the increased burdens on the planners at headquarters in the republics and in Moscow the federal Committee was to be enlarged by the establishment of departments for groups of industries, and these were to be headed by some of the newly displaced ministers.

The scheme became law in May, 1957. *Sovnarkhozy* were established in 105 economic regions, as defined by the republics. Small republics created but one, to administer industry absorbed from the abolished ministries. Large republics created many, following generally the boundary lines of their provinces but occasionally combining two provinces within a single economic region. Relatively small industries not desired for the *Sovnarkhoz* systems were transferred to the long-existing departments of local industry in the provinces and counties and large cities to be co-ordinated with the small brickyards, gravel pits, glass factories, and repair shops which these local soviets had long been permitted to develop as being solely of local interest.

A trend toward recentralization developed soon after the 1957 reforms had been put into effect. The State Planning Committee

(*Gosplan*) and its republic agencies attached to the republics' Councils of Ministers began to demand so much information from the *Sovnarkhozy* and dictated so many details affecting operating decisions that the chairmen of *Sovnarkhozy* complained that their operating duties were being absorbed by central agencies through the planning mechanism. In July, 1960, the three largest union republics, each with several *Sovnarkhozy* functioning in their provinces, namely the Russian, Ukrainian, and Kazakh Republics, were provided with a republic *Sovnarkhoz* to co-ordinate the work of the provincial *Sovnarkhozy.*

Chairmen of some *Sovnarkhozy* began to suggest at the same time that there was no good reason to retain production enterprises under the direction of the executive committees of provincial soviets. They proposed that all production activity be placed under *Sovnarkhoz* direction, leaving only service activities under the provincial soviets. Another indication of the attitudes being developed is found in a 1960 handbook declaring that the *Sovnarkhozy* must not be considered either as local or republic organs but only as organs of the central economic leadership on the local level.

Further centralization occurred through expansion in numbers of an institution called a state committee or "board" attached to the Council of Ministers of the U.S.S.R. These boards had been created in limited numbers in 1957 to co-ordinate planning primarily of defense industries. In 1961 new ones were created to deal with nearly all branches of heavy industry in planning and implementing policy on investment and technical advancement. This step returned to the federal government authority lost in 1957, when the newly created *Sovnarkhozy* received administrative direction of the industrial enterprises formerly under the control of the various ministries which planned investment and technical advancement of the enterprises under their authority. It was not a complete reversal of the 1957 reforms, for ministries had assumed before 1957 direction of the enterprises in many details, but it represented a significant shift in policy.

By 1961 the signs were multiplying that further recentralization was in progress, but the formal decision to retreat from the advanced position of 1957 was withheld until the party Central Committee's meeting in November 1962. The party's decision, when implemented by legislation in the following month, accomplished several steps toward further centralization: it created state committees in the Council of Ministers of the U.S.S.R. to plan investment and technical advancement for light industry, the food industry, the electro-technical industry, and in wholesale and retail distribution; it withdrew from the executive committees of the provincial and large city soviets jurisdiction over the producing industries leaving them only the service industries; it enlarged the geographical area of a *Sovnarkhoz,* thus reducing their number from 103 to 42; it removed from the *Sovnarkhozy* jurisdiction over construction activities, placing them under a construction committee (*Gosstroi*) within the Council of Ministers of the U.S.S.R., with subordinate committees in each union republic; it created a new Economic Council of the U.S.S.R. (*Soiuzsovnarkoz*) to become the chief implementer of the annual economic plans and restored to *Gosplan* its historic function of preparing long-range perspective plans; it revised the system of state control and audit to combine the long experienced state agency with the Communist party's internal control mechanism. A strong man trained in the Komsomols who was later head of the security police, was placed at the head of the amalgamation.

Explanations accompanied these changes. The *Sovnarkhoz* districts were criticized as having been too small for efficient operation and for having given too much thought to local rather than national interests. The enlarged *Sovnarkhoz* districts were designed to bring under one administration all production drawing upon a common raw material base such as iron ore deposits or conducting within a given region a single type of activity such as textile manufacture, petroleum refining, or food processing.

Sweeping as were the reforms of late 1962, they proved to be no more than forerunners of further change in March, 1963. A Supreme Council of National Economy, bearing a title that had become well-known in Lenin's time in designation of an agency that served as the co-ordinator and planner of all industrial activity performed by state enterprise, was established and subordinated to the Council of Ministers of the U.S.S.R. to become in effect its economic committee. To it were subordinated the recently created *Soiuzsovnarkhoz, Gosstroi* and *Gosplan,* all of which in the November, 1962, reforms had reported directly to the Council of Ministers.

The very important investment planning committees or boards that had been established in the Council of Ministers from 1957 to 1962 to intensify centralized control over economic growth during the period of decentralized operation of the economy were divided into two groups. One was subordinated to *Gosplan* to control investment in long established industries such as metallurgy, food processing, and textiles. The other to control investment in the vital spheres of defense and new industries such as atomic energy was directly subordinated to the Supreme Council of National Economy without the intervention of *Gosplan*. Presumably for these activities where priorities might be required over investment in established industries, political considerations necessitated that the highest political-economic body of the land should make the decisions, subject to ratification by the Council of Ministers.

Finally, both *Gosplan* and *Soiuzsovnarkhoz* were given firmer authority with regard to activity in the republics than they had been assigned in November, 1962. An editorial explained that under the 1963 scheme they would exercise direct control over the republic agencies of like name rather than the limited co-ordinating authority envisaged previously.

The Communist party indicated in its maneuvers of 1962 and 1963 that it was still seeking a workable balance between local operation and central planning. The pendulum, which had swung toward increased authority for administrators at the republic and provincial level in 1957, started on a return swing because such local autonomy as had been granted was hampering planning.

The sheer size of the planning task in the U.S.S.R. has been likened by Gregory Grossman to the square of the number of commodities plus the square of the number of economic units. In his view the task of the planners swells much faster than the growth of both products and producing units. Given this situation it is no wonder that there has been further experimentation with administrative structure; the wonder is that it had to await Khrushchev's ouster. Apparently, his determination to conduct the economy with emphasis upon centralization only in planning could be weakened only in small degree. His opponents moved slowly to undermine him: first by centralizing both planning and operations of key defense industries, then by instituting central investment planning and capital construction, and finally by creating new co-ordinating instruments above the economic regional organizations which he considered to be his "trade mark."

He could not be made to return, however, to any semblance of Stalin's centralized ministerial system. This led eventually to his undoing. Within weeks of his ouster the first steps were taken by his successors to pull down his novel structure, but the architects of the new pattern were careful to claim that they were not returning to Stalin's system. There was to be recentralization, but with a difference.

The Post-Khrushchev Administrative Recentralization

As a first step toward recentralization, and before the complete scheme could be prepared, the Presidium of the Supreme Soviet reformed the various planning and co-ordinating committees for key industrial segments of the economy into All-Union Ministries. Thus, in March of 1965 there emerged ministries for the industries concerned with aviation, defense, radio, shipbuilding, electronics, and the catchall categories which have included in the past some military components, such as "medium and general machine building." Clearly, for these key industrial activities there was to be immediate central planning and direct command of the enterprises concerned.

The major change took longer to prepare, not being submitted to the Supreme Soviet until its session of October, 1965. It constituted a sweeping upset of Khrushchev's economic regionalization. All *Sovnarkhozy* and their superior co-ordinating bodies were liquidated, and in their place emerged centralized ministries of both the All-Union and Union-Republic types. For those industries requiring standardization of parts, united research and design efforts, and close co-operation generally, the All-Union form was chosen; these were machine tool and other tool industries, the manufacture of equipment for construction, road building and civil engineering, tractors and farm machinery, motor vehicles, chemical and petroleum equipment, automation, control systems and industrial instruments, and the manufacture of machines for light industry, the food industry, and household appliances.

For the activities that use rather than manufacture equipment the Union-Republic form of ministry was chosen, these being: electrification and power, fishing, installation and specialized construction, geology, trade, and land reclamation and water resources. Not every republic was to be required to establish a ministry in each field, but only those where the volume of output and the number of enterprises to be directed warranted such an administrative center at the republic capital. If only a few industries were located in the republic, they could be operated by the ministry of a neighboring republic or by that of the federal government.

A subsequent meeting of the Supreme Soviet in December, 1965, cleared up some details that had been left untouched, the most notable administrative one being abolition of the title of minister for executives who were not in fact ministers. Under Khrushchev's system some division chiefs of the State Planning Committee had been seated in the Council of Ministers of the U.S.S.R. with the title and rank of minister so that their expert knowledge might be utilized without making formal recognition of the problem of co-ordination presented by Khruschev's plan.

The post-Khrushchev reforms looked to many like a return to Stalin's system of industrial administration, but the new government was at pains to quash any such suspicion. It admitted that the reform restored centralization, but it was to be of a new kind. It was designed not to discourage individual initiative among directors of the producing units, the state enterprises. Attention was focused on these enterprises to create in their directors a willingness to act without an order from above, and for this purpose draftsmen set to work on a new model charter. To understand the problem one has to look back over the years of industrial history.

Administration of the Industrial Plant

Administrative problems at the industrial-plant level have become entwined in Marxist countries with popular conceptions of democracy. Before the Russian Revolution, bolshevik writers had argued that nationalization of factories would take from the owners the power they had enjoyed of operating their factories without consulting the workmen. In Marxist terms, industrial management would be democratized because the workers themselves would be brought into the process of management. When the Revolution occurred, many workmen seized the opportunity to oust or even to kill the owners of the factories in which they worked. In other factories the managers were retained but were subject to the control of the workmen.

Workmen understood the operation of their own machines in a factory, but they did not comprehend the co-ordinating function performed by management. In consequence, it became necessary for workmen to form committees to manage the plants, or to check upon the decisions of managers in those plants in which managers were retained. This system became known as "workers' control," and it epitomized for the workmen the democratic plant management for which they had fought.

Difficulties developed early out of the system of workers' control. It satisfied the workmen to have managerial decisions made democratically by vote in committee, but it did not make for industrial efficiency. The new Russia needed production, especially at a time when production was hampered and even disrupted by the dislocation and destruction of the civil war. As had been indicated already, by mid-1921 Lenin found himself forced to abandon his program of complete nationalization of industry and channels of distribution. Among the measures instituted in an effort to restore the economy was the system of industrial management that had been traditional in capitalist Russia. Many factories were to be restored to the original owners or leased to other persons willing to accept managerial responsibilities. In the key industries that seemed to the bolshevik leaders too important to the retention of their own political power to be restored to private ownership or management, the pattern of industrial management was to be made like that of capitalist industry. A public corporation was to be formed, and a single man was to be placed in charge. State-owned industry was no longer to be operated as a bureau of a ministry. Factories were not to be run by a committee of workmen.

Lenin's policy for nationalized industry came to be known as the policy of the "trust." The policy of vesting responsibility in a single state manager, rather than in a committee of workmen, came to be known as "one-man management." The new approach was incorporated in a decree of 1923 that grouped all nationalized industry in related combines, to each of which was given independent economic status like that of a corporation. The state treasury allocated to each group of industries such nationalized property as was necessary to its functioning, and this property was inventoried and attached as a schedule of property to a "charter," in which the purposes for which the trust was created were enumerated. Thereafter, the trust was required to operate as best it could in competition with the newly revived private enterprise sector of the economy. It was to buy its raw materials, pay its labor, amortize the value of its buildings, and sell its products to make a profit. At the head of the trust was to be a single individual named by the ministry under which the corporation was to function. In exceptional cases the industry might be run by a committee of workmen, to be called a "college," but Lenin wanted the new principle of one-man management to apply universally as soon as possible, because he thought it made for efficiency.

The system did prove successful in improving the efficiency of operation of state-owned industry, although it was years before the managers' complete authority was accepted by the workmen. In 1927 the system was extended by reducing the size of each corporate unit. The groups of related industries were broken up, and each unit within a combination was given the status of a public corporation in its own right. This means that each unit was charged with property responsibilities and held accountable for its property through a system of cost accounting like that in use in capitalist countries. It could bring suits in courts of law, and it was, in turn, subject to suit by creditors. Judgments against it could be collected from its current assets, and it could be put through bankruptcy if these assets were insufficient for all creditors.

By 1927 the private enterprise sector was being taxed out of existence, and the first of the five-year plans for the expansion of the state-owned sector of the economy was being put into operation. A decree provided that the state corporations were no longer to buy and sell in the open market as best they could with the aim of making a profit. They were now required to help fulfil the national economic plan. They had no choice but to do their part.

Capitalist-like Techniques Serve Planning Purposes

To assure that costs would not mount, as they probably would have if all the economic controls developed for the trust in 1923 had been dropped, the system of cost accounting was retained. But now there was no free market in which the state enterprises could function. Their economic activities were to be planned by the central authorities. They were to be informed of the prices at which to buy their basic raw materials and of the prices at which to sell their finished products. Wages were set in collective bargaining agreements arranged by management with labor unions and under the eye of the Communist party so that no undue advantage would be taken of the workmen by ambitious managers. Later, even wages were set by law. The corporation was expected to make a profit between the planned costs and the planned selling price. If a profit was not made, the auditors of the Ministry of Finance could presume that management had been lax, and inspection would follow. Sometimes it would be found that the fault lay not with management but with those in the state planning commission who set prices, and a revision in the price schedule would be made.

Incentives to efficiency were created through the cost-accounting system required of each public corporation. If a manager could reduce costs by rationalization of production or the elimination of waste, he could increase the profits of his corporation over the expectation of the planners. When profits increased, the inspectors of the Ministry of Finance, upon receipt of the corporation's profit-and-loss statement, would investigate to see whether the unexpected profits were really the result of skill or rather of error in the fixing of prices. If the latter, the error would be corrected, but, if the former, the successful manager would be promoted to a larger plant or to a ministerial post.

Incentives were made even more concrete, in the form of bonuses for management, and for workmen who increased production beyond established norms. These norms were measured on a piece-work basis whenever the type of production permitted such a system, and charts kept the workmen informed of their success or failure. Through such incentives some of the more intelligent workmen developed their own schemes for rationalizing production, and some even invented new machines or combinations of existing machines. To encourage such inventiveness, there was devised a system of "authors' certificates" which entitled an inventor not only to a share in the financial saving resulting from the use of his invention over a period of one year but also to a waiver of personal income tax on his bonus and to priority in the allocation of the coveted positions in research laboratories and training schools.

It is on this system of incentives that the post-Khrushchev government is now building, to create in the directors of enterprises and in their staffs the will to innovate without command from above or constant reference to headquarters for approval. Planning in detail has been reduced for all but key items such as steel, copper, and aluminum, and manufactured components of a unique kind, such as hydroelectric generators. Today most goods are produced under global figures involving overall volume of production. Within this global figure, the director is authorized to manufacture to meet consumer demand, whether it be the demand of other state enterprises or the citizen directly. If he can sell his product in greater quantity by altering specifications to reduce cost, or if he can make it more attractive to consumers by improving design features, he is free to do so. Such profits as he makes from the resulting savings accrue to the enterprise, and are distributed as bonuses to the workers and the administration directly and also indirectly to all through improved communal benefits on which the profits are spent.

Those who know the methods by which capitalism encourages management and workers alike to exert themselves will see in the adoption of these incentive methods the aping of the most successful of the schemes employed in American industry. Soviet authors admit that they have copied American industrial methods, but they claim that they use them in more democratic fashion. They can no longer claim that Soviet industry is administered by committees of workmen, but they claim that the labor unions share in setting norms of work. They claim further that the state itself, which owns the factories, is the creature of the workmen and that hence there is democracy in determining the policies of the owners.

Such arguments as this sound persuasive to those who have not investigated the character of the Soviet trade union or the counterweights established within the Soviet political system to neutralize the influence citizens might exert through the ballot box in choosing the leaders of the state. As was indicated in earlier chapters, the controls are so inclusive that Soviet industry cannot claim to be operated more democratically than American industry. On the contrary, it can be said that throughout American industry today the labor unions, with their enormous influence upon management and the considerable pressure they have been able to exert at times at the polls, provide a more democratic instrument to the workers of American industry than do the laws of the Soviet system.

Centralized Planning Remains Paramount

In a review of developments in the Soviet administrative apparatus, centralization stands out as Stalin's remedy for inefficiency. Through it he expected to exceed production rates in the private enterprise economies, but he met difficulties. He could plan through a centralized apparatus, but rates of production failed to rise because the local managers came to fear innovation, the more so when many of them lost their lives in the great purge of 1934–37. Instead of imaginative directors, centralized planning created bureaucrats who risked as little as they could. It also led to lack of response to consumer tastes, and even needs. Central planners could not foretell them as they were too far from the markets, and the local directors did not care so long as they met the plans established for them at headquarters.

Khrushchev's scheme, adopted in 1957, was an attempt to overcome these evils, but some colleagues, imbued with the centralized and detailed planning concept, were so doubtful of its success that they sought to oust him. When he turned the tables and successfully expelled his opposition, he created his *Sovnarkhoz* system, but it soon demonstrated that what it gained in fostering local initiative it lost in lack of co-ordination. He had to turn quickly to devising panaceas. These violated his original theses by calling for increasing co-ordination of key industries through state committees, although leaving operating functions in the economic regions. Still he obtained little increase in production.

His colleagues in the top party circles came to the conclusion that the schemes of their leader were ill-devised, even harebrained, and they ousted him, but still they were uneasy. They felt the need for reform of Stalin's system, so their revision was made in an effort to strike a balance. They would centralize planning and even some operating direction, but through the use of incentives and a release of enterprise directors from minute direction from above they would create conditions in which they hoped for innovation to meet consumers' demands. In this way they expected to institute the democracy of consumers' choice and break away from the bureaucracy which Tito of Yugoslavia has called the "cancer of socialism."

Discontent with the results of the 1965 reform became apparent in the early 1970's. Centralizers indicated that they thought the industrial enterprises too small to permit managers to exercise individual initiative in innovating while reaping the advantages of economies of scale. As a compromise between bureaucrats in the ministries and high level Communist party generalists, a new program was instituted by the President of the

Council of Ministers, who had chosen to favor the local managers in 1965.

Under the compromise, the smaller enterprises were amalgamated into two types of "combines": industrial and production. In these mergers the smaller enterprises lost their legal independence as public corporations, under which they had been able to control costs and use of income. They became subordinate to the combine's management, which alone enjoyed legal personality, budgetary autonomy, and direct managerial links with ministries.

While experience suggests that administrative structures evolve constantly, the formula currently in use has been stabilized by the 1977 Constitution, whose Article 16 requires maintenance of a balance between centralized planning and managerial direction on one side, and operating independence of managers on the other. The latter are encouraged to devise techniques to stimulate production while cutting costs. Communist party leaders suggest that new vistas have been opened to management by the scientific and managerial revolution.

CHAPTER 8

FOSTERING THE COMMUNITY SPIRIT

The peasants of Russia have always presented the Communist party's leaders with a problem. They have wanted to own their own land, and they have been individualists. The Russian Marxist has felt that the success of his system requires eradication of both desires. Land, together with other productive resources, has to be nationalized, and the community spirit has to be fostered. Some of the early Communists thought it unlikely that the peasant mentality could be changed, therefore the peasants would not make good partners in the revolutionary movement, and plans for revolution should be prepared without peasant participation.

Lenin foresaw the difficulties but felt that victory could be won more easily with peasant participation in the revolutionary movement than without it. He believed that the very poorest peasants, especially those who were hired hands on the farms of the well-to-do peasants, could be relied upon politically to form the farm core of the Communist party. He expected that the middle-class peasants, who owned their own farms but hired no labor, could be neutralized in the revolutionary struggle and eventually won over to the Communist cause. Only the well-to-do peasants, who hired labor, seemed to be beyond the reach of the Communists, and Lenin was prepared to leave them out of his organization and eventually to declare war upon them.

Lenin's view triumphed early in Communist party circles. Peasants were represented at meetings, but they were always considered weak partners. The workmen were expected to carry the burden of the revolution and to be its enthusiasts. The peasants were to provide the mass support in the villages, but were to be subject always to the leadership of the workmen and of those of the educated classes who had thrown in their lot with the revolutionary chiefs.

The peasants of Russia resembled the peasants of Eastern Europe generally, except that they were even less familiar with problems of government on a national scale. Until 1861 they had, in their vast majority, been serfs, tied to the land of the great landowners and sold like slaves for domestic service. They had lived in peasant villages in which the landowners left them to manage their own affairs through their own elders, but they were subject always to the control of the landlord. In cases of serious disorder, the representatives of the Tsarist state entered the scene. After liberation in 1861 by edict of Alexander II, who had come to realize with his advisers that industrial progress and military strength required a free labor market and an army of free men, the peasants were given large portions of land for their own use. The landowners from whom the land was taken were provided compensation by the state, and the peasant communities were bound, as communities, to reimburse the state over a period of forty-nine years for payments made to the landowners.

Although individual peasant families tilled the land, all the families of a community shared in the village government, and some of the village pasture was given over to common use. In this arrangement there were aspects of both individualism and joint operation. It was because of the latter aspect that some of the educated people from the cities who hoped for abolition of the Tsarist system sought to enlist the peasantry in their movement. A Populist party, called the *Narodniks*, was organized in the countryside by intellectuals who went out as schoolteachers, blacksmiths, and in other disguises. The hope of this group was to play upon the long-smoldering hostility of the peasants toward the system from which they had only recently been freed formally and to which they were still bound by the duty to make payments in redemption of the land taken from landowners.

To facilitate their economic battle for existence, the peasants liberated from serfdom fell in with the peasant co-operative movement that was sweeping Europe at the end of the nineteenth century. With the model of Western European co-operatives to guide them, the peasants joined in co-operatives to buy agricultural implements, to disseminate information on new agricultural methods, to market their products, and finally, to finance capital development. In some cases they even formed agricultural co-operative associations to farm the land. These co-operative associations aroused the fear of Tsarist officials, lest they serve as a medium through which the peasants, in pooling their resources, might also evidence collective hostility toward the Tsar's government. In consequence, the co-operatives came under strict regulation by statute, and the consent of provincial governors was required before they might be organized. In spite of these limitations, the co-operative movement thrived, and by the early part of the twentieth century, leagues of the various types of co-operatives had been organized in each province. These leagues were composed of delegates sent forward by the various local co-operatives. The provincial leagues finally formed a national association with its seat in Moscow, thus creating a co-ordinate system with considerable economic strength and some political influence as a pressure group.

To strengthen the Tsar's hand against the mounting community sense of the peasantry, one of his prime ministers, Stolypin, had sought in 1907 to create a strong well-to-do peasant element. His legislation provided that peasants were free to leave their village communes and to divide their family property, and he made available tracts of state land for sale to such peasants. He hoped that through this process the natural individualism of the peasants might be strengthened at the expense of their community spirit, which was being fostered through the need of the peasants to combine to become successful farmers in an age of costly farm implements beyond the reach of a family purse.

Peasants and the Revolution

The early revolutionary events of 1917 brought the peasant into great prominence. Most of the soldiers in the weary Tsarist army were peasants, and they wanted to stop fighting and go home. The countryside had been disrupted by the war to such an extent that food was in short supply. Finally, the continuing peasant demand for complete expropriation of the landowners had been fanned by a slogan of the most popular peasant political party, the Socialist Revolutionary, namely, "socialization of the land." After the abdication of the Tsar in February, 1917, the provisional government sought to meet the peasant demands to the extent that it could. Yet there was strong sentiment in the provisional government for continued support to the allies against the central powers, and this sentiment was so encouraged by the leaders of the allies that no peace could be considered. The only promise that the provisional government could hold out to the peasants was ultimate socialization of the land, but this moved slowly. Many of the participants in the new regime were opposed to this; there was no clear meaning of what the slogan meant, and the country was in such chaos that it would have been difficult to organize distribution in orderly fashion even if there had been a real will to socialize and agreement upon a program. In consequence, nothing was done effectively by the central government, and peasants began to take the law into their own hands.

The bolsheviks seized upon the growing unrest and unfurled their banner of "Peace, Bread, Land." These three catchwords appealed to the peasants, and when the coup d'état was effected in October, 1917, many peasants were prepared to co-operate. But they were not in complete sympathy with the bolshevik platform: peace was wanted as was bread, but the land scheme of the bolsheviks was not acceptable. The left-wing Socialist Revolutionaries, who stayed with the bolsheviks in the Congress of Soviets after the fall of the Winter Palace, wanted all ownership of land, private and state, to be abolished and the use of the land to be passed to those who worked it. This program now seems hard to understand, but to the peasant mind it seems to have been an effort to free him from all restraint. He wanted to be free of state interference in the use of his little family plot. On that small plot of land the peasant wanted to be king, and the party that represented most of the peasants forced Lenin, in drafting his land program, to make a concession on that score. Thus the first land decree did not expropriate all land but only that of the great landowners. It was not until February, 1918, that Lenin felt strong enough to push his program to the limit and declare all land to be state-owned.

Even after the bolsheviks had found themselves strong enough to put into effect their basic idea of state ownership of all land, concessions to the peasantry still had to be made. There was yet the problem of land use. No one had thought out a system of land use that could accord with the Marxist principle of community use of resources. Lenin's colleagues, indicating that their ideas would be best, now fostered as their preferred form of land use the "commune"—a peasant society in which the component peasant families would pool their land and their tools and their cattle and their buildings and use these resources as the group decided in general meetings.

Less communized forms of land use were also offered to the peasantry. A second form would pool land, herds, and heavy agricultural implements but retain private ownership of small tools, houses, and barnyard cattle. This would be called the "artel," and it followed the general pattern of an agricultural co-operative that had found favor with some peasants prior to the Revolution. The third form of land use involved co-operation in the purchase of heavy tools and in planning the use of the land, but everything was privately owned. This was called the "toz."

While the three forms of co-operative use of the land found a good many adherents, especially under the enthusiasm of the moment for communal types of economic activity, the vast majority of the peasants wanted nothing so much as to be left alone. They wanted to have their own plots of land to do with as they pleased. Though the ownership of land had been taken over by the state, the peasants had the use of the land, and to their minds the legal difference between ownership and unmolested use was small. Peasant families had lived on small plots of land for decades since liberation from serfdom, and they had no intention of moving about and buying and selling farms, such as has come to be the custom among American farmers. So long as a peasant family had the unmolested use of a plot of land, it had all that it considered vital. The Communists knew this, as a result of their close study of the peasant mentality, and they were prepared to humor the peasant for a time, even though the goal of community use of the land remained high on the priorities list of the leaders of the Communist party.

A New Soviet System of Land Use

After the civil war of 1919–1920 had been won, and the economic and political life of the country had quieted, the Communist party fostered a new land law. As put into operation in 1922, it set forth policies that had become the rule during the early years of experimentation. It reaffirmed the first rule of the Communists that the land would be state-owned. The use of the land would be distributed to peasants by their local land committees in accordance with the peasants' desires. Peasants might apply for land family by family or as communities. Though the code declared that communities be given preference in the allocation of land use, families could apply singly. In fact, most peasants decided to apply for land by family groups. Many of the existing village communities were broken up in the general swing toward individualism that came in the villages along with the evolution of limited private enterprise in the urban areas, as permitted by what Lenin called a "New Economic Policy" for the restoration of the economy.

To dramatize the rights of the peasantry, the new land law provided that, whether peasants obtained the use of the land on a family or on a community basis, they obtained it in perpetuity. This sounded almost like ownership, for a primary feature of ownership is the right to own in perpetuity. Yet the new Soviet land code revealed its special character by placing limitations upon the use in perpetuity. This right, as allocated by the village soviet's land committee, could not be sold. If a peasant family decided to give up farming and move to the city to work in a factory, it was required to return the land to the village soviet's land committee for reallocation to another family. It could not lease the land or any part of it to another family or to a community, except for short periods of time when members of the family were called into military service, or went to the city to experiment with factory work, or became ill. Moreover, it could not use the land for purposes other than those for which the land had been allocated. In short, it was not to be permitted to stop farming and to build upon the land a slaughterhouse or a sugar-beet refinery. It could not inconvenience the neighbors by committing a nuisance, and it could not use the land in such a way that its agricultural value was impaired.

Since an individual plot was allocated to a family, there was no problem of inheritance so long as the family did not die out entirely. Following long-established peasant custom, there had developed during the Imperial period rules for the passage of land and of other family property from generation to generation within the family, as well as rules for the partition of property in the event that members of the family married out of it or decided to move away. These rules were continued in force by the land code, and the village community was to settle disputes in its customary manner. Only if, as a result of division, the family became too small to work the land was reallocation considered by the land committee of the village soviet.

Stalin continued Lenin's policy of concessions to peasant sentiment on the use of land, but he seems always to have had his eye upon the goal of community use. Foreign students of the subject have thought that Stalin realized that in the peasantry he had the principal source of opposition to his rule and that this opposition was strongest when peasants were organized by families rather than as communities; so he determined to do what he could to bring about the communalizing of land use. If this was his aim, he did not have to lay it bare, because events played into his hands.

Pressures for Collectivization

As urbanization of the U.S.S.R. developed with the increase in industrialization under the first of the five-year plans in the late 1920's, the demand for agricultural products grew in the cities. The fragmentation of the land among millions of small peasant families, brought about by the swing to family use during the period of the New Economic Policy, caused agricultural production to fall. The little farms could not be operated as productively as the large-scale communes or the artels, or, at least, so Stalin could convincingly argue. He decided that the time was ripe to press for communal use. The workmen were crying for more food, and thus he had a sufficient pressure group behind him to support his plan.

In late 1929 a drive for "collectivization of agriculture" was instituted. Stalin chose as the instrument for his purpose not the commune, with its very great communalization of property, nor the "toz," with its minimal communalization, but the "artel." In 1930 his government enacted a model charter for this artel and then required all communities of peasants setting up the new artels to conform to the pattern. The charter set forth in detail the manner in which the government of the artel was to be organized, the rules for membership, and the purposes for which the artel was created. The artel's colloquial name became "kolkhoz," which is a Russian abbreviation for what has been universally translated as "collective farm."

Having established the pattern, Stalin determined to force as many peasants as possible into it. While taking a public position that formation of such collective farms should be voluntary and no family should be required to participate, Stalin allowed his officials at the village level to use violent compulsion in their recruiting tactics. Between January 20 and March 1, 1930, the number of farms was increased from 59,400 to 110,200, and the number of collectivized peasant families, from 4,000,000 to 14,000,000. Obviously no ordinary recruiting program could have produced such results among such hostile people. The violent nature of the compulsion is evident.

Strong opposition to forced collectivization took place in the only manner left open. Many of the peasants felt that in pooling their livestock in the collective-farm herd they were being asked to contribute more than a fair share, and they preferred to slaughter the cattle and sell them. The result was a large drop in livestock herds. Other peasants refused outright to enter the farms.

Stalin saw his mistake and published on March 2, 1930, a much advertised policy directive in which he accused his subordinates of being "dizzy with success" in forcing peasants onto the collective farms. He called for a relaxation of recruitment pressure, but, at the same time, he took means to see that pressure of a different kind continued. He spoke out against those who would not enter the farms, on the ground that they were wealthy peasants trying to wreck the Soviet system. He called them "kulaks," although many of them were not in fact as well-to-do as a kulak was normally supposed to be. Finally, he had his government adopt a law "liquidating the kulaks as a class." This meant adoption of a system of guilt by association. It became unnecessary for a local official to prove in court that an individual peasant had committed a crime in destroying state property or in injuring a state official trying to organize the farms. It was enough that an individual be classed in the ill-defined category of "kulak" to give cause for him to be turned over to the local officials of the Ministry of Internal Affairs for imprisonment in the Siberian hard-labor camps. Foreign experts have estimated that large numbers of peasants were imprisoned in this manner.

Even this pressure, however, was not enough to achieve the purpose of complete collectivization. Stalin therefore seized upon the opportunity of proving his point that the system of individualized farming was inadequate to the needs of the country, when the harvests of 1931 and 1932 proved to be bad in large regions of the southwest and south central parts of the U.S.S.R. Famine conditions prevailed, and over a million peasants are estimated to have died. Foreign observers who lived in the U.S.S.R. at the time felt that food could have been shipped to the famine areas from some of the less arid provinces, but it was not. The conclusion has been reached by some students of Soviet policies that Stalin let the conditions develop into famine so as to teach his lesson that collectivization was necessary to meet the food requirements of the nation. Other students have thought that famine was not planned but was the result of excessive food-collection quotas imposed on the new collective farms.

The Collective-Farm Structure

While using pressures of various kinds, Stalin was not such a fool as to miss opportunities to bring the peasants into the collective farms of their own free will. He made the organizations sound democratic and hence attractive. Under the provisions of the model charter, each farm was to be run by a general meeting of all members. As members entered the farm, they relinquished the use of the plot of land that they had been farming and pooled it with the plots brought in the farm by other members. The peasant families retained, however, private ownership of their peasant homestead, of their small agricultural tools and barnyard animals, of their furniture, clothing, and supplies of food. They were even to be assigned for personal family use a small plot of land, varying with the fertility of the soil, on which they were to be permitted to do what they pleased and from which they might sell the surplus produce in the open market.

The general meeting of the collective farm was to set the general policy for the farm, but the execution of that policy was to be in the hands of an "administration," presided over by a president, which was to be audited in its financial activities by an "auditing commission." All these officials were to be elected, on a democratic basis, although voting was to be by a show of hands rather than by secret ballot. In operation, the voting method enabled the Communist party to introduce a nominee for president to the general meeting and see that he was elected.

In theory, the members of the collective farm were like members of the co-operative agricultural societies of Europe generally. They were co-operating private owners rather than employees of a state institution. This was evidenced primarily by the system under which they were paid for their work. No one, except the bookkeeper and the agricultural expert, who were employed by the farm, received a salary. All others received their compensation in the shape of a share of the farm produce left after taxes had been paid to the state. These taxes took the form of fixed quantities of produce that had to be delivered to the state at the end of each harvest and for which a purchase price was paid.

The reason why the deliveries can be considered taxes is that the price paid by the state was much less than the same goods would have brought if sold in the open markets that the state permitted in all villages and cities.

Decisions on the farm were lent a democratic flavor by making one of them the determination of each member's annual share of the farm surplus. To provide a statistical basis for payment at the end of each season, every job on the farm was rated according to its difficulty. For example, the most difficult was running a gang plow through virgin land; the least difficult was sweeping up in the dairy. The unit of measurement was called a "labor day," and for every full working day, from morning to evening, the labor of a peasant who plowed was rated in units of, let us say, one and three-quarters labor days, while the labor of a sweeper in the dairy was rated in units of three-quarters of a labor day. The bookkeeper would record the number of calendar days actually worked by a member of the farm, this figure would be multiplied by the labor-day equivalent of the calendar day, and the quotient would represent the share in the total produce of the farm, after taxes, to which the individual had a right.

At the end of the season the total number of labor days to which all members had a right would be divided into the total produce of the farm to achieve the "value" of one labor day. At one farm visited during World War II, this value was given as the following: cash, 7.50 rubles; grain, 4.4 pounds; potatoes, 6.6 pounds; cabbage, 6.6 pounds; beets, 2.2 pounds; carrots, 2.2 pounds; other vegetables, 4.4 pounds; and honey, 2 ounces. The "labor day" would then be used as a multiplier in determining the share of each member. Naturally, peasants could not wait until the end of the growing season to eat, and an advance based upon indicated earnings was given them from time to time. In 1956 the system of advances was formalized as routine practice, and some farms began to make guaranteed cash payments without distribution in kind.

Without changing the system of computation a 1966 order required payment of "labor days" at the same rate as farm wages for corresponding work on state farms. Bank loans for up to five-year terms were provided to facilitate payment during periods of lean harvests. The system was heralded as providing security and at the same time incentive to work by demonstrating the relationship between toil and return.

While instituting on the farm what he hoped would be accepted as democratic procedures in decision-making, Stalin was not prepared to permit the process to continue without regard to the interests of the state. In 1933 he expressed the view that while it was the purpose of the collective farm to induce the peasant to accept socialism voluntarily because of its high rate of productivity, the overlaid democratic procedure could not be permitted to function if the farm became unprofitable. If it did, it was the duty of the state, in Stalin's opinion, to step in and assume the direction. This could be done by introducing to the collective, and requiring its election of, a president believed by the experts of the community or of Moscow to be capable of finding the trouble and restoring sound economy on the farm. Many such persons were imposed upon the farmers in the years before the Second World War. Even more were imposed after Stalin's death, in Khrushchev's effort to increase production. In this practice lies one of the great differences between cooperative farming associations in the West and in the U.S.S.R. In the West, the members are left free to ruin themselves if they prove to be incompetent in administration. In the U.S.S.R., the social good, as specified by the Communist party, is used as justification for intervention by the state to prevent the members from suffering because of their incompetency, even if the intervention destroys democratic determination of policy and choice of leaders on the farm.

Further controls over the farms took the form of dictated sowing plans. Each farm was told what it must produce for the state, and until Stalin's death a farm's entire production was dictated in some areas, notably those growing cotton. Only after Stalin's death were rules established under which local authorities were to share in such decisions. Some reasonableness was exhibited, however, even under the system prior to Stalin's death, for example, in a case in which the Moscow authorities had ordered a farm to concentrate on a single breed of cattle. The local farm officials had experimented with this breed in the past, had figures to show that it did not prosper in the northerly latitude at which the farm was located, and were able to support effectively their recommendation that the order be rescinded.

Centralization of Agricultural Controls

After 1930, the collective farms were brought under other important controls. Prior to 1930, the artels provided a channel of co-operation and interchange of information by means of a pattern of relationships similar to that characterizing the co-operative associations before the Revolution, namely, a pattern composed of leagues of artels in each province and a "center" in Moscow. When the state wished to influence the artels, it had to work through the center, which passed down through the provincial leagues to the operating co-operatives the suggestions made by state agricultural experts.

In 1932, the Ministry of Agriculture of the U.S.S.R. was given the task of co-ordinating the collective farms, and the artel system of leagues and center was abolished. The ministry was of a Union-Republic type, so it did not communicate directly with each collective farm. When it wished to institute a program, it communicated the program to the ministries of agriculture in each of the union republics. These, in turn, fanned out the directive to the provincial executive committees. Where it went from the provincial level before reaching the farm varied. Up to the war's end it went to the county soviet, which sent it through the land department of the soviet to each village soviet. By 1950 the counties were bypassing the village soviet with agricultural orders, and in 1953 they in turn were bypassed, for the provincial soviet communicated directly with the machine tractor stations as the administrative channel to the farms. From 1958 to 1961, the county soviet's executive committee was again made the main link between the central apparatus and the farms, but in 1961 a series of changes in administrative organization was initiated, leading to the radical reforms of late 1962.

A major form of control over the collective farms was provided prior to 1958 by the machine tractor stations. Except on a few isolated farms in Siberia, heavy agricultural equipment was kept in tractor parks in which it was maintained by mechanics and from which it went forth each morning in the hands of expert operators. In a country in which mechanical skills were not widely distributed, there was logic in maintaining mechanical agricultural implements in such stations. On this logic the system rested, but it had wide political advantage as well. Since the farms could produce almost nothing without the machines, those who serviced and drove and therefore controlled the use of the machines could, by withholding them, enforce the will of the stations.

The Communist party saw to it that its members were strategically placed in the machine tractor stations, in greater numbers than on the farms themselves. An incipient peasant revolt could be precluded by the strategic distribution of farm machinery, and Stalin is believed to have had this in mind in setting up these stations. In addition, he may have had a reason arising out of his Marxist training. It was Marx's thesis that the ultimate success of his system required the worker and the peasant to be brought closer to each other so that the former's industrial methods and psychological acceptance of collective work would be widely diffused. Through this union of city and village, Marx expected to stamp out the individualistic approach of the peasant.

The machine tractor station represented the first step in the spreading of the industrial communal approach to the farms. Those peasants who were brought into the stations to be trained as mechanics to service or drive the machines could be expected to become shop-minded like their counterparts in the shops of the city factories. Being of the peasantry and in close contact with it, these peasant mechanics were expected to serve as a conduit of industrial attitudes and thus to hasten the day when the peasants think like workmen.

Collective Farm Reform

The year 1958 marked the reorganization of the controls over the collective farms with conversion of the machine tractor stations into repair and technical stations and transfer of the ownership of their farm equipment to the farms. On its face the change was an electrifying restoration of a measure of autonomy to the collective farms, presaging perhaps a return to the system of collective farm leagues abolished in 1932 to provide for the centralized system created by Stalin within the Ministry of Agriculture. On reflection, however, the change might have been anticipated, for the system of controls had changed, making the machine tractor station unnecessary if that was its major function.

Reorganization of the collective farm system had really begun as early as 1950 when Stalin inaugurated a program of amalgamation. Prior to his order each farm coincided in area generally with a traditional peasant village, as it had come down from the pre-revolutionary period of the Empire. Under the system of division of administrative function the farm management conducted the economic life of the village, while the village soviet saw to the political and cultural life. It was the soviet that provided a link with the administrative departments of the county soviet, under whose direction the local school, clinic, store, and fire department were run. Administrative instructions to the collective farm management were funneled through the village soviet on their way down from the Ministry of Agriculture.

The large number of villages throughout the vast expanse of the U.S.S.R. required that there be a large number of collective farms; there were 254,000 farms before 1950. Stalin changed this by ordering farms combined in the interest of agricultural efficiency under modern mechanized conditions. The number of farms fell during 1950 to 123,700 and by the end of 1952 it was 97,000. The number continued to fall, and the size of farms was increased by degrees through mergers. This began a trend which had gone so far by 1978 that only 27,500 farms remained, uniting 13,300,000 peasant households farming 230 million acres. Collective farms had come, even by 1952, to include several villages, and the village soviet lost importance. Some were combined as the farms had been, and the county soviet became the primary link with the administrative mechanism of the Ministry of Agriculture, although even that link was soon replaced by the machine tractor station operating until its abolition under instructions from the provincial soviet.

The amalgamation resulted in the co-operation of farmers who still lived in their own familiar village but who worked together in common fields with relative strangers. More than a thousand families were counted as members of a single farm instead of the fifty or one hundred of earlier times. The general assemblies of a farm became too large for intimate discussion and policy-making. They fell, as do all large groups, to the manipulation of the skilled chairman. The Communist party was strengthened in the countryside, for there was now hardly a farm that did not contain some party members, whereas the smaller farms often had had none. The dictation of elections of chairmen and executive boards was thus facilitated, and the party provided the candidates from its own ranks of skilled agronomist-administrators.

Confidence in the administration of the newly amalgamated farms was evidenced in an order signed jointly by the Central Committee of the Communist party and the Council of Ministers of the U.S.S.R. in March, 1956, authorizing farms to depart from the rigid provisions of the Model Charter of 1935 governing farm organization. Each farm might now amend the charter to meet its own concrete problems, and specifically might alter the amount of land permitted for the private use of each peasant household. The size of such garden plots had been rigidly set in the older charter. The government indicated by the reform that it no longer feared that farmers would arrogate to private enterprise large parts of the farm, and practice showed that the zealous chairmen were prepared to move too far in the other direction. Some got their general assemblies of members to eliminate private plots, thus causing such discontent that an order had to be issued to proceed more slowly.

Chairmen of the new amalgamated collective farms began to argue in the press that the machine tractor stations were impeding efficiency and duplicating what the farm could now do for itself. There was no longer need to put machines in a depot from which they could go forth on successive days to various farms. Their entire work was now for a single farm. No chairman suggested that the machine tractor stations were no longer necessary as instruments of political control, but that was the implication of the argument centered upon efficiency alone.

What the chairmen did not say about politics, the Communist party was soon to add. Following a resolution of the party's Central Committee issued on February 28, 1958, Khrushchev declared that while the machine tractor station had previously been necessary as the state's instrument of leadership, the state could now exercise a direct effect upon the farms through the supply of machinery. In short, control could be exercised with the help of farm management alone. Efficiency needed to be the only consideration, and that dictated ownership by the farms. The task remained only of transferring the machines to farm administrations and arranging for payment, on credit terms where needed.

The machine tractor stations were abolished by a law of March 31, 1958, but the desired results were not obtained. Experimentation was again initiated. Repair tractor stations, created in 1958 with the mechanics formerly employed by the machine tractor stations and given the task of servicing the agricultural machines of the collective farms, proved a failure. A new organization called The All-Union Farm Machinery Association was formed in early 1961 to procure machinery for both collective and state farms and to service it through its own county machinery associations. Representatives of the farms were placed on its boards of directors.

The Ministry of Agriculture was completely changed in function at the same time. Its activities were reduced to guidance of experiment stations and training of personnel. It was no longer the supreme pinnacle of the entire agricultural administrative structure. No single agency was established to assume these functions until March, 1962, when an All-Union Committee of Agriculture was formed in the Council of Ministers of the U.S.S.R. charged with the duty of co-ordinating agricultural plans with the nation's requirements and of assuring performance of party and state directives.

The chain of command of the new All-Union Committee ran through committees established in each republic's Council of Ministers to the provincial level, where a committee under the chairmanship of the Communist party's first secretary for the province was formed. At the bottom of the administrative pyramid a "territorial production administration" was organized. This combined what had been the agricultural responsibility of several county agricultural executive departments, thus eliminating county government entirely from the chain of command. Collective and state farms in the district over which the new administrations exercised control received their plans and orders from the new agency.

Khrushchev indicated his annoyance with both the party and soviet authorities at the county level for their lack of skill in handling agricultural affairs, and therein lay the reason for the change. The small counties were accused not only of being too small for efficient direction of agriculture, but the personnel available at this level was declared inadequate for the complex problems of modern mechanized agriculture.

Khrushchev's annoyance bore further fruit, for in November, 1962, the boundaries of the county soviets and their associated county party committees were redrawn to correspond in size with the areas placed under the territorial production administrations eight months earlier.

Khrushchev's administrative structure was upset within a year after his ouster. The Ministry of Agriculture was restored to its traditional role of planner, financier, and supervisor of all farms—both collective and state. The grass-roots supervisor was the county production agricultural administration. A new collective farm charter, adopted in 1969, provided a framework of organization for the large amalgamated farms; a representative assembly replacing the now unwieldy general meeting; an extension of the executive committee's term from two to three years; a substitution of a secret ballot for a show of hands to select the president and committee members; the introduction of a guaranteed wage and pension system; and the placement of increasing restraints on the size of household plots.

More surprisingly, at the same time "unions" or "leagues" of collective farms were reinstituted at every administrative level of the state. None had existed since 1932, when they had been replaced by the Ministry of Agriculture's chain of command. Although the new "unions" were at first only agencies of recommendation and were strictly controlled by the requirement that Ministry of Agriculture officials preside at all levels, by 1971 a model charter stabilized their role, and in 1973 in the Moldavian Republic, as an experiment, the Ministry of Agriculture was replaced by the "union" as planner and economic manager of farms. Ministry officials still presided, but a body probably more responsive to farmers' desires was emerging. Clearly, the farm problem continued.

The State Farm Becomes Favored

Since the Revolution there has existed alongside the collective farm a different type of agricultural unit, known as the "sovkhoz," or state farm. Such farms have been primarily experiment stations and demonstration farms and, more recently, farms raising specialized crops. The sovkhoz is a form of agricultural factory operating under the same laws as industrial enterprises, and the farmers within it are employed at a wage rather than given shares of the annual farm produce as are members of a cooperative association. The management is not elected, even nominally, by the farmers themselves, but has been appointed by the Ministry of Agriculture of the U.S.S.R. in the same fashion that managers of steel mills are appointed by the ministry in charge of steel mills.

Communist party leaders seem to have a predilection for the state farm as the farm of the future. After Stalin's death, his severe restraints upon the collective farms were reduced as a concession to the peasants, but the new leaders indicated that wherever they were not hampered by old customs they would introduce the state farm rather than the collective farm. Their opportunity came in developing a program for expanding agriculture in the fringe lands of the country, known as "virgin lands."

In these territories, where no form of agriculture had been conducted before, there was no old-fashioned opinionated peasantry with which to deal. Great numbers of Soviet youths were organized by the Komsomols to move to these regions to begin farming, and most of these came from cities to work under agricultural specialists provided by the agricultural schools.

Most of the agricultural units operating in the "virgin lands" are state farms rather than collective farms. Even in European areas of the U.S.S.R. state farms are absorbing collective farms, especially in regions close to large cities where market gardens prevail. Forty-seven per cent of the vegetables and 43 per cent of the grain produced by the state in 1960 came from state farms. In late 1962 there were 8,571 state farms which represented nearly double the number of 1953, and these employed 6,860,000 persons.

At the end of 1965 a new program was introduced without fanfare, one calling for quicker transition from collective farming to state farming as well as movement of farmers away from the traditional village into modernized agricultural towns. On Khrushchev's ouster in 1964 both programs, which had been dear to his heart, and had even been outlined in 1952 by Stalin as the desirable agricultural structure of the future, were halted by the Central Committee of the Communist party. Apparently the party's leaders feared peasant resistance and thought a tactical retreat necessary. The retreat ended in 1965. Transformations were rapid: by 1970 there were 14,944 farms, and by 1976, 19,639, employing nearly 11 million persons farming 278 million acres, devoted largely to grains, dairy and beef cattle, sheep, goats, and pigs.

The transfer of populations from the small villages had been proceeding since 1953 at so fast a rate that a study of one farm showed departures from 119 out of 164 farm families of all able-bodied members by 1965. In addition, planned transfers were to be speeded. Kyril Tidmarsh of *The Times* of London reported interviews held just prior to the fiftieth anniversary indicating that 580,000 rural settlements out of the total of 700,000 had already been marked for eventual extinction with transfer of their inhabitants to new, modernized agricultural towns. All new building in the condemned villages is currently forbidden, and permits withheld even for adding a room or heating facilities.

The Future of Agricultural Management

Article 12 of the 1977 U.S.S.R. Constitution promises continuing promotion of collective farms, but its third paragraph declares that co-operative property is "to approximate state property." In a few words this restates the 1961 Communist party program's forecast, which read, "Life itself has been bringing public and co-operative forms of ownership closer together and will ultimately lead to the establishment of a single, communist form of ownership and a single communist principle of distribution."

Statistics cited above suggest that the state farm structure is fast overtaking the collective farms, both in area farmed and in numbers of farmers engaged. Also, the transition to guaranteed wages, old age pensions, and increasingly distant association with management as farms expand in size, indicates approximation to state farm conditions. Further, many collective farmers have moved from their cottages to farming towns with small scale apartments and distant private plots on the edge of town. The difference between farmers in the two types of farms is now primarily a legal formality.

While the alternative to collective farming for most of the countryside remains state farming, a new experiment is being introduced, primarily in the Moldavian Republic. It is built around a new institution, called an inter-farm agro-industrial organization or association, created by collective farms, state farms, and local state enterprises to conduct specialized farming. It engages in cattle fattening, ownership and maintenance of farm machinery, chicken raising, fruit orchards and canning factories, and large scale fish production. These entities numbered 3,355 in 1965, and by 1976 they had more than doubled. They function as public corporations under a charter, their 104,085 shareowners being the farms and industrial enterprises that created them.

Structurally, the new entities are directed by a board, chosen by the shareholders, to which their managers are responsible. Thus, they are outside the traditional chain of command from the Ministry of Agriculture through the provincial soviets' executive committees. They bring together farms and industries subject to various ministries whose policies are no longer mandatory, and thus need reconciliation by the new board meetings. In Moldavia, because the collective farms were already in an experimental structure under which the collective farm "unions" had assumed administrative direction from the Ministry of Agriculture, the new entities are farther from the reach of the central ministerial bureaucracies than at any time since abolition of the former collective farm "unions" in 1932.

Soviet commentators show themselves puzzled as to how these entities will function and what impact they will have on farming. One reporter has stated that in Moldavia some collective farm chairmen are figuratively packing their bags because they expect their farms soon to be absorbed. They have transferred their machinery, their beef cattle, their fruit orchards, their chicken sheds, and their fish hatcheries out of the collective. The old-fashioned farm, raising a little bit of everything, is yielding to highly specialized inter-farm associations, who draw away the most skilled specialists from the collectives. This leaves the collective farms specializing in large-scale market gardening and intensive agriculture, which produce high yields.

In a sense the remaining collective farmers will now perform on the common lands, in much expanded form and with machines, the intensive agriculture they have been conducting successfully on their private garden plots. They are even to be permitted to draw on the grain supplies of the inter-farm entities to feed their private livestock so as to increase the national meat supply. In short, the giant activities of the collective farms are now in other hands, and the farmers today, in Moldavia at least, are to be engaged in the production of vegetables, specialized meat products, dairy specialties, honey, and milk products.

The experiment in a transition from collective farms to this new form of state property has been limited largely to Moldavia. There are few inter-farm entities elsewhere. Perhaps Moldavia has been chosen because its Communist party is known for successful innovation, or because its farming conditions are superior. With its expansion of the authority of collective farm "unions" and its development of inter-farm entities, it is leading the way to what may become a nation-wide agricultural revolution as profound as that of 1930, when Stalin suppressed the private farms of peasant families and drove the peasants into collective farms.

CHAPTER 9

STATE INTERVENTION IN PRIVATE AFFAIRS

Democratic currents of thought, awakened by the American and French revolutions, developed in the nineteenth-century West the concept of a minimum of state intervention in private affairs. The state was to be separated from the church, so that citizens might be free to worship as they pleased. Those laws that had to do with property and with family relationships were placed in a separate category called "private," to indicate that the state had only the instrumental function of regulating and enforcing private agreements. The state was not to utilize family and property law to achieve political ends. The spirit of the era was exemplified by the statement, "He governs best who governs least."

Marx set out to undermine this attitude in his *Communist Manifesto* of 1848. He began by attacking the society in which he lived, the society of Western Europe. He tried to show that the state was not really leaving its citizens alone. He argued that the nineteenth-century western state was the creature of that minority of its citizens who benefited most from a laissez faire policy because it left them free to exploit private property and to make profits. In short, to Marx the very absence of laws and of state intervention in private matters constituted a policy advantageous to a ruling class. Marx argued that the state was not democratic in its non-intervention because it left the economic stage free to a very small group of capitalists. He called for a state that would intervene in economic and social relationships for the benefit of the masses, and this he believed to be necessary to achieve democracy in the sense of government for the great mass of the people.

The Russian revolutionaries seized upon this principle of Marxism. They began to intervene very soon in what had been private matters of citizens. Lenin expressed the idea succinctly, when he told a friend in 1922 that all law must be considered public. He saw no possibility of developing the type of society he envisaged unless the state used every relationship, even those between citizens, to its advantage.

Controls on Religious Practices

Religion offered Lenin his greatest problem in social reorganization. He inherited Marx's view on the subject. Marx had opposed religious belief as unscientific because it could not be proved in a laboratory that there was a God. Since his interpretation of historical evolution rested upon his claim that he had found the motivating force of social development in discernible factors such as the invention of tools of production and the changing ownership of such tools, he could not accept the thought that a divine force influenced social development. It would have upset his theory and the argument for revolution which he was making. There are those who now suggest that Marx would not have been so hostile toward religion if he had not faced a practical problem presented by religious institutions.

The practical problem Marx faced when he considered religion was that the church of the nineteenth century was both very powerful in much of the West and certain to oppose him. Over the centuries it had been accustomed to associate itself with the status quo, and Marx conceived of it as a very strong instrument for preserving the structure of nineteenth-century society against which he was issuing a call to arms. Because of this fact, he opposed the institution of the church bitterly. The Russian revolutionaries had more cause than Marx to look upon the church similarly as a barrier to the success of their plans. The Russian Orthodox Church, to which the great bulk of the Russians and Ukrainians belonged, was favored as a state church under the Tsar's regime; its resources were provided in part from the state treasury; its large landholdings were protected by Tsarist laws; its bishops were named with the consent of the Tsar; and, on occasion, its priests were required to report on the political activities of members of their congregations. To oppose the Tsar often meant to oppose the church as well, and revolutionaries had difficulty, consequently, in winning converts among those who were religious and who accepted the discipline of the church.

While recognizing that hostility was to be expected from the Russian Orthodox Church and, in a measure, from the Moslems, the Jews, and the Christian denominations with fewer communicants, Lenin could not overlook the potential danger to his regime if he aroused fanatic hostility on the part of those who were religious. Russian history had been dotted with incidents of fanatic opposition to state authority from religious groups. No leader could attack the church, or religion generally, without risking ultimate otherthrow. Lenin approached the matter cautiously.

The core group of the Communist party was small and disciplined. Within this group Lenin could, and probably had to, enforce the rule of the Communist party program that no member of the Communist party could profess religious belief. To make certain that his colleagues in the party did not limit themselves to lip service, Lenin's organization carried out a vigorous program of antireligious propaganda on the theme that religion was not scientific and that the church, its handmaiden, was a threat to the success of the Communists' program.

For the general public, no such dogmatic approach was possible, for violent hostility toward such an approach could be expected. The article on religion in Lenin's first bill of rights in the Russian Constitution of 1918 guaranteed to all the right of freedom of conscience, yet it placed the official attitude of atheism on record by guaranteeing freedom of antireligious propaganda though also the right to propagate religion. The constitution's article on religion, like the others having to do with freedom of speech and of press, was limited by the general prohibition against assertion of any right to the detriment of the program of socialism; thus it was not an absolute guarantee of noninterference, such as that in the First Amendment to the Constitution of the United States.

Separation of Church and State

To indicate that the Orthodox Church had lost its position as a state church, the 1918 constitution declared the separation of church and state. This made necessary an immediate change in the mode of keeping vital statistics and of performing marriage ceremonies and the granting of divorces. Under the Russian Imperial laws, the various religious communities had maintained the records on birth, marriage, divorce, and death. There had been no records office in a city hall run by the state, as there is everywhere in the United States. But the early Soviet laws created a state registration bureau at which all were required to register events having to do with status and vital statistics. Soviet citizens might still register births in church, but such registration had no probative value. There had to be registration also in the state bureau.

Marriages, under the first Soviet decree on the subject, might still be solemnized in church, but the parties had also to declare their intent in a civil marriage ceremony and to register in the state bureau. The ecclesiastical courts to which the Tsar had delegated sole jurisdiction over divorce were abolished. Divorces were thrown into the newly created peoples' courts, to be handled on the basis of a state law uniform for all.

The new state laws relating to vital statistics and family relationships sought to remove the necessity of going to church to contract or register these basic relationships. In this way the Communists hoped to wean the people from the church by reducing the opportunities of the priests to see citizens. The move toward secular control of marriage and divorce was revolutionary in Russia, although it had long before been completed in Western lands, where the state maintains the records of vital statistics and requires licenses for marriage. Western states even require that marriage be solemnized by a state civil servant or by a religious dignitary authorized by the state to perform marriages and thus given the status of a state official. In some Western democracies, ecclesiastical courts still pass upon the marital status of the faithful, but generally no divorce or annulment is recognized by the state unless there has also been a state divorce or unless the ecclesiastical court is given the sanction of the state to grant divorce.

Lenin's steps separating church from state were cautious. They went very little beyond what had been accepted in Western democracies years before the Russian Revolution. His other step touched a subject which he believed to be of greater importance, and it aroused more hostility. He deprived the church of its property. While churches were permitted to collect funds from parishioners, they could no longer own land and receive rents, nor could they own their buildings and the vestments and sacramental vessels necessary to the performance of religious rites.

The use of the nationalized church buildings and sacramental vestments and vessels was allocated to religious groups for the purpose of religious services, but ownership remained with the state. Under this arrangement, the state could withdraw use at its pleasure. To hamper the church further, religious communities were no longer permitted the status of a juristic person or corporation. The church building and its contents were allocated to the congregation as a partnership composed of the elders of the community. This legal form established personal responsibility for preservation of the property. Since this property was now state property, local soviets, as guardians of the state's interests, were authorized to close a church at any time in deference to the wishes of the toilers, as these wishes might be determined by the local soviet.

Local soviets were protected at the same time from expected attempts by priests and monks to influence them. This was done by depriving clerics of the right to vote in elections for the soviet or to be elected to any state office. In practice, local soviets very often decided to pre-empt the church building in a village from the elders and to turn it into a grain-storage warehouse or local club.

Forbidding Religious Education

Religious education has always been thought by believers to be essential to real freedom of religion, for without the right to propagate the faith the religious community must die out. The Mass or morning prayer has been found insufficient to win converts or to hold the allegiance of children of religious believers. Experience has shown that there must be religious instruction, as well as freedom of worship, to make meaningful a guarantee of religious freedom. The bolsheviks seem to have realized this fact, for in 1921 they put a stop to religious education of persons under eighteen years of age. The criminal code forbade the teaching of religious beliefs to children in public or private schools, which, in effect, prevented the establishment of parochial schools. Another article forbade the collection of a tax for the benefit of the church. A third forbade the conduct of ecclesiastical courts and the assumption by them of administrative functions, presumably the keeping of vital statistics for other than church purposes. Still another article forbade the exercise of religious ceremonies or the placing of religious emblems in state institutions or in places such as trade-union or co-operative-association offices.

The narrowing of the right to teach religion found its way into an amendment to the Russian Republic's bill of rights in 1929, when the right to religious propaganda was removed while the right to antireligious propaganda was allowed to remain. The amendment was soon copied by the Ukrainian, Turkmen, and Uzbek republics and was made a part of the U.S.S.R. constitution in 1936. It was repeated in substance as Article 52 in the 1977 Constitution, which reads, "Citizens of the U.S.S.R. are guaranteed freedom of conscience, that is, the right to profess or not to profess any religion, and to conduct religious worship or atheistic propaganda."

To carry out this guarantee, an article was inserted into the criminal code to make it a crime to interfere in the performance of a religious service, but a loophole was provided in that the article makes intervention a crime only if the service does not violate the public order and does not encroach upon the rights of citizens. The concept of public order has been broad in all European countries, and particularly so in the U.S.S.R., so that the article provides a basis only for punishing a hoodlum who breaks into a church and commits an indignity at a time not deemed wise by the state officials. The article suggests that the problem of quieting the religious people of the U.S.S.R. has been found to be a difficult one. The leaders of the U.S.S.R. apparently wish to keep in their own hands decisions as to when interference shall be encouraged and to prevent overly zealous individuals from pressing antireligious acts at the wrong times or in an undesirable manner.

The conflict between religious communities and state officials during the late 1920's and early 1930's is well illustrated by some of the judicial decisions of the times. A group of elderly peasants who caused a riot in attempting to prevent the arrest of their priest were sentenced for "mass disorder accompanied by pogrom." Their sentences were commuted by a higher court, however, on the ground that most of the peasants were old, all were working and came from poor and middle-class groups, all were ignorant, and no serious consequences resulted from what they had done. Yet, when a peasant conducted religious meetings in his home, preaching that collectivization of agriculture was an invention of the devil and that any peasant who entered a collective farm would suffer in purgatory, he was convicted of crime.

The Effectiveness of Soviet Antireligious Measures

The effectiveness of the Communists' efforts to reduce religious belief in the period prior to World War II may be gauged from interviews conducted by a research team sent by Harvard University to European camps after the war. The camps contained persons who had fled the Soviet Union or who had refused to return to it after wartime servitude to the Germans. After studying the replies and the possibility that they were not truthful, the scholars have concluded that the replies can be trusted as reliable indications of family attitudes in the U.S.S.R. in the 1930's, which was the time most of the informants left their homes.

To determine the effectiveness of the antireligious campaigns among Soviet citizens, the informants were first placed in three age groups: those under thirty-five years of age, who had been born under the Soviet regime; those between thirty-six and forty-five, who had straddled the two eras, since they were in their teens at the time of the Revolution; and those over forty-five, whose habits and beliefs had been formed during the Tsarist period. In appreciation of the fact that before the Revolution the peasants had always been predominantly religious while the educated class had included many who scoffed at religion, the three age groups of informants were again split into two groups: those who came from worker-peasant stock and those who came from white-collar and educated families.

The report on the interviews indicates the following: in the worker-peasant group, persons over forty-five numbered no "atheists" or "agnostics" but fell only into the classes of "mildly religious" or "deeply religious." Fifty-three per cent claimed to be mildly religious, while 47 per cent claimed to be deeply religious, although their deep religious feeling might be manifested by prayer at home rather than by attendance at church. Of the middle group, aged thirty-six to forty-five, there were 3 per cent atheists, no agnostics, 71 per cent mildly religious, and 26 per cent deeply religious. In the youngest group, which had been reared under the Soviet regime's influence, there were 14 per cent atheists, 2 per cent agnostics, 62 per cent mildly religious, and only 22 per cent deeply religious.

The white-collar and educated group showed even greater in-roads of atheism. The group over forty-five years of age reported 6 per cent atheists, 6 per cent agnostics, 65 per cent mildly religious, and 23 per cent deeply religious. The middle group, of ages thirty-six to forty-five, showed greater response to Soviet propaganda, for 9 per cent were atheists, 15 per cent agnostics, 56 per cent mildly religious, and only 20 per cent deeply religious. The greatest effect of Soviet propaganda was found among those under thirty-five, in which category 16 per cent reported an atheist position, 11 per cent agnostic, 51 per cent mildly religious, and 22 per cent deeply religious.

The interviewers concluded that the over-all generational trend among workers and peasants has been away from the traditional "deeply religious" position toward a "mildly religious" orientation, with a total religious rejection appearing only among those who were both born and reared during the Soviet era. The conclusion on the white-collar and educated group was that the over-all trend during the Soviet era has been away from a "mildly religious" orientation toward a more complete rejection of religion.

Relaxation of Controls during World War II

The instability caused by World War II forced upon the leaders of the Soviet state the adoption of a less militant antireligious policy. In the face of threatened national disaster, the Russian Orthodox Church modified its attitude of hostility toward Stalin's regime and called upon its communicants to defend "Russia" and to contribute to the fund-raising campaigns to pay for the war. Priests fought with the armies, and the campaign funds swelled. Stalin grasped at this opportunity to strengthen his political cause at a time when military defeat was close. He relaxed his campaign against the church and against religious belief. The League of Militant Godless in which he had enlisted those prepared to fight religion, and in which 3,500,000 persons were listed as actual members in January, 1941, ceased to function. Although it was never formally abolished, the league ceased to publish periodicals in the autumn of 1941, within three months after the German attack on the Soviet frontiers began. In 1944, the government consented to the restoration of organized religious instruction for those who wished to enter the priesthood, and parents were permitted to give their children to the priest for religious training, although not in schools.

In October, 1943, a Council for Affairs of the Orthodox Church was established within the Council of Ministers, to be followed soon after by establishment of a similar council for all the other religions, including the Moslems and the Jews. These two councils provided the first formal channel through which religious communities of the Soviet Union could present their grievances and difficulties to state officials and to seek redress. In the same year the Orthodox Church was also permitted to call an assembly of bishops to elect a patriarch and to form a Holy Synod to serve under him. The church was even allowed to publish a periodical for the first time since 1929.

In spite of the relaxation of pressure on the church during the war, there was a later return to many of the old positions, if not to the old fervor. During the war period, the Komsomols had been infiltrated, apparently, by persons holding religious beliefs, for after the war a question was raised in the Komsomol journal about religious members. The answer given was that no religious youths should be permitted to remain in the Komsomols or permitted to join. The organization was not to retain such persons while efforts were made to change their minds. Persons being trained in the Komsomols for Communist party membership when they reached maturity could not be permitted to hold religious beliefs.

While the League of Militant Godless was not revived, there was created in 1949 the Society for the Dissemination of Scientific and Political Knowledge, which preached the doctrine that religion and science are incompatible and that youth must be informed of this fact. Museums attempting to prove this incompatibility were opened, as they had been prior to the war, and frequent excursions to them by school children became the rule.

In spite of these efforts, manifestations of religious conviction linger on. Two reports indicate the situation. A 1966 study by the Orel Pedagogical Institute established that 36% of those questioned on three collective farms were believers. A more detailed analysis by the Moscow University Sociology Laboratory revealed comparable figures in a study of a Ukrainian village in which 51% were collective farmers and the rest were divided between workers in a lime plant, civil servants, school teachers, and white collar workers in the stores and service institutions. The Moscow investigators looked for religious icons hanging in the homes and discovered the following distribution: 21% of the families whose heads were employed as civil servants had icons; 34% of the families of white collar employees had icons, and 47% of the families of collective farmers had icons.

The Moscow study, based on 1964 figures, sought to correlate icons with age and education. In the age distribution, 60% of the pensioners and 75% of the retired collective farmers had icons. In the education sequence the families where heads were engaged in predominantly mental skilled labor had icons in only 7% of the cases; in families where the heads were slightly skilled mental workers the rate rose to 24%; in families where heads were engaged in skilled physical labor 34% had icons, and in the families of unskilled physical laborers the rate was 57%.

Because of findings such as these the Communist party has intensified its atheist indoctrination campaigns, setting up in the Ukraine and Byelorussia what are called "schools of elementary knowledge" designed to teach materialism to elderly people of low levels of education. The lessons are also taken into their homes by what is called the "Knowledge Society." Among children atheism is stressed, but not adequately, in the party's view, for the Ministry of Higher and Specialized Secondary Education was accused in 1967 of showing little concern for such study in the key schools of pedagogy, agriculture, and medicine whose graduates will have close association with peasants.

The campaign has left voids, as indicated by a meeting of Soviet philosophers in 1967 who indicated that their atheistic studies were being accompanied by examination of problems of ethics and humanitarianism. Evidently, these qualities, which accompany religion, are being lost, and a new base of inspiration must be sought if social relationships are not to degenerate.

State opposition to religious institutions is currently most noticeable in the attitude toward Roman Catholics and Jews, although the trend in each case is different. For the Catholics there is less tension, probably because the Vatican has chosen to depart in the 1970's from its long-standing show of hostility toward Communists in an effort to eliminate the obstacles placed in the way of worship by the Lithuanians and Poles who were brought within the U.S.S.R. following the territorial adjustments made after World War II. The Soviet Foreign Minister has visited the Vatican to indicate symbolically the Soviet government's policy of peaceful coexistence, albeit with ideological struggle. Although exchange of clerics, increasingly common between the Russian Orthodox Church and Protestant denominations abroad, has not occurred with the Roman Catholic Church, except in the case of Papal investitures, relations seem calmer than in earlier years.

With members of the Jewish community in the U.S.S.R. the trend has been different. Although Communists were as hostile toward the Jewish faith as toward all other faiths during the 1920's, the policy of fostering minority cultures was extended to the Jewish secular community. A Yiddish theater was authorized and subsidized. Yiddish newspapers and books were printed. A Jewish ethnic territory was created in the Far East and immigration invited, although it was never heavy. But the policy of cultural support began to change during Stalin's era of purges in the late 1930's when he indicated distrust of Jews, ostensibly because many had relatives abroad, and he feared foreign penetration through them. Following the war, Israel's diplomats were received, but came to be treated as if they were agents of an enemy power. Diplomatic relations were severed finally as Soviet policy upheld the Arab side in Middle East conflicts. Harassment of Jews was intensified, resulting in protests and demonstrations. Arrests and imprisonments followed. Those wishing to emigrate to Israel were hampered by onerous bureaucratic procedures and discriminatory exit taxes. Currently no ethnic group is more disfavored in Soviet society and no religion more harassed, unless it is the traditional militant minority Christian cults who for centuries have resisted state restraint upon their practices.

Controls over the Family

The immediate Soviet attack upon the influence of the church, exerted through the monopoly granted to religious institutions by the Tsar to keep vital statistics and to marry and divorce citizens, was interpreted by some Soviet authors in the early years as an indication that in family relationships the state was going to refrain from intervention. It was even argued that in this sphere of private affairs there should be no state intervention at all, except for the maintenance of statistics and records. People were to be permitted to marry as they wished, to beget children without responsibility or social disapproval in the absence of marriage, and to consider themselves divorced when they found themselves incompatible. Some even argued that the family as an institution was no longer necessary in Soviet society.

Lenin seems always to have opposed such sexual freedom in

principle, although his political instinct persuaded him to give rein to such an approach, at least so long as the family remained the inculcator of attitudes that he associated with the old regime. He considered the mothers and fathers reared prior to the Revolution to be dangerous to his program. They taught their children religious faith, respect for the status quo, and a feeling that the days of the past provided much that should be preserved. Lenin could change the schools and separate the church from the state, but he had a very hard time entering the home. His only hope for changing social attitudes normally developed in the home was to split the family asunder.

Lenin's policies took form in encouragement to children to report on the anti-Communist teaching of their parents, to reduce parental disciplinary authority, to eliminate all but health restrictions on marriage, and to do away with all restraints on divorce. By 1927, the court was removed from the procedure required to obtain a divorce; the parties, or even one of them, could report their desire to be recorded as divorced to a state registration bureau, and the divorce became valid when the entry was made. A new family code permitted parties to marry without the necessity of recording the marriage in a bureau. In 1929, the court recognized a factual separation as a divorce, without the prior necessity of recording it. When after this change of rule it became necessary to determine for inheritance reasons whether marriage had existed, a court heard evidence on the relationship of the parties and declared that a man or woman was considered to have been married or divorced at the time of death regardless of the state of the official record.

Social attitudes changed slowly in spite of these measures. Evidence of this fact is found in a 1935 judicial decision by a Siberian court where a mother had been indicted for the murder of her new-born child. It was proved in her defense that she had not been married and that the child's father had deserted her. Her lawyer rested her defense upon old social attitudes. He pointed out that her baby had brought great social opprobrium upon her from her family. If the lawyer's statement was true, it meant that pre-revolutionary social attitudes were persisting nearly twenty years after the Revolution. As might have been expected, the court turned a deaf ear, saying that such social attitudes had been discouraged and could not mitigate the mother's crime; yet the penalty was withheld because of the mother's poor health.

The mid-1930's brought a radical change in state attitude toward the family, for intervention of the state in all family relationships was restored. Contemporary authors indicated that new reasons of social concern were responsible for the new approach. Fathers of children born out of wedlock were deserting their offspring and leaving them penniless. The state was not in a position to care for them. In fact, statistics of the time show that children reared without the influence of a home tended to become juvenile delinquents more frequently than those with a home environment.

Measures were taken in 1936 to discourage divorce. Parents were permitted to register as divorced only when both parties had had a chance to appear and to settle the care of the child. Fees for such registration were graduated from 50 to 300 rubles, and each successive divorce cost more. Parental discipline was strengthened, because parents were fined if their child was rowdy in the streets and were responsible in a civil suit for any damage caused.

The problem of homeless children was accentuated during the war, and a divorce law of 1944 went much further in coping with the broken home than the measures taken in the mid-1930's. The law now required that parties wishing a divorce go before a court as they had not had to do since the first years of the Soviet regime. A desire for divorce was no longer to be sufficient reason for granting the divorce. The court was required to make every effort to reconcile the parties, and it was not permitted to grant a divorce even if its effort failed. Only the next higher court was to have jurisdiction for this purpose.

No grounds for divorce were provided in the 1944 law. The second court, the one having authority to grant divorce, was required to summon both parties and to hear witnesses on the cause of the quarrel. It was then instructed to deny a divorce if it thought that there was, or ought to be, a reconciliation. Only if the home had been irrevocably broken should the divorce be granted. As with other laws that contain no precise definition of the circumstances in which they should be applied, the courts have had to develop their own rules.

Published judicial decisions indicate that what might be called a common law of divorce emerged. No divorce was granted solely because both parties desired it, or because a husband infatuated by another woman abandoned his wife, or because a husband was absent in the army or fought with his wife's relatives. Finally, in 1949 the Supreme Court ordered lower courts to grant divorce only if convinced that the application rested on deeply considered and well-founded reasons and that continuation of the marriage would conflict with the principles of Communist morals in preventing the conditions necessary to family life and the rearing of children.

The 1944 law also sought to discourage divorce by increasing fees over those charged in 1936, setting them from 500 to 2,000 old rubles, the exact sum to be decided by the court. At the same time the law seemed to foster births out of wedlock, for it relieved a father from a duty to support his illegitimate child and denied the child the surname of the father. Support of such children became the responsibility of the state.

Opposition to restraints on divorce forced a change in the law in 1968. Parties mutually desiring termination of marriage were authorized to apply to the Civil Registry Office, which could, after an attempt at reconciliation, issue a certificate without a court hearing, unless there was a dispute over custody or support of children, the distribution of marital property, or the termination itself. In such cases a court decree had to precede registration. Fees were continued at existing rates. Children born out of wedlock were given new rights: the right to registration of paternity, to the father's surname and patronymic, and to paternal support, if both parties agreed to registration. In the event of paternal resistance, the mother had a right to obtain a court hearing and determination of parentage.

Changes in Family Attitudes

The extent to which the policies of the 1920's and early 1930's influenced the thinking of Soviet citizens on the family is indicated in answers to questions directed at the same group of Soviet refugees as were interviewed by American scholars in connection with religious attitudes. The interviewers sought to determine whether Soviet parents felt that there were values that must be instilled in their children by authoritarian techniques, within the family circle if need be. As with the answers to the questions on religion, the answers on this point were classified according to age and according to worker-peasant or white-collar-intellectual stock. The results were as follows.

In the peasant-worker group, those under thirty-five who would be willing to be authoritarian in instilling in their children treasured values were only 1 per cent of those interviewed in this age group; those between thirty-six and forty-five who would use authoritarian methods were 37 per cent of those interviewed in the age group; those over forty-five who would use authoritarian methods were 48 per cent of those interviewed in the age group. In the white-collar-intellectual group, there was less variation for each age category, those under thirty-five who were prepared to be authoritarian constituting 22 per cent of those interviewed in this group, those between thirty-six and forty-five constituting 27 per cent of those interviewed in this group, and those over forty-five constituting 21 per cent of those interviewed in this group. The other parents in the main preferred to use extensively democratic, or mainly democratic, measures in persuading their children to accept their value schemes. Only a very few were indifferent to their role as parent.

The interviewers noted that in their sample the role of parent had developed before adoption of even the relatively mild laws of the mid-1930's strengthening the hands of parents, and well before the 1944 law. In consequence, their results do not reflect any trend toward parental authoritarianism that may have resulted from the 1944 legislation. Also, they caution that attitudes of parents are often a carry-over from childhood experiences with their own fathers, and not the result of law. Yet they find that "like father, like child" is a less strong pattern in the younger generation than in the older, and so they are prepared to put more emphasis on the influence of the state with youthful groups than upon the influence of childhood experience.

More recently Soviet sociological studies on the family have focused on broken and fatherless homes. Juvenile delinquency is traced in sample studies made in 1964 to neglect in 80% of the cases. It is found particularly characteristic that about half the crimes committed by young people occur after 10 P.M., when the investigators assume that attentive parents would require their children to be at home. Much of the neglect comes from the fact that for 10% of all Soviet children there are no responsible fathers, as the children have been born out of wedlock, and mothers find themselves unable to care for them. Even when families are intact with both a mother and father at home, the studies indicate that there is heavy drinking in from 25% to 30% of the homes of juvenile delinquents, and there is constant family quarreling and even fighting in 50%. Of the juveniles who committed crimes when intoxicated 90% had learned to drink under the influence of their parents or their everyday environment, not after they had gone to work.

Family degeneration has accelerated since 1964. The divorce rate in 1974 climbed to 28 out of 100 marriages. Births out of wedlock reached 1 in 10, and in the Ural city of Perm, it was 1 in 3. Pre-marital sex increased according to a Leningrad University study, showing that 52% of the males and 14% of the females had intercourse before 18. Extramarital sex was common: a Leningrad survey indicated that about half the married women responding claimed a right to have extra-marital affairs. Government efforts to strengthen the family seem to have been no more successful than the laissez-faire policies followed elsewhere.

State Intervention in Private Law Matters

Intervention in private affairs is indicated by the Soviet leaders' attitude toward what would elsewhere be called "private law relationships" such as are normally governed by a civil or commercial code. When the New Economic Policy was established by Lenin in mid-1921, it became evident that the restorative qualities of private enterprise would not be felt on the nation's economy unless there was developed a set of laws defining civil relationships. A buyer and seller had to know what would be the expected result of a contract. A lender had to know whether he could expect to recover the principal of his loan. A property owner had to know whether his ownership would be protected not only against theft but also against damage by a careless or wilfully harmful person. No one would risk capital in private enterprise unless he could be sure of what would happen in a law court. He had to know that agreements made in good faith would be performed in most instances out of fear of the law, and that in those cases in which performance was refused by the opposing party there could be enforcement in court.

Lenin himself was trained in the law, and he had with him in his Communist party some skilled lawyers. They knew what was necessary to restore confidence in law and order in the civil-law field, but they were ardent Marxists, and they feared that if they devised rules within which citizens might make agreements that would be enforceable under all circumstances, the way might be opened for agile capitalists employing skilled lawyers to act within the letter of the rules but to the detriment of the community.

All systems of law have to guard against misuse of the law to the disadvantage of society, and legal procedures have been developed under which persons who can establish a real interest may gain injunctions against activity which appears to be legal on its face. It is usually left, however, for the interested parties to bring the matter before a court when a smoky chimney from a neighborhood factory belches forth excessive smoke, or when a zealous municipality seeks to widen the streets at the expense of a historic tree, or when a board of directors decides to use corporation assets in a manner deemed wasteful by a stockholder. Most systems of law give no relief unless someone can prove specific damage to himself and to his legitimate interests. There is no state official who has the duty to evaluate every lawsuit in the name of the community and to file his views on the subject with a court charged with hearing the matter.

The Soviet code-makers decided to be specific and prominently so. They wrote into the civil code that they enacted in 1922 a first article denying the protection of the code to those who claimed rights under the code but in violation of the social and economic reasons for the establishment of those rights. To implement this denial, the code of civil procedure was made to include a provision permitting the state prosecutor to intervene in any civil case at any stage, or, if no case was in progress, to instigate an action to prohibit the enforcement of a right guaranteed under the code if the interests of the state or of society would be injured.

Reliance upon Article 1 of the civil code was frequent by courts refusing to enforce a right in litigation by a capitalist of the period of the New Economic Policy. There were also cases in which property owners were deprived of their ownership because they were not using their property in what the prosecutor believed to be the interests of the community, as when they let it fall into serious disrepair although they had funds to make repairs.

Other articles of the code provided that no contract should be enforced if one party had knowingly taken advantage of the extreme want of the other party in making the contract. Thus a sale was set aside when it was proved that a party had been starving and had sold his home for a small quantity of food.

In the articles of the code relating to suits for damages for injury, it was provided that in setting the amount of damages the court should take into consideration the relative wealth of the parties involved, so that no wealthy person might obtain a judgment against a poor person who had damaged his property and thus ruin him. It was even provided that a rich man who caused injury to a poor man's property or person might be held liable in damages although there had been no fault on the rich man's part. This doctrine of liability without fault is not unique to the Soviet system. It has become popular in many Western countries, sometimes because juries have found fault on the part of a defendant in cases in which it seems hardly to have been present. It has been suspected that juries in the West have sometimes been moved emotionally by some serious hardship situation to provide a remedy to a poor man at the expense of an insurance company or of a railroad for which they had no sympathy. What has been unusual about the Soviet system is the clear-cut espousal of the doctrine of liability without fault in the code, not only in cases of extra-hazardous activity, when even Western codes make such provision, but in all cases where a poor man suffers damage.

Social Change Requires a New Approach

A considerable change in the attitude of Communists toward the preservation of loopholes in the law began to appear in the 1930's. No application of Article 1 occurred after 1930 to withhold enforcement of a right formally established by the code. Judgments for damages no longer took into account the relative wealth of the parties involved in the dispute. State officials seemed to be prepared to let the law take its course and to intervene less against property owners.

The explanation of the change lay perhaps in the same factor noted so often in earlier chapters, namely the emergence of a managerial and technical class. The property owners of the 1950's were not those who carried over property from pre-revolutionary times. The attitudes of the past when property ownership was considered a means of making profits were thought to have been discarded. The new rich had earned their wealth as managers of state-owned industry, as inventors, as authors and poets whose artistry had propaganda value, and some were workmen whose high level of production had set the pace for a factory. The new Soviet man was expected to avoid what the Communists considered to be "misuse" of property.

The 1960's proved disillusioning to the architects of the new society. Owners of private homes leased rooms at exorbitant rentals. Automobile owners charged fees as taxis. Private vehicles were used to speed away from scenes of crime. A campaign against abuse of property ownership was begun by the party in reaction to these developments. In the Supreme Court it took the form of the first application of Article 1 in thirty years in order to deprive a woman of ownership of a home because she had leased rooms at high rentals. In spite of the argument from jurists some years earlier that Article 1 need no longer appear in Soviet codes, its principle was placed in the 1961 Fundamentals of Civil Law by those who feared that the new owners would abuse their privileges.

Criminal prosecutions against those who utilized private automobiles as taxis were initiated, and thieves who used vehicles to facilitate theft found them confiscated as part of the penalty. Private homes built after 1958 had to be of smaller proportions, and the allocation of plots of land for new private construction of cottages was stopped in 1960 as well as the sale of such cottages to individuals by local soviets. Talk was heard prior to the twenty-second Communist party congress in 1961 of the formulation of a policy against private ownership of any dwelling, and a flurry of sales by frightened owners followed, but the prohibition did not materialize.

No one can doubt that Soviet society has created a new rich since the war, and law is required to protect their wealth. It is not, however, a group comparable to property owners in the West, for no one is permitted to own land or factories or to become a merchant. All are on wages and salaries, and all are deprived of the right to own property of the type from which Marxists argue political power springs. Nevertheless, in spite of limitations the new rich have received substantial wages; they could and did buy large quantities of consumers' goods—private homes, summer cottages, automobiles, motorcycles, television sets, furniture. To be enjoyed these had to be protected, and there was strong support for a stability in the law.

The 1960's, however, witnessed proof that it was illusory to expect cupidity to have become a thing of the past and understanding of social duty to have become universal. Exploitation of property for personal gain gave rise to retaliatory measures; to the extension of the death penalty to speculation and even to bribery. More importantly, attitudes toward personal property ownership began to change, and these challenged the concept of personal property privileges for the new rich. Letter writers asked why there need be private ownership of homes and why property inheritance was necessary in a socialist society. While such challenges are only those of letter writers to the press, they are not without significance. Changes in official policy have frequently emerged in the U.S.S.R. after letters, whether inspired or genuine, have appeared in the press as trial balloons.

State intervention in private affairs may be lessening in the 1970's. Although radical reformation of society into a self-disciplined community remains a formal aim of Soviet leadership, the increasing stability fostered in the 1970's suggests that less effort will be exerted to discourage the remaining religious practices unless they are so eccentric as to harm health or relate in Soviet eyes to hostile political activity. Less effort will also be expended to discourage accumulation of wealth so long as it is not gained illegally as bribes or from the rental of living space at high rates or from merchandising. While Soviet editorial writers can be expected to inveigh against what Communists believe to be abuses of the concessions made to foster stability, the practical implementation of austere policies through suddenly adopted new measures seems unlikely.

CHAPTER 10

THE ARMY AND POLITICS

The army has always been related closely to domestic politics by the Marxists. It has been considered more as an instrument for a ruling class to maintain its power at home than as a tool of international combat. To the Marxist, the soldiers in any country are the second line of defense when the police are pushed to the ground. It was the army that moved into position to save the king at Versailles, and the army which was called upon to defend the regime in Petersburg, when a mob threatened the palace. Lenin said often that a revolution could not be successful under modern conditions of warfare if it did not win to its side enough of the army to neutralize the effectiveness of this strongest weapon of the rulers.

Soviet experience with the army has tended to emphasize the conclusions of the Marxists. It was because of the disaffection of large segments of the troops in the capital of the Russian Empire that the revolutionaries were able to win the day in 1917 and force the abdication of the Tsar. It was because of the abandonment of Alexander Kerensky by his commander-in-chief, Kornilov, later in the same year, that the Soviet regime, led by the Military Revolutionary Committee of the bolsheviks, was able to seize power. Only the women's battalion fired from the galleries of the Winter Palace when the mob closed in.

There followed after the Revolution a short period of liquidating the First World War's international military obligations of Russia. In concluding the peace of Brest Litovsk, Lenin had made major concessions to Germany to prevent defeat of the bolshevik regime and a German occupation of Russia. Thereafter Lenin planned a new army, not to take revenge outside of Russia by regaining what had been lost but to save the domestic situa-

tion for his party. With the important help of Trotsky, he organized a "Red Army" to serve as the strongest arm of the new
regime in saving itself from its domestic opponents. Within little
more than a year after the successful Revolution, this new army
was tested in the battles of a civil war.

Unlike the war between the states in the United States, the
Russian civil war involved no massive blocks of north and south.
It was not regional but universal. Some people in all parts of
what had been the Russian Empire rallied to the officers of the
old regime and sought to unseat the new regime. Like all military
struggles, the dramatic battles were fought in a few specific regions, but less dramatic episodes occurred throughout the land.
This civil war was a class war and not a regional war, and class
lines cut across the social fabric of the entire country.

Because of their concept that armies are maintained to protect
class interests, the new Soviet leaders built their army on class
lines. They permitted only members of the working and peasant
classes to enlist, and their first draft law followed the same line.
Only those presumed to be loyal to the aims of the bolsheviks
were to serve. To popularize the army, and probably also because they had confidence in the good sense of the natural leaders among the workers and peasants in the ranks, Lenin developed the army's organization in an unusual pattern: he attempted
to make of the army a thoroughly democratic institution in which
the men in the ranks would elect their own officers.

Controls within the Army

The army presented the same problem to the new leaders as
did industry. War was a technical matter, like the operation of
industry, and the workers and peasants who were to fight in the
new army had not mastered the technique. While it was politically attractive to espouse democracy within the army in the
selection of officers, it was not practical. Military commanders
had to be skilled professionals, and the solution to a dearth of
professionals in the army was the same as it was in industry.
Those professionals of the Tsar's army who were willing to continue in the new army were retained, and some were even con-
scripted; together they totaled 48,000 in number, constituting 76
per cent of all officers in 1918. They were not trusted, however.
They had to be watched lest they betray their units to the armies
fighting under their colleagues of yesterday, who were now trying to reconquer the country from bolshevik rule.

The Provisional Government of Alexander Kerensky had introduced the institution of commissars to watch those Tsarist officers who were not trusted—and with some reason, as the Kornilov affair had disclosed. The Soviet government continued to use commissars, from the beginning, although the first order on the subject, stating that the new commissars were the direct organs of the Soviet government in the army, appeared only on April 6, 1918. These commissars were charged with the duty both of keeping the army closely knit to the Soviet system and of preventing the army from becoming a focus of conspiracies against the workers and peasants. The orders of a military commander were to have no force until counter-signed by a political commissar.

With the April order, the Red Army adopted formally the system of dual control that was to plague its efficiency in later years. It was obvious that decisions in warfare had to be taken quickly and that speed was difficult to obtain if a second commander had to be convinced, before an order could be executed, that it was wise. The bolsheviks took the risk of delay and confusion inherent in their system of dual control because they thought that the risk of loss of troops by treason of the officers was greater.

The political commissars were not only to watch for treason but also to spread bolshevik ideas throughout the ranks. They were to be teachers as well as policemen. Their work was co-ordinated through an All-Russian Bureau of Military Commissars, later to become the Political Section of the Revolutionary Military Council of the Republic to which the conduct of all military operations fell. In 1919 this central control section became the Political Administration of the Republic, directly subordinate to the Central Committee of the Communist party.

Party membership increased within the army with the passage of time. The growth of party influence was facilitated at the end of the civil war by reduction of the army from the 5,500,000 that it had been at its civil-war peak to a cadre army of 562,000 men. A campaign was conducted to prepare the officers to become members of the Communist party, and by 1928 all corps commanders in the cadre army were members of the party. Those below included a large number of party men, with the end result that 55 per cent of the total officer corps belonged to the party.

Under peacetime conditions and in view of the increase in presumed loyalty of officers due to membership of so many in the party, the role of the political commissar was changed. In 1924 he was placed in secondary position and no longer required to approve the commands of the military commanders but rather to concern himself with party-political and cultural-educational work. Yet the organization of political commissars continued to be independent of the People's Commissar for Military and Naval Affairs, of the Revolutionary Military Council of the Republic, and even of local civilian Communist party organs in the territory in which the military unit was garrisoned.

The Stalin Purge within the Army

Many Soviet citizens and outside observers believed that the political loyalty of the Red Army had been assured in the mid-1930's by the increasing number of party members within the army. They did not reckon with a new factor that was not evident to the public generally—if it was to those below the highest policy-making circle of the Communist party. This was Stalin's determination to strengthen his role as dictator, not only over the masses, but over the party itself. The world, including the rank-and-file Soviet citizen, was shocked in 1936 by the first of the purge trials. On the face of them, and even allowing for distortion of evidence to prove disloyalty to Stalin, these trials indicated a new resistance to Stalin's authoritarian direction of the Communist party on the part of those of the original small groups of party leaders who had shared with Lenin in planning and directing the events of 1917 and who had opposed Stalin quite vigorously in party meetings from time to time after Lenin's death.

The purge swept through the highest party circles, marked in each of the years 1937 and 1938 with another dramatic public trial of an additional group of defendants. Forced confessions, recanted in one case on the second day of the trial only to be reaffirmed after what must have been the pressures of another night in jail, went well beyond the realm of credibility for foreigners. Yet they were dramatized so well for a people who had little factual knowledge against which to check the charges that in all probability they were believed by most Soviet citizens.

Finally the purge reached the army, with a secret trial in 1937 of the Deputy Chief of the Red Army, Marshal M. N. Tukachevsky, and of seven colleagues. The suicide of the head of all political commissars was reported at the same time. The accusation against all of these men was collaboration with the

Germans, who, under the leadership of Hitler, were at the time declaring their increasing hostility toward the U.S.S.R. After Stalin's death, the army trial was denounced as a falsification, and the reputations of the executed generals were cleared.

Notwithstanding that the allegations against the accused officers were untrue, Stalin seems to have been frightened. In the face of the proved inefficiency of the military commissar system as it had existed during the civil war, he restored this system within two months after the announcement of Tukachevsky's execution. The political commissar was made equal to the commander, though not superior to him, and all orders had to be countersigned by the political commissar although they were issued to the troops only in the commander's name. The authority of the commissar extended even to approving all awards, promotions, and demotions, and to the preparation of a report on the political training and reliability of all commanding personnel in his unit.

The inefficiency of the dual command was demonstrated again in the first military operation after its reintroduction, namely, the winter war with Finland in 1940. As a result of early Soviet defeats in this war, the political commissar was again moved back to second place. He was given a new name symbolic of his position, "Deputy Commander for Political Affairs," and was charged with political propaganda.

The German attack against the U.S.S.R. on June 22, 1941, again frightened Stalin, to judge from the record on political commissars. In less than a month after the German invasion of Soviet territory, the political commissars were returned to their civil-war status and adjured to concern themselves not only with propaganda but with military decisions as well. It is now known that defections from the Red Army were numerous in the early days of World War II, before the Germans proved to the Russians that they had more than the ousting of Stalin in mind and planned complete subjugation of the Slavs as a race. The political commissar system, as it had existed during the similar peril of the first years after the Revolution, was Stalin's answer to the defections of 1941. In spite of the proved inadequacy of such a system of political control under conditions of modern warfare, the peril was deemed sufficiently great to dictate the system's restoration.

Soviet officers who have since fled to the West have written that military operations on the Soviet front necessitated constant movement and thus made the countersigning of orders by a political commissar often impossible. Military and political commanders were often widely separated, yet swift decisions were necessary. The refugee officers have pointed to the character of modern warfare as a primary reason for a decree of October, 1942, which declared that the military commanders were to be solely responsible for the conduct of the war and that the political commissars were to be reorganized and made subordinate to them. The system adopted in 1942 remains in force today.

Party Membership in the Army

Reorganization of the political commissar system, so that it became a chain of command subordinate to the military commanders, did not mean that the Communist party had relinquished its control within the army. Two factors account for the conclusion that no military caste beyond the reach of the party was being permitted to develop. One was the extension of party membership and education within the army to bring in large numbers of men and nearly all the higher officers, and the other was the expansion of a system of police officers responsible to the Ministry of Internal Affairs. Each will be considered in turn.

The extension of party membership was dramatic and in sharp contrast to the policies in force before World War II. In 1939, there had been only 1,000,000 party members in all branches of civilian and military activity. Just before the German attack in 1941, the party reported 3,876,885 members. Immediately after the war began, the requirements for admission of soldiers and officers were relaxed so that by January 1, 1945, there were 5,760,369 members. Refugee officers have reported that the required three recommendations for membership were made by the political commissar of the unit, the company commander, and the company political commissar. Soldiers were being accepted at what is said to have been the rate of 100,000 per month, and during 1942 over one million members of the armed forces were admitted. Since many were killed or captured because it was they who were required to assume the role of leader and hero, a considerable campaign of recruitment was necessary to keep the party ranks full.

Such rapid recruitment of party members from the armed

forces did not give time for the careful training and disciplining characteristic of peacetime, but it did place many of the new members emotionally on the side of the regime as a part of the elite. Political commissars thus gained many men in their units on whom they could usually rely for desired political attitudes. For those who fell outside their propaganda net, there was the police net of the agents of the Ministry of Internal Affairs.

Both the political commissars and the agents of the Ministry of Internal Affairs, later transferred to the Committee on State Security, have had, and now have, organizations throughout the military apparatus. Thus, there is the Chief Political Administration of the Armed Forces, which is responsible both to the Central Committee of the Communist party and to the Ministry of Defense. It has various departments to provide educational materials, to edit military journals, to teach in military schools, and to work among the Komsomols in the army and the fleet. The Chief Political Administration works through a branch established in each of the military districts into which the country is divided and in each fleet area. These district branches channel their activities down through political sections of the corps, division, regiment, battalion, and company and through the corresponding units in the navy.

A political commissar, called *zampolit*, is appointed by, and responsible to, the next higher political commissar, but he is also subordinate to the military commander of the unit over whose political education he presides. Thus, in theory, political commissars are subject to dual subordination. They are said, in practice, to demonstrate considerable independence of the commander and even, at times, to make suggestions as to military tactics. This attitude is fostered by the requirement that they pass the usual technical examinations for any military promotion in grade, so that a major in the political corps is supposed to be as able a military leader as a major having primarily military duties.

Since all members of the Communist party within the unit in which the *zampolit* operates are expected to carry on their usual party work, there is a party organization within the unit to which they all are required to give service. This organization, as in the civilian organizations of the Communist party, elects its executive committee and its secretary. The party secretary's role is played by the *zampolit* at the level of military district, corps, and division. At the level of the regiment, and below, there is a separation of functions, in that a separate party secretary is elected, but, reportedly, he is invariably controlled by the *zampolit*, who recommends his election and who, at the regimental level, is generally one grade above his party secretary in military rank. During the war there was no pretense of democratic election of the secretaries, and they were simply appointed under a special directive, as were the members of the party executive committees for the military organizations at the various levels. In 1946 the system of elections was restored within the party apparatus of the armed services.

The schedule of activities of the *zampolit*, as reported by Soviet refugees, indicates that these political commissars are required to use every opportunity to imbue their charges with party doctrines, their major educational work being done among non-party men. Formal class discussions on political doctrine are held at regular intervals each week, if need be under trees near the front. Classes focus on basic political doctrines, but there are also current-events classes to apply these doctrines to contemporary situations. At periods which might be called "recreational," it is the political commissar's duty to see that Soviet novels, with their political messages couched in romantic terms, are read aloud. It has been reported that sometimes a *zampolit* has quarreled with a military commander because the latter called for a maneuver at the hour of political education.

The Komsomols are organized at every military level and in the same way as is the party. There is a Komsomol section in the Chief Political Administration of the Armed Forces and at each unit level a Komsomol organization that is subordinate to the *zampolit*. In theory, the secretaries of the unit organizations of the Komsomols are elected, but, in practice, they are chosen by the *zampolit*. Their work is primarily with the enlisted men, 50 per cent of whom are estimated to be members of the Komsomols. All Komsomol members are expected to be good examples to the other soldiers and to try to stimulate the interest of these men in cultural and political development.

Many of the poorly disciplined party members of wartime campaigns have been eliminated from the army since the war, for most of the rank and file has been demobilized and subsequently replaced by new draftees, who are admitted to the party only after the usual scrutiny. The officer corps also has been brought more firmly within the party. In 1952, the party congress was told that 86.4 per cent of all officers were members of the party or of the Komsomols. By the fiftieth anniversary 85% of the entire Army personnel were members of the party or of the Komsomols, while 93% of the officers were similarly affiliated. Under such conditions of development of disciplined party members within the armed forces, the influence of the political commissars is said to have been reduced because they can no longer claim a near monopoly on loyalty. They are surrounded by men whose loyalty is also presumed to be high.

Police Controls in the Army

No presumption of loyalty eliminates in Soviet minds the need for a security police. In all Soviet agencies, as has already been explained, there exists police supervision. It is provided by a Special Section, which appears on the organization chart of every ministry and public corporation, and even of the universities and professional schools. In keeping with the initials of the Russian words for "Special Section," these sections have been called the "OO." In the army they were designated in the same way before World War II, but during the war they became known as "SMERSH," an abbreviation of the Russian for "death to spies."

All such police sections, which exist in units parallel to those of the political commissars down to the division level, are subordinate to the Chief Administration for Counterintelligence of the Armed Forces of the U.S.S.R. This Chief Administration is today a bureau of the Committee of State Security, known as the "Third Central Administration" of the KGB. There is no simultaneous subordination to the Ministry of Defense or to the Chief of Staff, as with the political commissars. A direct line is maintained to the KGB. The Chief Administration's work is coordinated with that of other security agencies of the government. Below the division level, the units operate by means of informers.

The officers of the OO are said not to have had military training but only police training. They live a separate life from the army personnel and even from the party unit in which they work, for they have their own party organization within which the work of the OO is discussed. While these men are believed to exert no direct influence on the commander with respect to military decisions, they do report on the military condition of the unit and on the political morale and material and medical welfare of the troops. They exchange information with the political commissars, and they may arrange for the transfer of an informer to a unit in which they have been unable to recruit one. Clearance from them is required before any officer within the army may be promoted.

When a violation of law is found by the OO, the matter is turned over to the military courts for action. If a charge arising before 1953 was not sufficiently supported with evidence to be taken before a court, the Special Board of the Ministry of Internal Affairs might have been called upon to eliminate the suspected person from the ranks by putting him in a concentration camp as a social danger. Since abolition of the Special Boards in 1953 this procedure has not been available.

Enhancing the Prestige of Officers

Controls such as those provided by the political commissars and the OO can be effective in eliminating the occasional dissenter from the army and in stopping plans for a mutiny or desertion before the organizers attract enough persons to be successful, but they are not enough. The long-range success of the Soviet leaders in holding the loyalty of armed forces must, and does, rest upon forces stronger than police and political commissars. To assure long-range loyalty, there must first be general emotional acceptance of the Soviet system by the great majority of the high command. Second, there must be sufficient military discipline within the armed services to permit the high command to maintain its authority over the rank and file.

The Soviet leaders have been active in both spheres. They have wooed the high command, and they have seen to the strengthening of discipline. Wooing of the high command took the form of reintroducing in 1935 military titles of the conventional type—lieutenant, captain, major, lieutenant-colonel, and colonel. Prior to this time, the commanders had been designated merely as commanding a squad, company, corps, or army. In 1940, the ranks of general and admiral were reintroduced, even though these titles, as such, had been the butt of revolutionary propaganda for so long as to make them synonymous with traitors to the bolshevik cause. The duty to salute officers, which had been abandoned in 1918, was restored, and in July, 1943, the title "officer" was reintroduced together with the epaulets of rank, which in themselves had been symbols of the old regime for all the years since the Revolution. Even the term "soldier" was reintroduced for army privates, to replace the title "Red-armyman." In 1946 the name of the whole army was changed from "Red Army" to "Soviet Army."

All these changes were intended to enhance the prestige of the officers. They could now feel that they were an elite, and the manner in which they bore themselves within the army and outside it indicated a great change in attitude toward their positions. There was also restored the Officers' Court of Honor, which resembled that of Tsarist times and was designed to guard the dignity and honor of the rank of officer by providing to the officers a means of punishing those of their own number who degraded the uniform.

Even within the officers' corps there were established notable practical distinctions. The scale of pay indicates that a sergeant receives 4.3 times as much basic pay as a private; a captain, 24.3 times as much; and a general of the army, 114.3 times as much. In addition, special privileges to buy scarce consumers' goods and to have prior right in the allocation of living quarters and in the choice of theater seats are granted the general officers.

Measures such as these are taken by the top Communist party policy-makers presumably to supplement the incentives to loyalty that they expect political indoctrination to instil in the ranks of the Communist party. If the ideological arguments do not succeed in assuring loyalty of army chiefs to the party, the favors showered upon them by the party can be expected to achieve the desired result.

Discipline has been strengthened markedly since 1940. The duty of obedience existed not at all prior to 1919, at which time soldiers were required only to execute "service" orders and "service" duties and were excused from performing commands directed against the Soviet government or obviously criminal in nature. In 1925 a new disciplinary code required performance of all orders, unless criminal in nature. The 1940 Disciplinary Code requires the execution of every order regardless of content. It allows no rejections on the basis of violation of law. To avoid a conclusion that subordinates may now have to execute illegal orders, a commentary has suggested that it will be presumed that no Soviet officer would violate the international law of war in giving an order.

To enforce discipline, the commanding officer is authorized to apply penalties ranging from personal reprimand, through extra duty, to confinement, and finally to reduction in rank. Such penalties are subject to certain procedural requirements: the penalty must be imposed within five days of the commission of the offense, it must be executed within a month, it must be proportionate to the offense, and it must not exceed the authority of the superior or he will himself be liable to disciplinary or judicial punishment. The subordinate is very much limited in his complaint on procedural grounds, for he may object to the immediate superior only on the basis of exceeded authority.

Military Crime and Its Punishment

If crime has been committed, as defined by the 1958 federal statute on military crimes, a trial is held before a military court. These courts of the federal government are organized by the Supreme Court of the U.S.S.R. in military districts, army corps, and army divisions. The jurisdiction of each is successively determined by the rank of the person prosecuted. For the highest ranks, there is a military college within the Supreme Court of the U.S.S.R., which may also take jurisdiction over any case that in its opinion is sufficiently complex or of great political or social importance. The courts are composed of one professional judge, trained as a military lawyer, and two non-professional judges, without legal training and chosen for each case usually from the ranks of the armed services.

Appeals from a decision are permitted to the court next above the one in which the trial was held. There may be no appeal from a decision by the military college of the Supreme Court, but this does not mean that there may not be a review of the decision, for the President of the Court or the Prosecutor-General of the U.S.S.R. may always request a review by the full bench of the Supreme Court, sitting as a plenum. To provide political control over decisions in the event of need, the decision of the Plenum of the Supreme Court may be taken to the Presidium of the Supreme Soviet by the President of the Supreme Court or by the Prosecutor-General of the U.S.S.R.

The military courts are required to follow the code of criminal procedure of the republic in which they are sitting. Thus, they are not outside the regular court system with a procedure of their own. This fact is not as remarkable as it might seem, because the criminal procedure established by the code for all courts, military and civilian alike resembles more closely the procedure used in military courts everywhere than it does the procedure of American courts of law. Discussion of the main points of the procedure will be reserved for the chapter following this one.

After reviewing the provisions and practice of Soviet military law, it has been concluded by two foreign students that Soviet criminal procedure does provide a basis for reasonable prediction by the accused of the outcome of his trial. It seems to these students, therefore, to contribute to stability within the army and to confidence that punishment will not be meted out unless it is deserved. For the officer corps, this is important to peace of mind, and it may not be chance that Marshal Georgi K. Zhukov, soon after Stalin's death, raised his glass in a toast to "justice." For the morale of the armed forces, the efficient operation of the military courts is necessary.

Army Officers' Fate since Stalin

After Stalin's death in 1953 the prestige of professional soldiers rose in the Communist party. Marshal Georgi K. Zhukov, a professional soldier, was named Minister of Defense in the first recognition of a career officer as minister. In February, 1956, he was elevated to the Presidium of the Central Committee of the Communist party as an alternate member, again an unprecedented recognition of a career officer as a political leader. In 1957 he provided the critical support Khrushchev needed in his power struggle with the faction seeking his ouster. By this act the Armed Forces were in a position for the first time since the days when officers were largely men inherited from the Tsar's army to challenge even the Communist party.

Zhukov in his new position manifested his desire for a strengthening of the hand of career officers to the detriment of the security police, the political commissars, and political education generally. There were many foreign observers who anticipated open conflict between Khrushchev and Zhukov, as the latter moved to separate the Armed Forces from the traditional control of party and police.

Making use of an opportunity to send Zhukov to Yugoslavia for consultations during the late summer of 1957, Khrushchev arranged Zhukov's removal during his absence. Jealousies among Zhukov's colleagues were nurtured by Khrushchev and party discipline was reasserted among the top officers. As he stepped from the plane on his return to Moscow, Zhukov was confronted with his demotion. Shortly thereafter he was removed from the Presidium of the party and disappeared from public notice.

Political education, although left in the hands of a *zampolit* subordinate to the military commander of each unit, was reaffirmed in importance by appointing a war hero as Chief of the Political Administration to command respect for military prowess and demonstrate a concern for political education. A career officer with no past history as a first-rank hero was made Minister of Defense. He was seated on the Central Committee of the party but not on its Presidium. Matters were restored to what Khrushchev must have considered normal conditions, namely, the unquestioning subordination of the Armed Forces to the Communist party and the acceptance of a program of political education within these forces designed to assure acquiescence in such a role.

By the events of 1957 the army marshals, who had been imponderables under Zhukov's command and provided potential support to the managerial class as it emerged in industry, agriculture, and channels of distribution, were shorn of any potentiality as a source of coercion hostile to the Communist party. They sank back to the status of an interest group able to exercise pressure only through persuasion.

Limitations upon their effectiveness even as an interest group were demonstrated in December, 1959, when the party's Central Committee voted to make a one-third reduction in the armed forces' personnel as a result of the decision to place reliance in the future upon a nuclear missile arsenal. The army opposed the decision, but without avail. When the U-2 incident occurred in May, 1960, stressing the extent to which the United States had been able to penetrate Soviet air defenses, military leaders again tried to obtain a reversal of policy, but they were unsuccessful, and before the end of 1960 some 500,000 men had been discharged from military duty. Not until July, 1961, was the reduction suspended, following growing tension in Berlin and increases in Western defense expenditures, which strengthened the army's arguments.

The establishment of missiles in Cuba in 1962 provided another opportunity to assess the army's influence. Some Western specialists thought that the move had been initiated by the army and that it was proof of the army's growing power in policy circles. Yet, when the missiles were removed under pressure from the United States, the party emerged as the agency that still dominated the strategy of the U.S.S.R.

The army's role as an interest group was again evaluated in 1963 with the establishment of a Supreme Council of National Economy to create a high command of production. A General of Engineers with long association with the defense industry was named chairman. It is possible to suppose that the military commanders together with the bureaucrats of the economic administration combined to force a retreat from a policy favoring local industrial autonomy which they thought was inefficient.

When Khrushchev's Minister of Defense, who outlasted his sponsor in office, died in 1967, there was speculation that Khrushchev's successors would seize the occasion to restore the Ministry to a civilian Communist party member. Soviet criticism of Mao Tse-tung's use of the Chinese Army in 1966 to wrest power from the main forces of the Chinese Communist party bureaucracy, which Mao thought to be a stultifying factor in his revolution, suggested that Soviet Communists were re-studying the relationship between Army and party. What transpired in the secret discussions on the subject is unknown to outsiders, but the outcome became apparent when another career officer was appointed to the Ministry. The Communist leadership had concluded that the Soviet Army was not moving in the direction of challenging the party leadership.

Questions were raised outside the U.S.S.R. in 1973 when the Minister of Defense, Marshal A. A. Grechko, a professional soldier, was named a full member of the Political Buro. Analysts asked whether this advancement indicated influence of the military in policy-making circles. Not since Zhukov's demotion in 1957 had the armed forces been represented among party generalists, although the heads of all major military services and nearly half the regional commanders had been sitting on the party's Central Committee. Specialists in group theory, notably H. Gordon Skilling and Milton C. Lodge, sought to determine how the interests of the military differ from those of party generalists. Their studies suggest that the military senses increasingly its predominant role as the specialist in military matters and resents the intervention of others in their field. Indeed, some foreigners doubt whether the party's Secretary General can compel military colleagues to accept armament levels desired by party generalists in bargaining with other governments over arms reduction. They believed that Marshal Grechko, during his ascendancy, strengthened the military's role as an interest group.

The party generalists may have sensed danger. At least, on Grechko's death in 1976, they reverted to party tradition. His place as Minister of Defense was filled by Dmitrii Ustinov, a Political Buro member and former party secretary in charge of supervising the armaments industry. He was given the rank of Marshal, but his presence indicated that the military's master remained the Political Buro.

CHAPTER 11

ENFORCEMENT OF LAW

Justice has been claimed as a major aim by the bolsheviks since their seizure of power. They have argued that the efforts of the West to create a system of courts independent of the legislative and administrative branches of government and to provide a fair trial are designed solely to mask the injustice of the Western systems. They have quoted Marx's stricture on the courts of Western Europe as he set it forth in the *Communist Manifesto* of 1848. Marx said that the justice that was so much praised by the men of his time was really only for the limited few who ruled. In keeping with his analysis of the state as an instrument of class domination, he said that the courts were no more than instruments of a ruling class. He declared that they could not be considered impartial and that they did not administer justice in any abstract sense.

The bolsheviks have never claimed to administer justice in any abstract sense. Their claim that their courts are more democratic than any in the West rests upon their claim that the Soviet system of government represents the masses. They declare openly that their court is an instrument of state policy and by no means impartial. In the earlier years of their regime they spoke frequently and proudly of "revolutionary legality," by which they meant the maintenance of order for the benefit of the aims of their revolution. The courts were thought to have as much of a duty to maintain order of the type sought by the Communist party as did the administrative branch of the state apparatus.

The bolsheviks have not constructed their system so as to utilize the courts as a check upon the legislature or the executive. They have formally discarded the concept of separation of powers so basic to the American system. In keeping with Marx's analysis, they have said that the separation claimed in the United

States is mere subterfuge and that American judges are as much subject to the pressures of the political party in power and its instrument, the executive branch of government, as are the judges in their own system. They have never appreciated the extent to which the American judiciary can and will check the authority of the executive branch, as it has done so often in history and not long ago in the case testing President Harry S. Truman's power to seize the steel mills and in the various cases limiting the power of the executive to dismiss individuals from the civil service and to issue passports.

In view of the Soviet attitude toward courts and their insistence that judges be politically alert in enforcing the policies of the Communist party, one may wonder why the Soviet system includes courts at all. It is possible to imagine an official of the Soviet Ministry of Justice presiding over an office before which the police could bring charges against those whom they believed to be in need of punishment and before which persons engaged in a dispute might appear for settlement of their quarrel. Such a system was common enough in feudal times, when the feudal lord settled the disputes of his vassals and decided on the basis of his own wisdom what penalties were desirable for those who displeased him. Even in more modern times there have been many administrative tribunals, often with power of punishment. In the United States we find no difficulty in accepting administrative boards that decide the right to open a radio station or fine those who violate administrative regulations.

The U.S.S.R. has made considerable use of the administrative tribunal to keep order. The special boards within the Ministry of Internal Affairs, the heirs of the *Cheka*, had a record of activity so vigorous as to indicate that the Soviet leaders found them useful as instruments of terror. A chapter has been devoted to these boards and the governmental function they performed. It might have been possible to extend the jurisdiction of these special boards to all charges of violation of law and even to disputes between citizens. This was not done, however, and in view of the Soviet leaders' practical approach to government, there must have been good reason.

Reasons for Establishing a Court System

Various reasons why Soviet leaders have preferred to establish a body that they have called a "court" rather than to utilize administrators of the Ministry of Justice can be imagined. Lenin inherited a society in which the court, in spite of Marx's criticism of its injustice, enjoyed considerable popular esteem. To have abandoned the concept of a court right after the Revolution would have caused apprehension among the people. Perhaps that is why within a month after the Revolution a decree established a new court system to replace the old. Ever since that time the court has been retained, and there has never been talk of abandoning it in favor of an administrative official.

With their ever present concern for world public opinion, the Communist leaders have probably also considered the effect upon that world public opinion of their attitude toward courts. They have not had to worry about negative reaction to their class approach, for those who welcome a system pledged to further the cause of workers and peasants have been ready to accept a court professing to administer class justice. A potential French Communist would not be displeased with a system that favors the poor man over the rich, but he could be expected to be unhappy with a system that is not established to provide justice as he understands it to members of the working class. Soviet Communists cannot overlook the fact that Frenchmen have had a violent fear of administrative officials ever since the declining days of the French monarchy. To return to arbitrary administrative determination of guilt, even though the determining official worked for a state under the domination of the Communist party, would worry a Frenchman. The Communists in the U.S.S.R. most probably take foreign public opinion into account.

In Soviet political literature, it is possible to distinguish another reason for maintenance of a court system rather than the institution of an official of the Ministry of Justice to administer the law. Administrative efficiency is said to play a part in the decision. It has been found that the judicial function is a specialized one, requiring a greater measure of contemplation and more time to determine facts than is customary in an administrative office. The denial of the separability of politics and law has not meant to Soviet leaders that the judicial function was not separable from the administrative function. Soviet judges are admonished to study their politics carefully and to keep in constant touch with political leadership. They are not permitted to separate themselves from the aims of the Communist party. In fact, three-quarters of them at the lowest level, and all of them at the highest, are members of the Communist party and subject to its usual discipline.

There can be no opposition in court to the policies of the party, but it is accepted that a judge has a special type of task to perform and that for this task he requires special training and special ability. In attempting to explain the Soviet attitude, Andrei Vyshinsky has written that the Soviet system rejects the concept of separation of powers as it appears in the United States Constitution but accepts the necessity of separating functions. By this he seems to mean that the court function is considered to be a specialized one. It is to be performed by experts, but these experts are not to think of themselves, nor is anyone else to think of them, as being a check upon the executive or the legislature. All three branches of government—legislative, executive, and judicial—must be considered to be members of the same team under the guidance of the Communist party.

To indicate this fact in constitutional terms, it is provided by the Constitution that the courts shall be responsible to the Supreme Soviet of the U.S.S.R. as the all-powerful authority within the U.S.S.R. In theory, the Supreme Soviet and the subordinate soviets could act as courts, but the draftsmen of the Constitution preferred to have the Supreme Soviet delegate its authority to settle disputes and punish offenders to a system of courts created by it, responsible to it, and in the final decision reversible by it, if the necessities of policy require.

Political Courts in the Early Years

Acceptance of the desirability of maintaining a system of courts has not meant to the Soviet leaders that all courts need be alike. In their fear of class enemies, the revolutionary leaders of 1917 decided to create two types of court in their first decree. One was to handle the routine cases of crime and civil dispute. The other was to try the cases involving the safety of the regime itself. This latter system was called the system of "revolutionary tribunals," to indicate that its task was to make certain that the revolutionary regime was not unseated. Its judges were chosen for their political training, and they were released from the limited procedural restraints created for the new regular courts.

With the passage of years, the revolutionary tribunals came to outlive their usefulness, in the opinion of some of the officials of the Ministry of Justice. It was felt that the major dangers of the civil-war period had passed and that it had become possible to concentrate all courts within a single system. To this view, some members of the staff of the Ministry of Justice objected. They felt that the new courts, called "peoples' courts," had shown themselves to be politically innocent and too much subject to local pressures, especially when they were called upon to punish such chronic evils of the village communities as the illegal manufacture of moonshine liquor and attempts at evasion of military service. It was argued that if the revolutionary tribunals were abolished, it would be necessary to improve greatly the political quality of the judges in the peoples' courts. Improvement of the quality of judges seemed impossible to the opponents of the plan to abolish the revolutionary tribunals. It was argued that it would take time to train judges who could resist local pressures and who would understand fully the aims of the new regime. Until the time came when this process of political education was completed, the separation of the two court systems was expected to be necessary.

A compromise was adopted in 1921, under which the number of revolutionary tribunals was reduced and their jurisdiction limited. Fewer types of crime were to be brought before them, but they were not to be abolished. They were to be reestablished as "military courts" and "military transport courts," subject to the control of the supreme court of each republic, through which there might be preserved the same standard of procedural protection as was to be enforced in the peoples' courts. This was thought to provide the desired unity of policy, if not unity of structure. The preservation of the revolutionary tribunal idea in its new form would make it possible to reserve for judges well trained in Communist party policies the cases involving attempts to overthrow the regime, whether committed by military personnel or civilians.

To take up the lesser cases of political importance that were being removed from the revolutionary tribunals in their new form, the political quality of the peoples' courts was to be improved. It seemed obviously impossible to the Ministry of Justice to develop enough skilled lawyers with political understanding in a sufficiently short time to staff all the courts. As a solution to their problem, the ministry officials seized upon a practice that had developed in 1920. They would establish two levels of peoples' courts, one for the routine criminal and civil cases and a second one with more experienced and politically qualified judges. The great bulk of the cases would be heard by the first court, and the fewer more complicated and more serious cases would go before the second court, which could sit in the provincial capitals rather than in the county seats close to each village community or even on circuit among the villages.

The two-stepped system of courts was carried one degree further, for the Supreme Court in each republic was given authority to try unusual cases of very great political importance. Thus there emerged a system of courts at different levels to meet the needs of different situations. At each successively higher level the political and educational requirements for the position of judge were more exacting. By the 1922 Judiciary Act, there was established a system of courts which has remained essentially the same to the present day.

The Courts in the New Federation

Federation in 1923 affected the court system in some measure. There was created a Supreme Court of the U.S.S.R., and to it were transferred the military and military transport courts that were the successors of the revolutionary tribunals. In this move, the protection of the state against acts designed to overthrow the regime became subject always to the jurisdiction of federal courts. With the passage of the years there were added to these federal military courts, with their jurisdiction over all types of revolutionary activity, whether committed by military personnel or by civilians, two other systems of federal courts. One of these had to do with crimes committed by employees of the water-transport system and by civilians whose acts affected the operation of this system. Its jurisdiction was the same as that of the transport courts concerned with railroad operations. The second new system had to do with crimes committed by inmates of the concentration camps maintained by the Ministry of Internal Affairs.

After Stalin's death all but one of the specialized federal courts were abolished and jurisdiction returned to the courts of the republics. The one survivor was the military tribunal, but even this was changed. Its jurisdiction was reduced to cases involving charges against men in the Armed Forces or charges of espionage brought against civilians.

The other courts of the republics having to do with criminal and civil cases were untouched by federation. All civil disputes between individuals were reserved for the courts of the republics. The federal courts were only criminal courts and treated only special situations. It will be seen immediately that the line dividing federal and republic jurisdiction in the U.S.S.R. is quite different from that dividing the federal and state courts in the United States. There is some similarity between the systems in the two countries as they relate to criminal law, in that federal law defines certain crimes in the United States, and offenses against such law are tried by federal courts. Such crimes in the United States include treason, just as espionage is a federal crime in the U.S.S.R., but they also include lesser crimes over which the federal government has jurisdiction because of its constitutional authority to control interstate and foreign commerce. Such lesser crimes are exemplified by the carrying of guns across state lines or by the smuggling of narcotics.

There is no similarity between American and Soviet federal courts in the civil field. While in the United States there are many civil suits brought in federal courts because the parties are citizens of different states or of different countries, in the U.S.S.R. there are no civil suits between individuals in the federal courts. Although in the U.S.S.R. there may be a suit by one republic against another, just as there may be a suit by one state against another in the United States, the similarity ends with the stating of the rule, for although states in the United States have sued each other quite often, especially over water rights, there is no public record of suits in the U.S.S.R. Supreme Court between republics of the U.S.S.R.

Soviet federal courts are subject to the same requirements as to structure of the bench and procedural rules applicable in a criminal trial as are the courts of the republics. Such difference as there is has to do with the problem raised in 1922 when the question of qualifications of judges interfered with the plan to create a unitary system of courts. The federal judges are all named by the Supreme Soviet of the U.S.S.R., not only those on the Supreme Court bench but also those on the benches of the lower courts in the federal system. The judges in each republic are named by the supreme soviet of the republic for the supreme court of the republic and by the provincial soviets for the provincial courts. The judges in the lowest courts of the republics have presented a special problem raised by the necessity of appealing to the confidence of the people.

Reaction to Democratic Pressures

Democratic pressures seem to have been felt in the judicial system as well as in the selection of deputies to the various soviets. These have been met in part by provision for the selection of judges at the various levels by the soviet at the same level. To the extent that the soviet itself was democratically elected, it could be argued that the judges represent the will of the people as expressed by their deputies. This argument is not without appeal. It is used also in the United States in support of direct election of judges. For example, public opinion polls in New York State, where judges are elected, have proved that only a very small percentage of the voters knows anything about the candidates proposed for judicial vacancies. People are thought to vote blindly for the candidates proposed by their political party. In consequence it was urged by the Bar Association leaders in New York State that the ballot be shortened to exclude judges, leaving only candidates for the political offices of governor, mayor, and other executive and legislative offices. It was argued that the governor should appoint judges, since opinion polls proved that voters study the careers of those proposed as governor, while they cannot be expected to study the careers of candidates for judicial office. Some other states have long provided that the governor should appoint judges.

The Bar Association's proposals met strong opposition, and finally a compromise was adopted. Judges in New York continue to be elected for all courts below the highest. The top judges are appointed by the governor with the consent of the state senate. This adopts at the state level the system prescribed in the United States for the appointment of federal judges by the President.

That the populist argument for direct election still persists suggests that there is public sentiment of this nature around the world, and it may even have reached into the U.S.S.R. Pressure for adoption of what the world accepts as a democratic choice of judges may have influenced the draftsmen of the U.S.S.R. Constitution of 1936, for it was provided therein that the judges in the lowest courts be elected directly by the voters rather than appointed by the local soviet. No change was made in the manner of appointment of judges at the higher levels, but the change was made for the lowest court.

Foreign students of the Soviet system recognized little difference between the long-established system of appointment of local judges by the local soviet and the 1936 innovation of election by the people. Since it was obvious that the Communist party had been able over the years to establish its complete control over selection of deputies to the local soviets, it was presumed that the party could control the election of judges as easily. The change in procedure seemed to be in form only, and presumably was instituted to present to the Soviet people and to the world evidence of increasing democratic practices within the U.S.S.R.

The elections to local soviets since adoption of the secret ballot in 1936 have produced few surprises, as has been indicated earlier. The Communist party has shown its skill in devising counterweights to democratic procedures so as to assure the choice of its candidates in almost all districts, regardless of democratic forms adopted for the elections. In spite of its success in controlling elections to the soviets, the Communist party seems to have been reluctant to put the choice of local judges to the vote. No judicial elections were held for thirteen years after adoption of the provision. No direct election of judges in the peoples' courts occurred until 1949. To be sure, World War II had intervened, but this cannot have been the whole explanation. When the first election of judges occurred, the pattern of elections to the various soviets was reproduced. The name of only one nominee appeared on each ballot. Voters were given no choice. Apparently, there were no large number of scratches, for all candidates were reported to have been elected for the constitutional three-year term. Similar elections have been held at the required intervals since the first election, with similar results. The elections of May, 1977, in the Russian Republic resulted in the seating of a group of judges 95% of whom were members of the Communist party or the Komsomols and 35% of whom were women. Judicial terms were maintained at five years by the 1977 Constitution, as they had been set in 1958.

Popularization of the Bench

The Soviet court system has borrowed from Germany a substitute for the jury of the Anglo-American common-law court. Together with the single professional judge, chosen in the manner just indicated, there sit for each civil or criminal case two lay judges. This is the rule not only in the peoples' courts at the bottom of the judicial ladder but also for each of the higher courts, including the supreme court of the republic, when these higher courts sit as a court of original jurisdiction, i.e., when they try a case that has not been heard in any lower court. This is the rule also for the federal courts, including the Supreme Court of the U.S.S.R., when it tries a case as a court of original jurisdiction.

The lay judges are chosen differently for each court. At the bottom level, they are elected, under the 1977 Constitution, for terms of two and a half years at meetings of colleagues at their place of work or residence. At the upper levels, they are appointed by the same soviet that appoints the professional judge. While they are, therefore, chosen to serve over a period of years, they sit for not more than ten days each year. They are not lawyers but laymen, who are supposed to add a democratic flavor to the bench. They are selected to bring to a case, whether criminal or civil, the common-sense approach of the members of the community, just as the jury contributes this element in the common-law court of the United States.

The lay judges of the Soviet courts have greater authority in a sense than the American jury, because they are permitted by law to share with the professional judge the decision of all questions, whether relating to the determination of the credibility of a witness or to the meaning of a statute. In the United States the jury is not permitted to determine the meaning of a statute. The American jury is ordered only to determine facts. Its task is usually to decide whether to believe a witness.

While he has greater formal authority than the American juror, the Soviet lay judge is subjected to more guidance than the American juror, for the Soviet professional judge sits with the lay judges to determine the court's decision. In the United States the judge may not go to the jury room with the jurors. He can tell them what law is applicable and sometimes what he thinks of the evidence, but cannot sit with them. They are free to do as they please when they are alone, and they occasionally make a finding which is quite contrary to what the judge has suggested.

Although Soviet lay judges can under their law outvote a professional judge, the outside world has been informed of only a very few cases in which this has happened. These cases have been recounted by former Soviet lawyers who have fled to the West, and one is reported in the Soviet official reports. Generally the lay judges are believed to be quite docile in accepting the proposals of the professional judge. They rarely ask questions at the trial or show any independence of view. Nevertheless, they provide an opportunity to the general public to share in the decision, and as such they may help the Soviet leaders to maintain popular support for the regime.

It is not entirely accurate to say that the Soviet lay judges represent the general public. While very few of them are members of the Communist party, they are selected by institutions in each district, such as factories, farms, universities, retail stores, and army units. The Communist party shares in the selection by these institutions, and the nominations are unopposed. In consequence, the panels from which lay judges are called for service are not cross-sections of the entire population as are the panels from which jurors are selected in the United States. For trials in the Supreme Court of the U.S.S.R., the panel of lay judges is even less representative, for it is small and is composed of the cream of Communist party leadership to be found in the various major institutions of the country, the army, and soviets, the administrative apparatus, the trade unions, the educational institutions, and the collective farms.

Procedural Guarantees and the Exceptions

Procedure within the courts has been made to correspond in general with what the world accepts as necessary for a fair trial. The code of criminal procedure established the basic principles of orality, publicity, confrontation of witnesses, the right to introduce evidence, the right to counsel, the right to be informed of the charge, and the right to appeal. The code of civil procedure offers the same opportunities to present one's case and to rebut the position of the other party in open court with counsel.

Some of the procedural guarantees are incorporated in the U.S.S.R. Constitution, such as the right to counsel, the right to public trial, and the right to an interpreter. In spite of this fact, these guarantees are made subject to such exceptions as may be established by law, and the law has, in fact, created exceptions. One of the exceptions established by law is that public trial not be granted when the offense involves a sex crime or when relevant military or diplomatic interests of the U.S.S.R. cannot be disclosed. Another exception which was kept until 1956 was that right to counsel did not extend to trials involving terroristic acts against Soviet officials or attempts to unseat the regime defined in that part of the criminal code devoted to "counterrevolutionary" crime. Further, there was in the law in effect until 1956 denial of the right to appeal in such cases, and in trials for terroristic acts or assassination of Soviet officials, the accused did not have to be present at the trial.

In the political exceptions to the usual rules of procedure, the

Soviet policy-makers again demonstrated their readiness to withdraw from the general pattern of protection espoused by all democratic peoples those cases which in their opinion threatened the very continuation of the regime. Their decision to maintain such exceptional methods until 1956 was the more remarkable because of the opportunities they have had to control the final outcome of any case. Through the appellate courts, they always have had the opportunity to bring an undesirable decision of a lower court before judges chosen for the appellate courts because of their extensive political training. There would seem to have been no danger in permitting a defendant to appeal through the usual procedure to the court next higher above the one in which his trial occurred. The appellate bench for the peoples' court is the provincial court, and appeals from the provincial court when it sits as a court of original jurisdiction go to the supreme court of the republic concerned. Perhaps in recognition of the protection provided by the appellate procedure, Stalin's heirs made their decision in 1956 to eliminate the political exceptions to ordinary procedural rights. In doing so, they have probably won praise from those who do not appreciate the controls remaining.

When a court hears an appeal, it has no lay judges on the bench. All three judges are selected from the panel of professional judges available at that level. Under such circumstances, the policy-makers' decision under Stalin to allow no appeals seems to have been a vote of no confidence in the political wisdom of the professional judges in the higher courts. This conclusion is fortified by the fact that, even if the appellate court should have taken a position contrary to the desires of the policy-makers at the highest level, the procedural code provided before 1956 and still provides another chance for the government to require a review. Under the code, either the Prosecutor-General of the U.S.S.R. or the President of the Supreme Court of the U.S.S.R. may ask for a review of the record by the appellate college of the Supreme Court of the U.S.S.R. Should the appellate college of the Supreme Court of the U.S.S.R. again decide against the interests of the state, as interpreted by the highest policy-makers of the Communist party, another review may be had by the Plenum of the Supreme Court of the U.S.S.R., on which sit all judges of the various colleges of the Supreme Court.

With so many possibilities to change the decision of the trial court on appeal to the next higher court and on subsequent review by courts right up to the level of the full bench of the Supreme Court of the U.S.S.R., the denial prior to 1956 of the right of appeal in political cases could have had only one object, to deter potential assassins and those seeking to bring about a new revolution by striking terror into their hearts. They were being advised that they could be assured of no escape from execution. In this is another example of the value the Communist party has found in terrorizing as an instrument of government to prevent the unseating of the regime. The good will of the people at home and abroad that was gained from the adoption of procedural due process for the routine cases was sacrificed when the vital cord of the regime was in danger.

The Status of the Presumption of Innocence

Another element of what the American court considers vital to the concept of due process of law is missing from Soviet codes. This is the presumption of innocence, which operates to require the state, through the prosecutor, to prove that the crime has actually been committed. Under the system in use in most Western countries, the prosecutor may not lay his charge before the judge and ask the defendant to disprove it. The prosecutor must prove his charge, even when the defendant refuses to take the stand and respond to questions. While this procedural protection of the defendant is often exasperating to a prosecutor who feels that he has a good case, so good in fact that he can presume the defendant guilty and especially if the defendant will not take the stand in his own defense, mankind throughout the centuries has reached the conclusion that the only fair trial is the one in which the defendant must be presumed innocent at the outset.

Soviet law contains no such written statement of presumption of innocence, but Soviet text writers have said that the presumption exists. They argue that it exists because the law guarantees the right of counsel and they say that such a guarantee is meaningless unless the attorney retained by the defendant can have an opportunity to present his client's defense. These authors seem to feel that if a citizen were presumed guilty, there would be no reason to give him any chance to defend himself, so that any right to defense naturally carries with it the presumption of innocence.

This view was restated in 1958 when new fundamental principles for criminal procedure were adopted. Although jurists on the drafting committee urged specific declaration of the existence in Soviet law of a presumption of innocence, non-jurists argued that common people would not understand what it meant, for they could not but suppose that when an accused was brought to trial, the prosecutor and the preliminary investigator must have had good reason to conclude him guilty. The presumption was not incorporated, although the President of the Supreme Court of the U.S.S.R. restated in his speech to the Supreme Soviet as a deputy, perhaps in an effort to make his point in the stenographic minutes, that the procedural guarantee of the new codes rested on the assumption of the existence of a presumption of innocence, even though it was not stated explicitly.

Westerners have been rather doubtful of the effectiveness of such an argument in times of stress. They would prefer having the presumption of innocence spelled out, and this is usually done in the West. It is particularly important in procedural systems structured upon the customary pattern of Continental European countries, as is the U.S.S.R., for in those countries there is always a lengthy preliminary investigation before trial, which is unknown to Anglo-American procedure. The Soviet preliminary investigation is a hearing before an investigator who is a civil servant subject to the administrative control of the prosecutor's office. Under the Soviet procedural code, he is supposed to conduct an impartial hearing like that of a judge, in spite of his administrative link to the prosecutor. He is required by law to hear not only those witnesses brought by the police and by the prosecutor but also all witnesses and evidence that the defendant wishes to introduce. On the basis of careful weighing of all of this evidence, the investigator prepares a conclusion supported by the record of his investigation, from which the prosecutor can prepare the indictment. The indictment and the record are then sent to the court for use in the trial, which means that at a Soviet trial the judges have before them a record, often in several volumes of typewritten and handwritten notes, of what every witness said on the occasion of the preliminary investigation. The judge has only to work through the material, calling the witnesses and seeing whether they adhere to their prior testimony.

It is a rare Soviet judge, on the admission of Soviet text writers themselves, who can resist the conclusion that the investigator's work must have proved guilt. While the judge is supposed to consider the accused innocent, he has a hard time approaching the case as if the accused were innocent. He is likely to try to prove the record before him rather than to verify it. Under Soviet rules of procedure, a judge may ask any question he wants and cross-examine witnesses himself. He is not limited to listening to the direct and cross-examination by prosecutor and defense attorney, as is the case in some American states. In consequence, the judge can, and often does, appear to be a second prosecutor acting on the basis of the record before him.

The great threat to the presumption of innocence presented by the preliminary investigation has caused even Soviet authors to argue that the accused should be permitted to have counsel at the preliminary investigation as well as at the trial. Their arguments were partially successful in obtaining reform in 1958, but only for juvenile delinquents. Later, the right to defense counsel was extended to physically handicapped persons. For other defendants, counsel will be admitted on consent of the prosecutor, but, if denied, counsel cannot aid until the indictment is presented.

The Soviet Lawyer

Such emphasis upon the importance of counsel must take into consideration the character of the lawyer in Soviet circumstance. In all systems of the law, to be permitted to practice, the lawyer must be licensed by the court or by some administrative body such as a ministry of justice. Such licensing is thought to be necessary as a protection to clients against incompetency or criminality on the part of attorneys. In the U.S.S.R., lawyers are licensed by the ministry of justice, the Council of Ministers, or the Supreme Court of each republic under an instruction issued by the controlling body. They must pass bar examinations. The major differences between the Soviet and the American lawyers are not in licensing. They lie in other places.

On the organizational side, the Soviet lawyer practices in an office operated by the republic's college of advocates, to which he is admitted after passing the requirements of an educational and character nature. These offices are placed in areas believed to be convenient for clients, by the appropriate authorities of each republic. Although no law prohibits private practice, there are now no private practitioners. All lawyers work in the offices of a college of advocates. Within these offices, operations are conducted like those of a partnership. One member is selected as manager by vote of all of the members. When a client calls for assistance, he may choose his preferred lawyer, and, if he has none, the manager assigns one. When fees are paid, they are allocated first, in a given proportion, to meet the operating expense of the office, and the balance is paid to the lawyer who did the work. Fees are set by regulation in accordance with a scale based upon time spent and type of work done. Since the scale has to be flexible to meet the varying demands upon an attorney, there is still some room for negotiation of the fee with a client. Fees may even be waived, if the client is too poor to pay.

From the organization side, it is evident that there is more control over the activity of a lawyer than would be found in an American state in which lawyers conduct their practice on a private basis. In actuality, a Soviet attorney is rather free to choose the cases he will accept and reject and to decide upon the measures he will take to represent his client, but he is always mindful that the success of his career is subject to the pleasure of his colleagues in the office, and they in turn develop attitudes which they believe to be favored by the Communist party.

In this effort to please a monopoly political party lies the major difference between the Soviet attorney and his American counterpart. The difference will be seen to be deeper than an organizational framework of the bar. It lies at the base of the Soviet one-party system of government, as a result of which the lawyer will be wary of unpopular causes. There is no large and powerful opposition to which he can turn for protection in the event that his client's case is unpopular politically. In the routine case involving no politics, the Soviet lawyer seems to feel free to defend his client's interest as he will, but in the political case he has to limit his activities to what the Communist party policy-makers feel is permissible defense.

In the early days of the Soviet regime, the lawyer's lot was more difficult. There was a tendency on the part of the public and even of Communist party members to feel that a criminal defendant and a civil plaintiff were politically questionable characters. It was presumed that the police would not have arrested a person unless he were guilty and that a civil plaintiff in bringing suit was taking advantage of some poor workman who could not pay his debts. A lawyer taking such cases was associated in the public mind with the unpopular position of the client.

In the early days there was no appreciation of the attitude that Western societies have taken toward the role of lawyers, namely, that no one can be sure of what really happened until after the trial, for if one could be sure, why should there be a trial at all? Westerners believe that the trial will not produce the true facts unless all interested parties are given a chance to state their case. This requires a lawyer, for few individuals are sufficiently alert in the excitement of a courtroom, even if they have knowledge of legal procedures, to make the decisions necessary to present their case well. All this experience of the centuries with the conduct of a lawsuit was discarded by the Soviet citizens of the early years in their attitude toward trials and lawyers.

A Changed Attitude toward the Bar

During the last twenty-five years there has been creeping back in the U.S.S.R. an appreciation of the lesson of the centuries. Soviet authors now attempt to explain to their public that society is harmed if the innocent are punished or if a negligent driver is not made to pay for damage as the result of a civil suit to determine fault. If an innocent man is punished, the guilty one is left at large to commit the same crime again, to the injury of the state and of the society that it professes to protect. If a negligent driver does not have to pay damages as the result of the civil suit, he feels no restraint for the future. In consequence, effective defense is beneficial to the state and to society and should be encouraged. It makes certain that those who are really at fault are punished.

Even prosecutors have written to the editors of the journal of the Ministry of Justice of the U.S.S.R. urging that a defense attorney be permitted to appear at the preliminary investigation. The argument they give is that errors can creep into the most carefully prepared prosecution, and it would help the prosecutor to know that a lawyer representing the accused was watchful against such errors. In short, defense is desirable because it protects the state.

As in other areas of Soviet activity, the position has lost support up to the present time in highest quarters when a terrorist act was committed or when there was a conspiracy to overthrow the regime. It may have seemed to Soviet policy-makers that in such vital cases the prosecutor's staff could afford to assign to the matter a sufficient number of men to review all possibilities so as to make certain that the accused was guilty. One of the prosecutors could take the role of devil's advocate to make sure that no stone was left unturned. In the case of an assassination, the would-be assassin was usually caught in the act, so that there could be no question of guilt anyway. In consequence, a defense attorney may have seemed unnecessary to protect the state.

The world's interest in the presence of defense attorneys at a trial is so great, however, that in the purge trials of the late 1930's defense attorneys were assigned to some of the defendants by the college of advocates at the request of the court. Being in a situation where Stalin's own hand had formulated some of the charges and knowing that guilt was dictated by him before the trial began, the defense attorneys limited their defense. They acknowledged that their clients were guilty. They argued only that their clients had not been instigators of the alleged plot but had been led into it because of their weak wills after years of exemplary living. Clemency was asked and nothing more.

This being the political situation as it affects the activity of the Soviet lawyer, it can be seen that there are limitations on him that are not to be found in Western society. The Soviet state has, apparently, appreciated this danger. To compensate for it, there is placed upon the prosecution a duty to watch out for the interests of defendants and of parties to civil suits. It has already been indicated how the prosecutor may, and does, intervene in civil suits when he believes that the interests of the state are jeopardized by the impending defeat of one of the parties.

A Special Role for Prosecutors

The prosecutor of a republic may, and often does, intervene also in criminal cases, after a sentence has been pronounced and after a provincial or county prosecutor has obtained a verdict against the accused. The higher prosecutor is supposed to be more than a prosecutor. He is supposed to see to the correct application of the law. It may be that a lower prosecutor has made a mistake, and it is the superior's task to verify from time to time the work of the lower courts and to select for review by higher courts those cases that have not gone forward for review on appeal because the defendant did not press his case.

To assure that the prosecutor will not be influenced by the Communist party politicians at the local level, the structure of the prosecutor's office is completely centralized. Unlike the judges, who are named by the process of election at the local level and by the appropriate soviet at higher levels, the prosecutors from top to bottom are named by the Prosecutor-General of the U.S.S.R., although on the advice of the prosecutors of the republics. The Prosecutor-General in turn is named by the Supreme Soviet of the U.S.S.R. for a five-year term. By this system, the prosecutors are always subject to influence by the highest Communist party circles, but they do not have to seek appointment by fawning upon local party bosses, nor need they fear for their jobs if they displease local party bosses who are tending to become local tyrants.

To the Western student of the Soviet system, it seems incredible that prosecutors, even under such structural protection, can think in two ways, as a prosecutor and as a defender. Yet the court reports are full of actions brought by prosecutors in the supreme courts of the republics and even before colleges of the Supreme Court of the U.S.S.R. to set aside a conviction of a trial court. The procedure does not appeal to those accustomed to a system that permits a series of appeals to the highest tribunals in the states of the United States, and sometimes to the Supreme Court of the United States, with the help of a fearless attorney who does not have to rely for his livelihood upon the political party in power. It is for this reason that the right to independent counsel in all cases and the right to appeal to the highest tribunal have been cherished so long in the West. These comprise some of the many marks distinguishing the Soviet system from those in the Western democracies.

CHAPTER 12

EMPLOYMENT BY THE STATE

State employment of labor has become a primary characteristic of the Soviet system of government, and it has affected vitally the lives of many Soviet citizens. To the Westerner, the result seems at times to be a new form of economic serfdom. To the Soviet propagandist, the system seems to provide the only way of achieving the maximum production that he believes essential to the working of a real democracy. An examination of the rules governing state employment and of the reaction of Soviet citizens to them will provide an opportunity to end this study of the Soviet system at a point close to the lives of individuals, where the impact of government is felt most strongly. In the final analysis, for a very large number of people in every country the ultimate acceptance or rejection of a system of government stems from the system's effect upon the job.

At the outset, it is necessary to recall that not everyone in the U.S.S.R. is employed by the state. The members of a collective farm are in theory co-owners of their agricultural enterprise, receiving not wages for their work but a share in the total net product of the farm. Although the activities of these farmers are prescribed by numerous laws and regulations, which are enforced in practice by the Communist party's discipline enforced on farm chairmen, the collective farmers are not state employees, as are their fellow farmers on the state farm.

There are still a considerable number of artisans at work in the U.S.S.R. Many of these perform their work as cobblers, tailors, repairmen, and wood-carvers at a popular crossing of two paths in a village or under the stairwell of an apartment house in a city. Those engaged in service trades are often organized in artisan co-operative associations that have much the same organizational structure as the collective farms. Membership meetings choose managers who conduct both the buying of raw materials available locally and the sale of the service in the repair of property which the state shops are not equipped to provide. Within these artisan co-operatives there is much more freedom than within the collective farms, because the government seems to feel that their service functions are not as essential to the well-being of society as is the produce of the farms. Nevertheless, the government relies on these artisans for service, and their contribution is considered in preparing economic plans.

Considerable numbers of domestic servants are employed by private families so that wives and mothers can be freed of the duties of the home to pursue careers in the professions. Also, herdsmen are employed by collective farmers to watch those flocks that remain the private property of the households. While the number of these private employees is even today of some statistical importance, private employment is believed to be diminishing. This is because nurseries, laundries, and dining halls are lifting from the professional woman with a family some of the burdens that she has up to now been passing to a domestic servant or to the children's grandmother.

There are still some categories of professional persons who can be said to be self-employed. Lawyers perform their services in co-operative associations of lawyers organized under the auspices of the college of advocates, as has been indicated earlier. They receive no wage but a share of the fees commensurate with their work. Occasionally, up to very recent years, the most skilful of them have conducted private practice from their homes, but this time seems to have passed. Home practice is also a feature of the life of the medical doctors, but today this is always an after-hours practice, for the doctors are employed in clinics and hospitals by the Ministry of Public Health and spend the greater part of each day as state employees.

To support prospecting for precious metals and the trapping of furs, citizens are still encouraged to take to the trails of Siberia and of the Far North. It is these prospectors and trappers who, perhaps, alone retain the characteristics of what Americans have called "rugged individualism." Yet, even these last of the individualists of the private enterprise era have no choice in the disposition of their hauls. The gold and platinum must be sold to the State Bank and the furs to the state enterprise dealing in this item. No fur trapper can seek independent bids from firms interested in his pelts. Many are now joined in co-operatives.

Such private enterprise as there is suffers further discouragement from the personal income tax statutes. While all Soviet citizens are required to pay an income tax graduated in accordance with the amount of their income, the private enterpriser is subjected to a higher rate than those employed by the state. In consequence, the doctor who is tempted to practice after hours in his home thinks twice about the extent to which he may be able to retain the fees he can collect. The social insurance rate for injury hampering employment is also lower by half for those domestic servants and herdsmen of collective farm households who choose private employment in the only areas still permitted instead of employment by the state, and there is no social insurance for the self-employed who loses his capacity to work.

Making a Career

For the ambitious young man or woman seeking a career in Soviet society as it is today, the only thought will be of state employment. State employment opens the road to power, prestige, a desirable apartment in the multiple dwellings maintained by state agencies, and a steady income followed by a state pension.

Schooling prepares youth for careers. During the 1950's and 1960's an 8-year program was extended by degrees even to the remote regions of the U.S.S.R. In 1972 the primary school having one teacher to a class was cut back from 4 to 3 years to introduce specialized teaching at an earlier age, and by 1975 the compulsory program was ordered extended to 10 years. The ninth and tenth grades are devoted to an advanced generalized program offered to the graduates of 8-year programs, 63% of whom are admitted. The rest enter a specialized or vocational curriculum, or begin work while studying nights. About 4% drop out.

Khrushchev's experiment of 1958 with a working recess in the educational sequence for all but students in mathematics, sciences, music, and graphic and performing arts, where continuity of study seemed necessary, was abandoned even before his ouster in 1964. Students now proceed from the eight-year schools immediately to the ninth grade, if admitted, but during the tenth they are expected to participate voluntarily in varying forms of socially useful labor in production, either in school shops or in neighborhood factories. This part of school experience is designed to orient them to the worker mentality of their state and to dissipate any tendency they might have to exalt themselves over their working fellows because of their educational advantage.

The narrowing of the passage to a professional career is accentuated on completion of the tenth year, when applications to universities or specialized higher schools are filed. The eighteen-year-old is subjected to a grueling set of examinations, especially for admission to the most noted institutes. The Plekhanov Economic Institute in Moscow rejected seven out of eight applicants in 1966. The high quality of those admitted was evidenced by the fact that for the specialty of economic cybernetics three-fourths of the successful ones had been medal winners in the secondary schools.

Medal winners are exempt from all but one examination in their specialty. Should they fail, however, to live up to their promise and receive a grade of less than "excellent," they must take all of the examinations and compete with those who have done less well in the tenth grade. The non-preferential requirements are four examinations, of which mathematics is required of all as a control subject. Two of the examinations must be in the specialist field chosen. The other one may be selected from a group including Russian language and literature, chemistry, physics, history, and government. A foreign language must be offered for admission to a career in linguistics or where a discipline requires it.

Preference in admission was accorded students coming to the universities and higher schools directly from production under Khrushchev and 80% of those matriculating had to be from this group. Practice showed that they were often poorly prepared, and the obligatory ratio was abandoned after his ouster. Today, the applicants from factories and farms are placed in a separate category within which there is a competition, and the directors of the institutes or rectors of the universities establish the percentage to be taken from this group as their proficiency suggests.

Oral examinations are required of those recieiving a three out of five average in the written admissions examinations, if there are vacancies left for candidates from that category. It is here that favoritism has been charged, for irate letter writers to editors claim that examining boards in some institutions have preferred athletes, musicians, and amateur artists to higher-standing students to round out a representative student body.

Graduate programs leading to higher degrees, including the

doctorate, are available for those who wish to proceed to academic circles.

The age of fifteen or sixteen is a momentous one for those hoping for a white-collar career. Very few individuals have been able subsequently to move into the coveted ranks of the "intellectuals" if they did not obtain entry at the point when professional education began. To be sure, there were much-heralded exceptions, as when a workman by some invention or rationalization of work proved his mental powers. In such cases he might be catapulted with great public acclaim into a professional school for further training, but these were the exceptions and not the rule. The separation of those who will eventually be favored as the technicians, the managers, and the intellectuals generally, from those who must remain throughout their lives at the level of the manual laborer, occurs at an early age.

Social Mobility

In the West, of recent years, the question has been discussed whether any real choice exists for the sons of workmen and peasants in the U.S.S.R. at the age of decision or whether they may be expected to continue their parents' activities at the workbench and at the plow. In an effort to determine whether the professed favoritism of Soviet leaders toward workmen and peasants in the new Russia had resulted in greater social mobility than is to be found in the West, the Harvard team of interviewers asked a series of questions of 2,725 refugees in Western Europe and in the United States during 1950 and 1951. The interviewers concluded that worker or peasant background had been a severe handicap to social mobility in the 1920's but that the situation had changed sharply in the 1930's.

The chances of a person who had been a worker or peasant before the Revolution to move into a white-collar or non-manual-worker group in the years between 1917 and 1929 were found to be only one-seventh as good as the chances for those who came from what the bolsheviks called the former "exploiter" classes. These had been the aristocracy, landowners, former Tsarist civil servants, intellectuals, army officers, merchants, and priests. While the interview sample may have been biased, in that probably fewer of those who had made the transition from one class to another had been sufficiently disgruntled with the

Soviet system to flee, the statistics for the 1920's are not thought to be unduly unrepresentative since in all functionally specialized societies the rate of mobility possible within a single generation has been found to be low.

The rate of mobility in Soviet society during the 1920's, to be specific, was found by the interviewers to be 12.1 per cent. This meant that 102 persons out of the sample group of 840 members of the working class had been able to change their status. This contrasted with the success of 607 out of the sample group of 705 members of the former "exploiter" classes in retaining their white-collar status after the Revolution. The interviewers concluded that the high rate of retention of status by the former white-collar groups was due in part to the decision of Communist party leaders to utilize specialists of the old regime in posts for which new specialists could not be trained quickly.

By the 1930's, the process of educating the masses had progressed markedly. The illiteracy rate, which had stood at 50 per cent as late as 1926, was pushed back to 20 per cent in 1939. The five-year plans were inaugurated to speed up industrialization, thus creating the need for large numbers of technicians and managers. The interview statistics indicate a reflection of these developments: the rate of mobility from the worker-peasant category to the non-manual category jumped from 12.1 per cent in the 1920's to 29.5 per cent in the 1930's.

The percentile increase is computed from the fact that 190 persons out of a group of 644 sons and daughters of working-class parents had been successful in moving into the white-collar or "intellectual" category. They did so, however, without pushing out the sons and daughters of persons who had been in the non-manual category before the Revolution, for the statistics show that 89.7 per cent of this group had been able to retain the favored position as compared with 73.9 per cent in the 1920's.

To determine how the Soviet rate of social mobility compared with a Western rate, the interviewers took a table prepared by Dewey and Anderson from a sample American community in 1933–34. This showed that 26.4 per cent of the persons who started their first permanent job as manual workers had been able to move into the non-manual category by the time of the investigation. Robert A. Feldmesser has concluded from his analysis of the Soviet statistics that social mobility in the U.S.S.R. has been the result of industrialization and that the figures are about what one would find in other industrialized societies. If this be so, the opportunity for choice of a profession at the age of decision in the U.S.S.R. is about what it is elsewhere. The children of parents who have the educational background associated with the non-manual categories of workers still have the greatest opportunity to gain admission to the professions. This is not because of any bias in their favor but simply because it is easier to maintain good records in school and to pass entrance examinations if parents are interested in such success and provide the environment in which academic pursuits find encouragement and stimulation.

The increasing success of children of educated parents in competition for university admission worries educators committed by Marxist doctrine to advancement of workers. Universities were directed in 1969 to establish remedial tutoring under which graduates could enter universities without competitive examination, but 1975 statistics show that many tutored students drop out after admission. Students from minority ethnic areas tend to fail because of inadequate Russian, or because they are overrated by ambitious teachers. In Armenia over half the medalists from secondary schools failed the first university examination in 1977.

Compulsory Assignment to Jobs

The Soviet youth who has been successful in placing his foot upon the ladder of the professions through completion of training at the university or at a professional school may have been chosen for his career through much the same process as is familiar to youths of the West, but at this point the structure of the Soviet system introduces a new feature. In the West, with the exception of students trained at state expense in military academies, a graduate is not required to pursue the profession for which he was trained, even if he has attended a state university. In the U.S.S.R. it is different.

Graduates of Soviet professional schools are required by law to serve for three years in the post to which they are assigned by the ministry for which they have been trained. It is argued by Soviet officials that it would be a social waste to do otherwise. Students have received stipends during their period of professional training, and they have been relieved of the duty to pay tuition. To a Soviet official mind, they owe service to the state in return for what they have received.

To avoid hardship, personal wishes are respected by the officials who make the assignments. Wives are not sent to cities apart from those in which their husbands are to work. Health factors are considered. Yet in most cases the jobs requiring recruits are in the remote provinces. It is the rare student who is assigned to Moscow, Leningrad, or Kiev, although the Soviet press has recently declared that some students have sought to use influence within the ministry to obtain the coveted posts in these cities. If a student refuses to go to the place of his assignment, or refuses to remain at the assigned post for the three years required, he is subject to prosecution.

From the foregoing, it is to be seen that the top ministerial administrators of the future, and the directors and technical directors of public corporations, are selected from the pool of experts created by the educational programs of the universities and of the professional schools. Those who have not been able to obtain admission to such schools are deprived of nearly all subsequent opportunity to cross the barrier between manual labor and the professional positions. These comprise the great pool from which employment directors meet their needs for unskilled labor.

A shortage of semiskilled personnel seems to have been felt just before World War II, for in 1940 a labor draft was instituted. Under the provisions of the labor-draft law, young men and women, on completion of their studies in the ten-year schools or at such time as they dropped out of school because of lack of ability or desire to continue beyond the required minimum of seven years, were subject to the labor draft. Local boards composed of the adult members of each rural and urban community decided which of the youths whom they knew were most suitable for a semiskilled education. Quotas were established for each community and filled from those young people who had not progressed to the university or to the professional school or who had not been drafted for military service under the conscription law.

The youths of both sexes who were drafted under the labor-reserve program had to serve four years. Their work began with a short course of technical training to fit them for an apprenticeship that led eventually to a position of foreman. They were uniformed and subjected to discipline only slightly less vigorous than that of the military. Eventually they were assigned to their place of work by the Ministry of Labor Reserves and its successor agency, to become the nucleus of a large industrial army of semiskilled workmen. In the first nine years of operation, the program trained four and a half million youths.

The labor draft was ended in 1955, and the labor reserve schools were absorbed into the general school system in 1958. Thus, skilled workers are trained today in one- or two-year programs of vocational-technical schools after completing the eight-year general education program. Emphasis upon the importance of these schools was increased by a Communist party resolution of September, 1977, which noted that 2 million skilled workers were being graduated annually although their preparation was inadequate. The party demanded better coordination of social science disciplines with practice. Also, the party ordered that students be imbued more intensively with "lofty ideological-political and moral qualities, love for their occupations, the desire to labor honestly and conscientiously for the good of the homeland."

The Komsomols and labor unions were directed to improve their patronage of schools, and universities were enjoined to help in staffing schools with graduates of engineering and technical training programs. Graduates were to be given opportunities to study further.

Civil Service Regulation

For the unskilled workmen and clerks, there is no national recruitment program. The employment officers on the operating level of each ministry and of each public corporation are left completely free to choose whom they wish for the jobs they have to fill. No panel of available candidates is prepared by a civil service commission, as is the case generally in the West with state employment.

Regulations on such recruitment are few. The criminal code punishes any discrimination on the basis of race, religion, or sex. This latter basis for discrimination has been the subject of much trouble in the case of pregnant women who apply for jobs. Employment officers hesitate to employ a woman in this condition, for they know that soon she will take maternity leave, during which time she draws her regular pay, and at the end of her leave she must be returned to her job. Under the system of budgeted wages established for all state agencies, there will be costs from which there will be no return.

The policy-makers of the state have set up a budgeted wage system to assure maximum value from the wages expended; yet in the instance of the pregnant-woman worker they are faced with a competing value, the desire to increase the birth rate to provide a larger pool of labor supply and to man the armed services at the levels desired. Further, there is a public opinion problem, for there would be considerable hostility on the part of the women of the land if they found themselves excluded from jobs when about to bear children. In the face of these considerations, the policy-makers have found it necessary to include an article in the criminal code punishing managers of state enterprises who discriminate against pregnant women in their employment policies.

Close relationship by blood or marriage is the sole basis for legal discrimination in employment, and then only if one of the persons would be subject to the supervision of another. From this exclusionary rule are excepted technicians in a post office and in a telegraph agency, teachers, artists, musicians, medical doctors, agronomists, meteorologists, and laboratory workers. Presumably kinship makes no difference in the performance of duties by such professionals, or the demand for them may be so great that the risk of influence must be overlooked in the interest of getting things done.

No civil service examinations are given for positions in the state services and public corporations, it being assumed that the records in the schools are sufficiently uniform to provide a basis for judging the relative ability of every applicant. Further reason for the absence of a standard examination may be that with the present shortage of labor there is no pressure for admission to state employment, with the result that few if any allegations of favoritism in making appointments are made. Conditions are different from those in some other countries, in which employment is the subject of stiff competition and in which the civil service law requires that every candidate for a job be rated against his competitors on the basis of a uniform examination.

The functions to be performed in every job are described, as they are in the public services of other countries, in a civil service manual that provides uniformity throughout the entire country. Each job is given a rating to which is attached a specific wage scale. The scale varies with the qualifications of the incumbent, so that the wage will be higher if the incumbent has specified academic qualifications such as the Master's or Doctor's degree, if he accumulates years of service, or if he works in a remote location or in an especially dangerous place such as the psychiatric ward of a hospital. By this means, incentive encouragement is given those to whom the piecework system is inapplicable, such as medical doctors, teachers, directors of administrative bureaus, and the like.

Dismissals are a source of friction in any society. Even in private enterprise economies, the circumstances under which dismissals may occur are becoming the basis of contract regulation as the result of collective bargaining between management and labor unions. While there is no law in the United States forbidding a private employer to dismiss whom he will, there have come into being strict laws governing employment by state and federal governments in their respective civil services. For such employment, dismissals are regimented so that they may not occur without a hearing, meeting the tests of due process of law, in which the facts meriting dismissal are proved.

With its wide application of a system of public employment, the Soviet government found it necessary to define the circumstances under which dismissals might occur. This was done in the Code of Labor Laws, adopted in each Soviet republic in 1922 to meet the needs of the New Economic Policy when limited private enterprise was being reintroduced. While the rules were designed to restrain private employers, they were made equally applicable to the state managers, and they are presently of concern only to these, as private employment for productive purposes is now constitutionally forbidden. Their validity under conditions of monopoly state employment was reaffirmed in 1969 when, after a decade of discussion, they appeared with little change in the fundamentals of labor legislation adopted by the federal Supreme Soviet.

The rules for dismissal are quite similar to those existing for the civil service of other lands. No one may be dismissed unless there is: complete or partial abolition of an office or reduction in its work load, termination of the position for which a person was employed, incompetency, recurrent failure without a satisfactory reason to perform duties assigned, commission of a criminal offense in connection with the work, failure to be present at work without excuse, failure to resume work for four consecutive months after restoration of capacity to work, or displacement by a reinstated person formerly performing the functions of the incumbent. During World War II absence for twenty minutes was made grounds for prosecution. While prosecution is no longer permitted, the twenty-minute rule probably represents the tolerance allowed before dismissal may occur.

Grievance Procedure

Established standards of conduct are always accompanied by disputes as to whether, in any given situation, the standards are met. A grievance procedure has been provided in private enterprise countries by management and labor, under which management and the labor union determine whether the provisions of a collective bargaining agreement relating to dismissal have been met. In the U.S.S.R. a grievance procedure is also provided, but it is established by law and not in collective bargaining agreement. Under the Soviet procedure, a system of grievance boards exists under the administrative supervision of each labor union's apparatus. These boards contain equal representation of the labor union to which the disgruntled workman belongs and of the management for which he works.

The very placing of the grievance boards under the supervision of one of the interested parties, namely, the labor union, rather than under an admittedly state agency such as a ministry of labor, which presumably would be impartial as between state manager and labor union, suggests the unusual position in which the labor union has been placed in the U.S.S.R. It has become in a sense a ministry of labor in the eyes of the policy-makers of the Communist party. Since 1930 it has been ordered not to take a position in defense of the interests of laboring men against those of the state managers, because the interests of both are supposed to be identical. To avoid development of any narrow syndicalist attitudes, the trade-union leadership has been related closely to the Communist party leadership, and, in consequence, the transfer of the grievance procedure to the trade-union organization is not the concession to labor that it appears to be. It is not the subordination of the state managers to the trade union, as would be charged in the United States if the Transport Workers Union in New York City were to be made responsible for the conduct of a grievance procedure to settle complaints brought by its members against the agency managing New York City's municipally owned subways. On the contrary, the Soviet labor unions have been so thoroughly absorbed into the state apparatus that the state managers need not ordinarily fear discrimination against them in the grievance boards. There would seem to exist an equal balance which permits decisions of a nature that both sides seem in the main to accept as fair, although some Soviet refugees have reported that management hesitates to tangle with the trade union before a grievance board.

The employee in a Soviet state agency is not bound under the 1969 general principles to bring his case before the grievance board in all situations. He may go directly to a court if he has been discharged from any but a supervisory position. In other cases, however, the law requires that he exhaust the remedy offered by the grievance boards, persumably on the assumption that the matter will usually be one of simple fact that can be determined quickly, informally, and accurately by men on the spot who know the conditions of employment. A disgruntled employee may appeal the grievance board's decision to the trade-union committee in the factory, shop, or locality concerned. Examination of the case is required by the trade-union committee if the grievance board is unable to agree on a solution.

If the trade-union committee fails to satisfy the employee or management, in cases unrelated to dismissal, the disgruntled party may take the case to court. Once he is there, he has available to him the usual route of an appeal to a higher court, and even intervention by a prosecutor or a president of a supreme court, to bring the matter before the supreme court of the republic or of the U.S.S.R.

Management is permitted to make some decisions without fear of review. Thus it may discharge employees who have the authority to hire or discharge other employees, and it may also discharge various officials having posts of such sensitivity as to preclude a public airing of their qualifications and their performance, such as, for example, agents of the Ministry of Internal Affairs.

Numerous judicial decisions having to do with labor disputes arising before the 1959 reform provide insight into Soviet society. In addition, there are reports of lawyers who have fled the Soviet Union after years of service as advisers on labor matters to Soviet managers. From these reports it is possible to conclude that, through the procedures provided to protect an employee in a job, the great majority of disgruntled Soviet employees have been able to obtain redress against a foreman who has been arbitrary in recommending a dismissal. The court will order reinstatement. Perhaps the most illuminating case involved the dismissal for incompetency of an elderly woman by the management of a village clinic. The case was pressed by the employee until it reached the Supreme Court of the U.S.S.R., which concluded that there had been insufficient study of the woman's qualifications by the lower tribunals through which the case had gone.

The Disadvantages of Monopoly Employment

The disadvantages of monopoly employment by state agencies would seem to be numerous, to one who is used to the private enterprise system. First and foremost is the disadvantage created by the Soviet government's attitude toward employees of the Soviet state. The government has tended over the years to treat employees as if they were resources, like cement or bricks or steel. The economic planners began their planning with control over the distribution of electrical power, on the theory that with limited control over a vital necessity of all industry they could influence industrial development as a whole. They moved into the planning of production and distribution of all key resources, leaving outside the allocation system only those locally produced and consumed. As Soviet planners have found themselves plagued by the tendency of employees to move from job to job in search of better conditions, they have tried to control labor turnover by prohibiting it, and, finally, under the strain of World War II, they moved to the allocation of labor to meet production needs.

In anticipation of war, all employees were frozen in their respective jobs in June, 1940, and became subject to prosecution if they left the job without permission of management. Management was required to give permission only if an employee was in ill-health or had been admitted to a school of higher learning to improve his or her skills. When entire factories were moved to new locations behind the Urals from areas of the Ukraine and western Russia threatened by the German advance, the employees were required to accompany the plant. Permanent cities were built for the employees, from which they were not permitted to depart after the war. From the state officials' point of view, production would have been lost if the individuals had been permitted to return to the Ukraine of their childhood. Since the welfare of all was thought to depend on maintenance of production, attention to personal desires was not permitted.

Mobility from one job to another was, therefore, reduced sharply in the U.S.S.R. after 1940. Reports coming from the U.S.S.R. as early as 1951 suggested that there was beginning even before Stalin's death a relaxation in the strict restraints formerly enforced against those who wanted to leave their jobs. In 1956 this suggestion was confirmed when the 1940 law was publicly repealed. There has been, however, a renewed propaganda drive to urge employees to remain on the job because of the wastefulness involved in labor turnover. Managers have been asked to discourage moving about, especially on the part of those employees whose training has involved time and expense.

Soviet reliance on the criminal code rather than on economic incentive is to be found in other situations. As in the case of preventing labor turnover by means of criminal law, penalties have been established to encourage faithful performance at the job. Thus, a manager of a state enterprise, as well as the chief engineer or the chief of technical inspection, is subject to prosecution if employees produce goods below standard quality. While the law was not enforced generally during the war, because of the difficulty of obtaining information from consumers in time to take the prescribed measures against the managers, and seems under postwar conditions to remain an almost dead letter, it indicates Soviet attitudes. In a private enterprise system, the quality of goods finds quick reflection in the action of consumers, who will boycott poor quality or demand a reduced price. Managers who are unable to meet consumers' demands will find their enterprise losing money, and they will either lose their jobs, if they are employees themselves, or find themselves insolvent, if they are owners of the establishment. In the U.S.S.R., they are prosecuted if they are found to have been personally at fault.

The Soviet planners have tried to introduce some of the economic controls that result from the application of consumers' choice in a private enterprise system. They have placed identifying symbols in the form of trade marks on state-produced products of different plants, hoping that consumers will boycott the products which they have found by consumption in the past to be poor and choose the ones they have found to be good. The difficulty has been that the rate of production has been so much lower than necessary to meet consumers' desires that the economic method of weeding out poor managers has failed. There have not been enough commodities to give the consumer a choice. The criminal code has been made, therefore, to bear the burden of policing the efficiency of the managers. Rising production may change this situation.

Enforcement of planning directives prior to Khrushchev's ouster also influenced industrial freedom, for the authority of managers to operate the plant as they thought best to achieve results was limited. It happened, apparently, that errors in allocations, or faulty deliveries of goods, resulted in the accumulation of machine parts or of other supplies that could not be used in the production process or in the operation of an office. Before 1940, if we may believe the statements of Soviet refugees, managers used to sell these surpluses to managers of other enterprises who had need of them in exchange for items for which they had need. This practice aroused the antagonism of the planning authorities, and an article was added to the criminal code prohibiting it on pain of prosecution.

The criminal penalty did not frighten the managers. They continued to do as they had done and to rely upon the results that they could show in terms of completing a job to justify their violation of the law. Reports of refugees, as analyzed by Joseph S. Berliner, indicate that flouting the details of the law in order to achieve production quotas became so common that scarcely a manager was free of guilt. Many were tried and sentenced, but it is indicative of the hostility that these prosecutions evoked that immediately after Stalin died in 1953 there was a general amnesty of certain categories of prisoners, prominent among whom were the managers who had been convicted of "economic crimes." Further, in 1955 the criminal penalty for disposal of surpluses was revoked, and a review of procedures for distribution of the unneeded products was ordered.

In view of the expansion of autonomy for plant directors since Khrushchev's ouster, the emphasis upon economic stimulation to highly productive work rather than penal sanctions for bad work is introducing a change in the situation. Consumers' desires have become a major criterion of planning, which leaves to the market the determination of style and design, setting only limits on the critical raw material allotted by central authorities. Under such circumstances, prosecution of managers for failure to follow strict rules will be unlikely. Poor work will result, as it does in market economies, in demotion or dismissal, and imaginative work in promotions and bonus payments.

Psychological Reaction to Controls

The post-Khrushchev emphasis upon market controls rather than control by law is being met with mixed feelings by the Soviet public. For many years they have accepted the restraints on job mobility and criminal penalties for violation of law as the reverse side of a coin of great value, namely guarantee of employment. Even among refugees from the Soviet system during Stalin's time, there was notable dislike of searching for jobs in the West under the free enterprise system. Many of them found themselves unable to accustom themselves to an economy in which individuals find their own jobs and enjoy the mobility that such freedom of choice makes possible. Some even chose to return to the U.S.S.R. rather than to remain in a free market economy.

Students graduating from professional schools in the U.S.S.R. have expressed to foreign students amazement that graduates of professional schools abroad have no assigned post awaiting their arrival. Much as they grumble about the obligation to serve in such a post for three years after graduation and the remoteness of some of them, they seem to require for their peace of mind the security offered them in the assurance of a job. Their objections during Stalin's time were not to mobilization of labor, but to the personal political risks to which they were subjected under Stalin's system of terror. They wanted to be assured of just determination of guilt when there was a charge of mismanagement, and they wanted to avoid the purge.

Questions are now being sent to newspapers asking whether the new system will not result in unemployment and less rigid planning of jobs. To many it seems highly advantageous to be relieved of fear of punishment for crimes they have not committed, but they are haunted by a new fear fostered by many years of propaganda about unemployment in a free market economy. They hope for the best, but they fear the worst.

To allay their fears Soviet leaders are telling them that when they become unemployed because of technological change they will be retrained at state expense and sent to labor-shortage areas if they are willing to move. This sounds attractive, but letters to editors have indicated that the retraining is slow, and the new jobs are often hundreds of miles from familiar haunts. There is no escaping the conclusion that Soviet citizens have taken literally the Constitution's guarantee of a "right to work," and they expect that pay envelopes will continue to arrive even if the job represents an unnecessary continuation of an outmoded practice. In a measure Soviet citizens have lost personal initiative at the lower levels of employment where ambition to advance to positions of prominence and good pay cannot be realistically encouraged for people who have not advanced sufficiently far in schooling to qualify for the rewarding posts.

Soviet leaders have much to overcome in re-orienting their people psychologically to meet the challenge of a new type of planning which relies heavily on market stimuli operating within the framework of a plan which is much less rigid than in Stalin's time.

CHAPTER 13

THE PERIL-POINTS

Democratic forms do not assure democratic government. History has proved that there are places at which counterweights can be placed to prevent democratic functioning of the forms. Modern dictators have shown that it is possible to combine democratic forms with counterweights. This has sometimes been done so cleverly at the early stages of a dictator's bid for power that the general public does not see the peril. It does not realize that it is losing the possibility of influencing policy and choosing leaders.

The blending of popular and dictatorial institutions in a fashion that fools the public may be said to be one of the characteristics of the modern totalitarian state. It is here that the totalitarians have been able to improve upon the system of the authoritarians, typified by the Tsars of Russia. The totalitarians have found a way to please the majority of the people, for a time at least, by giving them a parliament, an electoral procedure, trade unions, co-operative associations, local autonomy, a bill of rights, and codes of law. At the same time they have been able to preserve power by the use of controls over the forms that they have established or inherited. The totalitarians have shown that a people can no longer feel safe from the loss of freedom merely because its system of government incorporates democratic forms.

Soviet experience provides an example of the points at which a dictator has been able to prevent the democratic functioning of democratic forms, and this example has importance because it shows the extremes to which it is possible to go. It is obvious that in those countries that have long enjoyed democracy the public would not easily be misled into thinking that its system was democratic if the forms were counterweighted as they are in the U.S.S.R. Yet, even well-informed leaders of established dem-

ocratic states have realized that there are points at which democracy can be counterweighted and eventually destroyed.
These points may be called the "peril-points," because they are
the places at which restriction of democratic functions imperils
the future of a democratic state.

Abraham Lincoln worried about such peril during the crisis of
the war between the states, when he wrestled with the necessity
of suspending the historic writ of habeas corpus. The Supreme
Court of the United States worried about such peril when it had
to pass upon the constitutionality of restraints on freedom of
speech and of the press enacted by state legislatures during the
First World War. During the Second World War and into the
subsequent decade, the issue has been faced in many lands. In
the United States, first in connection with the problem of protecting society against potentially dangerous individuals of German
and Japanese stock living within the United States, and later in
connection with the problem of removing Communists from positions in which they could cause harm, the Supreme Court has
again been testing these restraints to determine whether they go
beyond the point of necessity and permanently endanger constitutional freedoms.

It is appropriate at the end of this study to review the principal
lessons of the Soviet dictatorship. It bears repeating that the
major danger to be avoided is the adoption of the underlying
philosophy of the Soviet leaders. The danger lies not in the acceptance of Marxist ideology, for few thinking people in the established democracies have been prepared to accept the limited
Marxist explanation of historical phenomena. The danger lies in
something deeper than the specifics of Marxism. It lies in the
philosophy of its high priests, namely, that one man or one group
of men can be infallible in their determination of political policy.

A Sense of Infallibility

In contrast to the leaders of the democratic states, Soviet leaders have professed since the days of their Revolution confidence
in their understanding of the forces of history. They believe that
Marx and Engels developed a method of analyzing history that is
unquestionably correct. They believe that only a small number
of thoroughly trained people can understand the method and
apply it. They do not imagine that the general public can be
taught to understand the method for many years. They conclude

for this reason that the public will require leadership for the foreseeable future and that the leaders must be selected from the narrow circle of people who have been reared in the Marxist method and who have the skill to apply it to an ever changing economic and political situation.

In contrast to the attitude of Soviet leaders, the men and women of the democratic states of the West who work their way to a position of leadership have no such purpose. They do not believe that a theory of history can be deduced with certainty from the events of past centuries, although they enjoy speculating on the plausibility of one or another theory as it is developed by men such as Arnold Toynbee. Having risen from the ranks themselves, whether it be from a farm, a haberdashery shop, or the rough and tumble of a British trade union, they do not believe that any group of men has a monopoly on wisdom or on leadership qualities. They believe that wise ideas may come from many sources, often quite unexpected and that these sources cannot under any circumstances be limited to a certain school of thought.

Although Western democratic leaders sometimes express the wish that they be let alone for long enough to apply their own schemes for national prosperity, they are prepared to bow, as did Winston Churchill during the Potsdam Conference at what seemed to be the very pinnacle of his career, to the will of the majority, and to step down for political opponents with quite different backgrounds, education, and aims. To men such as these, a major purpose of democratic government is to maintain a route through which new views may be aired and new men chosen to give them a trial.

Discipline for Party Members

The Soviet leaders, with their belief in the special wisdom granted to them by their mastery of the Marxist method, have constructed a matrix of government that assures their retention of power. Its core is an apparatus called a political party within which there is preserved a discipline like that within an army. Yet, to win and maintain the adherence of the rank and file members of this apparatus, the leaders have had to devise a procedure that can be thought to give the membership an opportunity to shape policy and to choose party leaders. Counterweights have been developed at the peril-points, namely, the selection of delegates to the higher echelons within the party and the manner in which minorities may express their views and organize their supporters within party meetings.

The counterweights to democratic elections within the party have been the establishment of the one-candidate ballot and the indirect election of delegates to the higher levels of the party apparatus. The counterweight to complete freedom of expression guaranteed by Communist party rules is the prohibition against the formation of voting blocs or "factions."

Western democratic parties usually provide that party members may vote for delegates to the national party conventions directly, in primaries, rather than indirectly. Further, Western political parties place no restriction upon the organization of voting blocs within a party, with the result that the world is often startled by such notorious party splits as that between the Clement Attlee and Aneurin Bevan factions in the British Labour Party, that between the Dixiecrats and the Truman leadership within the Democratic party of the United States, and the schism over Pierre Mendès-France in the Radical Socialist party of France.

When one moves beyond the political party to the representative bodies of the state, the contrast between the Soviet system and that familiar in Western democracies is even more noticeable. The principal feature of the contrast is the Soviet denial of the right to form a political party other than the Communist party to function within the representative bodies. The right of association in political parties is specifically limited by the Constitution itself. In Western democracies, the multiplicity of parties is fundamental. It is appreciated by students of politics that influence upon choice of leaders or determination of policy can be had only by association with like-minded persons, and this means, in political terminology, a political party. The right of association means, therefore, the right to form political parties without hindrance.

Yet, even in democratic countries there are occasions when a single political party in fact exists for a long period of time for some historical reason. While the right to form other parties continues, the right has little practical value because of the traditional situation. Thus, in India, the Congress party gained such prestige in its battle with the British prior to liberation that for a considerable period of time it remained the dominant factor in

Indian politics, although smaller parties won some important local victories. Yet, no one questioned the fact of Indian democracy before 1975 because the Congress party permitted its members to influence the choice of leaders and even to split the party. Faith in the democratic process was shattered when the stronger faction of the Congress party silenced all other parties in 1975 by arresting their leaders on charges of conspiracy. Still, the dictatorship was not to last, for the Prime Minister herself called new elections in 1977 (thinking, perhaps, to legitimate her power), freed opposition leaders, and was defeated.

The same possibility of change not only in personalities but even in party domination is true in those regions of other countries in which one or another political party holds power for many years. The important factors are the freedom given small parties to organize and seek votes and the establishment by law of the duty to select candidates for office through primaries permitting party members to choose their own candidates. Voters tend to move from faction to faction and even from party to party as sympathies change. The Supreme Court of the United States has recognized that a one-party system can be democratic in practice if the party that has an effective monopoly of power preserves a democratic structure within itself. The Soviet system provides no such safeguard.

Having eliminated any possibility of effective challenge to their authority from a second political party, or from a faction within the Communist party, the Soviet leaders have turned their attention to other possible sources of pressure upon their determination of policy. One gains the impression that Soviet leaders have sought to find the points at which they are unable, because of public opinion either at home or abroad or, sometimes, both at home and abroad, to eliminate a source of power and hence of pressure. They have then made arrangements that have neutralized the actual or political pressure groups, and sometimes they have been successful in bringing a group within their own orbit to exert pressure upon segments of the population or upon workmen throughout the world for the benefit of the Communist party leadership.

Limitations on Potential Pressure Groups

Organized religions have presented a real challenge to the Soviet leadership's monopoly of power, both because of the tenacity with which many Soviet citizens hold to worship of their God and also because foreign pressures have been great. The Soviet leaders have sought to dissuade those nearest to them from religious attitudes by expelling them from party member-ship if they practice religion. They have sought to win others away from religion through a vigorous campaign against religious belief on the ground that the natural sciences disprove the exis-tence of God. They have sought to restrict the influence of those who will not be frightened away from their beliefs or pro-pagandized out of them by limiting religious education and de-nying legal status to church communities. Only during World War II, when the Russian Orthodox Church gave its support to Stalin, was a respite granted. It is likely that if the church should become again, as it was in the early days after the Revolution, a strong pressure group against the government, it would find its activities circumscribed as before. By intensifying atheistic pro-paganda since 1956, the Communist party is losing no opportu-nity to weaken the church.

The trade unions have also presented a grave problem to Communist party leaders. The trade unions could not be abolished as they were by Hitler, for their strengthening had been one of the slogans of the Revolution, and their vigor was looked upon by many workmen outside Russia as evidence of the healthy policies of the Soviet government. Yet, they could not be permitted to function as a force capable of challenging the policies set by the Communist party. When they appeared to be moving in that direction in 1928, their leaders were purged. They were provided with new leaders and directed to support governmental policies calling for increased production.

The co-operative associations have also been a potential politi-cal threat. For economic reasons, the Communist leaders have had to expand the co-operatives in the agricultural field and in the artisan field also to fill the gaps in state-organized production. Such expansion has created a source of pressure. Yet the co-operatives have been prevented from becoming a national pres-sure group. The agricultural co-operatives have been sub-ordinated to the Ministry of Agriculture and have been con-trolled by dictation of the choice of officers whenever the mem-bers' choice was undesirable to the Communist party. They were further controlled until 1958 by a system of machine tractor sta-tions to which was transferred maintenance of the mechanical agricultural implements used by these co-operatives. Since abolition of machine tractor station control the party has relied on intensification of party activity within farms amalgamated to create large agricultural enterprises. The artisan co-operatives were controlled by limiting their sources of supply and by regulating the services they performed, and finally they were abolished except in service trades.

Any pressure that might have been exerted upon leaders by an industrial lobby, a chamber of commerce, or a real estate lobby has been eliminated by the expedient of abolishing private ownership of industrial establishments, of land, and also of merchandising enterprises. Those who manage the public corporations that operate state industry, sell its produce, and use that part of the land not allocated to the co-operative societies are permitted to form no independent associations such as the National Association of Manufacturers or the United States Chamber of Commerce.

No associations in other fields, even for ostensibly cultural purposes such as the propagation of literature or music, are permitted to organize without state authorization, nor can meetings of any group concerned with members in an area larger than a county be held without a license on each occasion.

Leaders of Western democracies have had a very different philosophy as to the value of pressure groups. They have believed that the functioning of the democratic process requires the existence of equally balanced pressure groups. When the balance has been unfavorable, efforts have been made to redress it; for example, the Wagner Act was adopted by the United States Congress to encourage the organization of trade unions, only to be superseded by the Taft-Hartley Act when the Congress thought it necessary to restore the balance between management and labor. When industry became so centralized as to threaten the development of monopolies, the Congress adopted antitrust laws to preserve competition and to fragment economic power. In the interests of fostering democratic practices, efforts were made by American experts in rebuilding Germany and Japan after World War II to limit the concentration of industry in a few hands and to prevent a return to the cartel system of prewar Europe.

Restrictions on Avenues of Expression

Having abolished the base for certain groups, such as those interested in the protection of productive property, and having limited severely the independence of other groups, such as the trade unions and co-operative associations, the Soviet leaders have taken great care to forestall the pressures that might be exerted by a free press. They have had to move carefully at this point, for one of the most obvious yardsticks of a democratic system of government is a free press. To satisfy their own people and win friends abroad, Soviet leaders have found it necessary to guarantee freedom of the press in the Soviet Constitution.

Having established the guarantee of a free press, Communist party leaders have provided counterweights to the guarantee. They have forbidden private citizens to operate even a mineograph machine, much less a great modern newspaper press. They have created a state printing monopoly and a state censor for all potential publications. Further, they have provided that freedom of the press may be exercised only to the advantage of their system of government, and they have drafted a criminal code that permits prosecution of those who attempt to use press or speech to damage that system.

In sharp contrast to Soviet attitudes toward the press, citizens at all levels of Western democratic governments will fight to maintain a free press. No legal limitations are created in Western democracies on ownership by private persons or corporations of the essentials to publish newspapers, magazines, handbills, and books. No censorship prior to publication is permitted by law, although civil servants who have accepted secrecy as a condition of employment may be silenced, and editors may be asked to keep secrets. Although censorship subsequent to publication has been permitted, by means of confiscation of the offending issue, and although in very unusual cases further publication of a newspaper that has been consistently endangering the security of the state has been prohibited, the administration of censorship is carefully controlled by the courts. It has usually been necessary for the executive to prove to a court that the danger to the democratic regime is obvious and that it is immediate.

The Soviet regime has not silenced its public completely. It has found it advantageous to permit citizens to write letters to the editors of the Soviet press in complaint against mismanagement of Soviet institutions. Such letters have value not only in suggesting to the people that its leaders permit free expression but also because they provide an important source of information for the leaders on the faults of subordinate administrators and on the temper of the people. Yet such letters to the editor do not meet the requirements of a free press, for they need not be published, and the pattern established in them over the years suggests that the writers have created for themselves a code of criticism that limits the subject matter that they will discuss and the personages whom they will subject to abuse.

No Independence for the Judiciary

The courts of the U.S.S.R. are avowedly an arm of Communist party policy. Soviet jurists accept no doctrine of separation of powers. While lower courts are insulated by law from interference by local party tyrants, the Supreme Court is always subject to control by the highest policy body in the state apparatus, the Supreme Soviet, in which almost 75 per cent of the deputies are members of the Communist party and, therefore, subject to strict political discipline. The courts do much to protect the citizen from mistaken application of state policy, and in so doing win the respect of many citizens for the fairness of the regime in matters affecting the employment relationship, family quarrels, and housing disputes, but they cannot be a bulwark against tyranny if the leaders of the party decide that some tyrannical measure is necessary in the interest of security.

The courts of Western democracies are not always considered an independent branch of government beyond the reach of the executive, for there is not always separation of powers in the West. Yet in countries such as England, in which the Lord Chancellor as head of the judiciary is at the same time a member of the government and the presiding officer of the House of Lords, there is a tradition of non-interference with the affairs of the judiciary by the Parliament and its government of the day. The courts of the West have indicated their willingness to enforce human rights, whether guaranteed in a written constitution or by tradition alone, against encroachment by the executive in the name of security.

Legal procedures in the U.S.S.R. exhibit many of the measures accepted by Western lawyers as constituting procedural due process of law and as helping to assure the defendant an opportunity to present his case. Yet, when the charge is one of attempting to unseat the regime, these very measures of protection had been withdrawn until the reform of 1956 by exceptions written into the procedural codes. It is at this point that procedural protections are needed most if democracy is to be preserved, and the West has always held to this view.

Again, the position of the Western democracies is not an absolute. There have been times when some of the elements of procedural due process of law have been withdrawn, as when the
writ of habeas corpus has been suspended during wartime. The
very torture of mind through which Abraham Lincoln went in
deciding whether to suspend it during the war between the
states, and the hesitation of the English prime minister when the
Battle of Britain was at its height, suggest that the difference
between the Western and the Soviet approaches is a matter of
degree. Yet, in that difference of degree there is an element of difference of quality. In the U.S.S.R., procedural due process has
been waived even in peacetime. The decision seems to have been
made with little reluctance in 1934, at the moment when one of
Stalin's aides was assassinated. In the Western democracies the
writ has been waived only in wartime, and after the passing of
the emergency it has been quickly restored.

Few Limitations on the Security Police

Both the U.S.S.R. and the Western democracies have found it
necessary to establish a security police. Both systems of government seem to have approached the institution with caution. The
Soviet security police, established in 1918 as the *Cheka,* was
limited at the start in its authority, and there were many Communist party members who disliked the idea of having such an
agency at all. Yet, it was established. It soon expanded its authority to such an extent that it aroused the anger of the Soviet Ministry of Justice and the Congress of Soviets. It was abolished in
1922 and replaced by an institution with more limited powers
and subjected to great control by the cabinet. The new security
police then expanded its power, until the leadership found it
advisable to abolish it in 1934 to create a still more limited instrument. Yet, this in turn expanded its authority. Since Stalin's
death the security police has been under attack, and measures
have been taken to control it through a strengthened Prosecutor-General of the U.S.S.R.

While recognizing that real danger, even to the regime itself,
lurks in a security police over which there is no line of supervision through an official in close touch with the highest policy-
makers, the security problem of the Soviet leadership has been
seemingly so great that the security police was permitted under
Lenin and Stalin to make arrests and to try those whom it had
arrested in its own tribunals without reference to the courts.

Only the Prosecutor-General of the U.S.S.R. has had the right to interfere, and even he, and his subordinates through whom he must operate in the daily situation, have been reluctant to intervene, because of the prestige developed by the security police in leadership circles. Since Stalin's death the Prosecutor-General has shown himself to be much more courageous. His office has published accounts showing the servile practice of the Prosecutor-General under Stalin, and the implication is clear that this servility will not occur again. It remains to be seen whether this post-Stalin approach can be maintained in the event of serious political crisis.

The Western democracies have been alert at all times to the danger that a security police may get out of hand. There have been efforts to provide checks upon assumption of authority greater than intended by the legislature by making the security police a subordinate part of a Ministry of Justice or responsible to an attorney-general rather than an independent ministry, as it has been in the U.S.S.R. There have been efforts in the West to limit the powers of the security policy by permitting it to make arrests only in wartime, rather than in peace and war as is the case in the U.S.S.R. There have been other efforts to check its activities—by making it deliver all arrested persons to the judiciary for trial within a fixed period of time or by denying to it the right to pass sentence of any kind against any person. This has been a sharp contrast to the broad rights granted the security police in the U.S.S.R. until 1953.

Perhaps the surest protection against unlawful assumption of authority by the security police in the Western democracies is the multiparty system. If the security police exceeds its authority to the point that it enrages the citizens, there is the opportunity in a democracy to vote out of power the party whose responsibility it has been to curb the police. This ultimate method of dealing with the problem through the ballot box is not available to the citizens of the U.S.S.R., as it was not available to the citizens of Hitler's Germany and of Mussolini's Italy, in both of which the excesses of the security police became symbolic of the character of the regimes.

Finally, among the agencies on which the Soviet regime rests for security when all else fails, there is the army. For the Soviet leaders, the army has been a necessary evil. Its existence is required to protect the regime at home and from foreign powers. It must be strong, yet in its strength lies latent danger to the political leadership, for it could unseat the regime if it were not controlled. The whole history of the relationship between the Communist party and the army has been dotted with experiments in control by the former over the latter so as to assure loyalty without reducing military efficiency. In contrast with the citizens' armies of Western democracies, the Soviet army seems to be under more formal and rigid political controls, although from Stalin's death in 1953 to Marshal Zhukov's ouster in 1957 its leaders appeared to be gaining more influence in policy-making circles.

The army was one of the two major forces that seemed after Stalin's death to be pressing for recognition in the formulation of policy and the selection of leaders. The other force, as has been indicated throughout this book, was the managerial and technical class. It was necessary for the Communist party leadership to expand this class, as it was necessary to expand the army. The managers and technicians were essential to the productive functioning of a modern industrial and agricultural plant. To encourage maximum effort, more was found necessary than exhortation on the basis of traditional political goals. It was necessary to give to the managers and technicians preferred status, not only in terms of greater monetary rewards but also in terms of medals, personal praise, and prestige.

Pressures for Change

Following Stalin's death it became evident that there was pressure for a lessening of the severity with which he had ruled and that this pressure was strong even within the Communist party. Statistics showed that this party had become under his regime a party predominantly of specialists, meriting classification as intellectuals. Most notable within this group were the senior officers in the Armed Forces, the managers of industrial enterprises, the agronomist-chairmen of collective and state farms, and the professional party functionaries.

As Marxist-trained individuals these intellectuals probably respected the doctrine that only the enlightened few were yet qualified to rule. It is unlikely that their dreams of the future contained thought of mass participation in the policy-making function. All evidence suggests that the new intellectuals held firmly to the necessity of maintaining the system of state ownership of production and monopoly political direction and rejected any thought of private enterprise or the multiparty system.

The new intellectuals exerted influence upon some of the senior members of the Communist party, if the outsider can judge by results. Khrushchev appears to have been frightened, for in 1957 he began to take a series of steps designed to reduce their power and reshape their thinking and the thinking of their children. The Armed Forces were returned to their completely subordinate position with the dismissal of Marshal Zhukov and the strengthening of political education. The industrial managers were subjected to audit by production conferences established by the trade unions and by supervisory commissions created within the factories by the Communist party.

A campaign was conducted within the Communist party to proletarianize its membership. Two-thirds of those admitted between 1956 and 1959 were bench workmen and dirt farmers. Within the Presidium of the Central Committee of the party Khrushchev reestablished at least the semblance of Stalin's authority to forestall the active resistance of dissenters tending to think in terms of factions.

Reshaping of the thinking of the intellectuals took the form of extensive revision of the education law with the professed aim of bringing the next generation into close familiarity with the shop and the field. All but the students needing uninterrupted study to master complex disciplines were required to undergo a period of schooling, including bench labor and dirt farming, before entering upon specialized study in the universities and technical institutes.

While moving to close the gates on potential dissension, Khrushchev continued to denounce Stalin's dictatorial rule as the "cult of the individual," although in less comprehensive form than his denunciation before the party in 1956. He and his colleagues within the Presidium found it desirable, if not necessary, to assure the intellectuals on whom they relied that personal safety could be expected. This assurance took the form of redefining criminal law in the interest of precision and expanding the procedural code to facilitate in some measure defense of the innocent.

With its 1961 program the Communist party made a dramatic move to gain support from the forces brought into being by the needs of a modern industrial society. It declared that antagonistic classes no longer remained and that the state had become representative of the entire people. It need no longer, and could not longer, be a dictatorship of the proletariat or of the toiling people over other classes.

To this position the Chinese Communists took vigorous exception in a letter of July, 1963, but the Soviet Communists refused to retreat. To strengthen their newly declared doctrine, they reaffirmed their intention to include large numbers of citizens in the activities of the government in all its functions—legislative, executive, and judicial. They revised the Communist party rules, with the declared intention of popularizing its leadership through a system of rotation of most of the members of the governing bodies of the party.

Khrushchev's ouster in 1964 was used to re-institute some of the features characterizing the Soviet system of government before he became its chief soon after Stalin's death. Even before his ouster, while his power was waning, the educational system was restored to its earlier form with elimination of the enforced experience in agriculture or industrial production which Khrushchev thought necessary to avoid emergence of a managerial class lacking in knowledge of and sympathy for the working man. Doctrine still called for an experience in production, but it was to be entered into on a voluntary basis and without massive organization of opportunities. Also, the Communist party, while continuing to emphasize the importance of admission of large numbers of workmen and collective farmers, expanded its rolls primarily with the new intellectuals trained as experts in disciplines as well as party leadership. The party also showed itself willing to increase its reliance upon the expert advice of civil servants in the state apparatus and university specialists rather than to create within its ranks a very large apparatus of specialists with the task of providing a political counterweight to what was being submitted by the technicians.

Restoration of the party to its Leninist structure in 1965, with revocation of the Central Committee decisions of 1962 inspired by Khrushchev, tended also to increase reliance on experts outside the party hierarchy for management of industry and agriculture. There was to be no bifurcation of party organs into agricultural and industrial for the very reason that the experiment had caused overlapping of party and state functions to the detriment of action. The party was to return to its status as the corps of generalists Lenin had created, albeit with a novel feature introduced without benefit of party orders: its leaders, though generalists, were, by virtue of the fact that education had spread widely among party members, possessors of broad knowledge of techniques as well as of politics. They were both "red" and "expert" as they had not been in the 1920's.

All of these features tended to bring to the foreground the intellectuals' influence as a stabilizing factor. Flexibility and dynamism of policy which had characterized the revolutionary period gave way to stability in production and personal relationships. The Chinese Communists were quick to seize upon this fact to charge that the spirit of the Revolution had been lost in a bourgeoisification of Soviet society, and Mao Tse-tung saw the same tendency within his own country, necessitating a revival of revolutionary enthusiasm and dynamism. The reaction of the Soviet Communists typified the new thinking in the U.S.S.R. To them the Chinese leader had instituted chaos from which no good could come. They denounced also his espousal of asceticism in personal living, which they felt undesirable as Soviet society increased its resources to the point where it could undertake a plan of consumers' goods production, notably in providing more adequate housing for a population long deprived of this basic asset.

The changes introduced since Stalin's death have obvious importance. They have required a re-evaluation of the potential power of the men who defend the frontiers and manage the economy and the lower levels within the Communist party, but they do not suggest an impending change in the Soviet system of government. The system remains, as it has been since 1936, the embodiment of some of the most publicized forms of democracy, but these are counterweighted to prevent their use to unseat the inner circle of the Communist party.

If one looks to the future, it can be predicted that the ranks of the educated will swell within the U.S.S.R. as elsewhere. Even given the Marxist formulation of Soviet instruction, this expansion of education cannot but have an effect upon the system. It is hard to imagine that the new intellectuals will be content for very long with a position as executives outside the circle that makes policy. Still, it is unlikely that the present system will be threatened in its essentials. At most there will be an expansion of the circle of the ruling elite.

There is as yet no hint that those who are moving to positions of responsibility as executives are coming to believe that the public generally can be trusted to choose leaders wisely or to formulate policy. There is no reason to think that Stalin's heirs intend to institute a democratic system of government.

STRUCTURE OF THE COMMUNIST
PARTY OF THE SOVIET UNION

All-Union Communist
Party Congress

All-Union Party
Conference

Politburo

Central
Committee

Secretariat

Party Control
Committee

Republic Communist
Party Congress

Republic Party Conference

Bureau

Central
Committee

Secretariat

Provincial Communist
Party Conference

Bureau

Secretariat

City or County
Party Conference

Bureau

Secretariat

Primary Party
Organization

Bureau

Secretariat

STRUCTURE OF THE SOVIET
GOVERNMENTAL APPARATUS

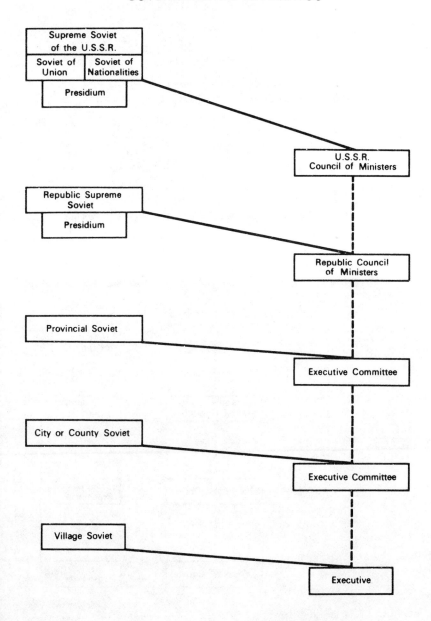

THE FEDERAL PATTERN

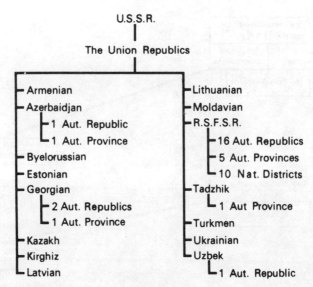

U.S.S.R.

The Union Republics

- Armenian
- Azerbaidjan
  - 1 Aut. Republic
  - 1 Aut. Province
- Byelorussian
- Estonian
- Georgian
  - 2 Aut. Republics
  - 1 Aut. Province
- Kazakh
- Kirghiz
- Latvian

- Lithuanian
- Moldavian
- R.S.F.S.R.
  - 16 Aut. Republics
  - 5 Aut. Provinces
  - 10 Nat. Districts
- Tadzhik
  - 1 Aut Province
- Turkmen
- Ukrainian
- Uzbek
  - 1 Aut. Republic

THE COURTS AND PROSECUTORS

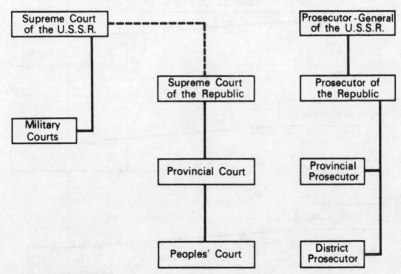

Supreme Court of the U.S.S.R.

Military Courts

Supreme Court of the Republic

Provincial Court

Peoples' Court

Prosecutor-General of the U.S.S.R.

Prosecutor of the Republic

Provincial Prosecutor

District Prosecutor

APPENDIX

CONVERTED HEADING:

CONSTITUTION
(FUNDAMENTAL LAW)
OF THE
UNION OF SOVIET
SOCIALIST REPUBLICS
Adopted October 7, 1977

The Great October Socialist Revolution, made by the workers and peasants of Russia under the leadership of the Communist Party headed by Lenin, overthrew capitalist and landowner rule, broke the fetters of oppression, established the dictatorship of the proletariat, and created the Soviet state, a new type of state, the basic instrument for defending the gains of the revolution and for building socialism and communism. Humanity thereby began the epoch-making turn from capitalism to socialism.

After achieving victory in the Civil War and repulsing imperialist intervention, the Soviet government carried through far-reaching social and economic transformations, and put an end once and for all to exploitation of man by man, antagonisms between classes, and strife between nationalities. The unification of the Soviet Republics in the Union of Soviet Socialist Republics multiplied the forces and opportunities of the peoples of the country in the building of socialism. Social ownership of the means of production and genuine democracy for the working masses were established. For the first time in the history of mankind a socialist society was created.

The strength of socialism was vividly demonstrated by the immortal feat of the Soviet people and their Armed Forces in achieving their historic victory in the Great Patriotic War. This victory consolidated the influence and international standing of the Soviet Union and created new opportunities for growth of the forces of socialism, national liberation, democracy, and peace throughout the world.

Continuing their creative endeavours, the working people of the Soviet Union have ensured rapid, all-round development of the country and steady improvement of the socialist system. They have consolidated the alliance of the working class, collective-farm peasantry, and people's intelligentsia, and friendship of the nations and nationalities of the USSR. Sociopolitical and ideological unity of Soviet society, in which the working class is the leading force, has been achieved. The aims of the dictatorship of the proletariat having been fulfilled, the Soviet state has become a state of the whole people. The leading role of the Communist Party, the vanguard of all the people, has grown.

In the USSR a developed socialist society has been built. At this stage, when socialism is developing on its own foundations, the creative forces of the new system and the advantages of the socialist way of life are becoming increasingly evident, and the working people are more and more widely enjoying the fruits of their great revolutionary gains.

It is a society in which powerful productive forces and progressive science and culture have been created, in which the well-being of the people is constantly rising, and more and more favourable conditions are being provided for the all-round development of the individual.

It is a society of mature socialist social relations, in which, on the basis of the drawing together of all classes and social strata and of the juridical and factual equality of all its nations and nationalities and their fraternal co-operation, a new historical community of people has been formed—the Soviet people.

It is a society of high organisational capacity, ideological commitment, and consciousness of the working people, who are patriots and internationalists.

It is a society in which the law of life is concern of all for the good of each and concern of each for the good of all.

It is a society of true democracy, the political system of which ensures effective management of all public affairs, ever more active participation of the working people in running the state, and the combining of citizens' real rights and freedoms with their obligations and responsibility to society.

Developed socialist society is a natural, logical stage on the road to communism.

The supreme goal of the Soviet state is the building of a classless communist society in which there will be public, communist self-government. The main aims of the people's socialist state are: to lay the material and technical foundation of communism, to perfect socialist social relations and transform them into communist relations, to mould the citizen of communist society, to raise the people's living and cultural standards, to safeguard the country's security, and further the consolidation of peace and development of international co-operation.

The Soviet people,

guided by the ideas of scientific communism and true to their revolutionary traditions, relying on the great social, economic, and political gains of socialism, striving for the further development of socialist democracy,

taking into account the international position of the USSR as part of the world system of socialism, and conscious of their internationalist responsibility,

preserving continuity of the ideas and principles of the first Soviet Constitution of 1918, the 1924 Constitution of the USSR and the 1936 Constitution of the USSR,

hereby affirm the principles of the social structure and policy of the USSR, and define the rights, freedoms and obligations of citizens, and the principles of the organisation of the socialist state of the whole people, and its aims, and proclaim these in this Constitution.

I. Principles of the Social Structure and Policy of the USSR

Chapter 1
THE POLITICAL SYSTEM

Article 1

The Union of Soviet Socialist Republics is a socialist state of the whole people, expressing the will and interests of the workers, peasants, and intelligentsia, the working people of all the nations and nationalities of the country.

Article 2

All power in the USSR belongs to the people.

The people exercise state power through Soviets of People's Deputies, which constitute the political foundation of the USSR.

All other state bodies are under the control of, and accountable to, the Soviets of People's Deputies.

Article 3

The Soviet state is organised and functions on the principle of democratic centralism, namely the electiveness of all bodies of state authority from the lowest to the highest, their accountability to the people, and the obligation of lower bodies to observe the decisions of higher ones. Democratic centralism combines central leadership with local initiative and creative activity and with the responsibility of each state body and official for the work entrusted to them.

Article 4

The Soviet state and all its bodies function on the basis of socialist law, ensure the maintenance of law and order, and safeguard the interests of society and the rights and freedoms of citizens.

State organisations, public organisations and officials shall observe the Constitution of the USSR and Soviet laws.

Article 5

Major matters of state shall be submitted to nationwide discussion and put to a popular vote (referendum).

Article 6

The leading and guiding force of Soviet society and the nucleus of its political system, of all state organisations and public organisations, is the Communist Party of the Soviet Union. The CPSU exists for the people and serves the people.

The Communist Party, armed with Marxism-Leninism, determines the general perspectives of the development of society and the course of the home and foreign policy of the USSR, directs the great constructive work of the Soviet people, and imparts a planned, systematic and theoretically substantiated character to their struggle for the victory of communism.

All Party organisations shall function within the framework of the Constitution of the USSR.

Article 7

Trade unions, the All-Union Leninist Young Communist League, co-operatives, and other public organisations, participate, in accordance with the aims laid down in their rules, in managing state and public affairs, and in deciding political, economic, and social and cultural matters.

Article 8

Work collectives take part in discussing and deciding state and public affairs, in planning production and social development, in training and placing personnel, and in discussing and deciding matters pertaining to the management of enterprises and institutions, the improvement of working and living conditions, and the use of funds allocated both for developing production and for social and cultural purposes and financial incentives.

Work collectives promote socialist emulation, the spread of progressive methods of work, and the strengthening of production discipline, educate their members in the spirit of communist morality, and strive to enhance their political consciousness and raise their cultural level and skills and qualifications.

Article 9

The principal direction in the development of the political system of Soviet society is the extension of socialist democracy, namely ever broader participation of citizens in managing the affairs of society and the state, continuous improvement of the machinery of state, heightening of the activity of public organisations, strengthening of the system of people's control, consolidation of the legal foundations of the functioning of the state and of public life, greater openness and publicity, and constant responsiveness to public opinion.

Chapter 2
THE ECONOMIC SYSTEM

Article 10

The foundation of the economic system of the USSR is socialist ownership of the means of production in the form of state property (belonging to all the people), and collective farm-and-co-operative property.

Socialist ownership also embraces the property of trade unions and other public organizations which they require to carry out their purposes under their rules.

The state protects socialist property and provides conditions for its growth.

No one has the right to use socialist property for personal gain or other selfish ends.

Article 11

State property, i.e. the common property of the Soviet people, is the principal form of socialist property.

The land, its minerals, waters, and forests are the exclusive property of the state. The state owns the basic means of production in industry, construction, and agriculture; means of transport and communication; the banks; the property of state-run trade organisations and public utilities, and other state-run undertakings; most urban housing; and other property necessary for state purposes.

Article 12

The property of collective farms and other co-operative organisations, and of their joint undertakings, comprises the means of production and other assets which they require for the purposes laid down in their rules.

The land held by collective farms is secured to them for their free use in perpetuity.

The state promotes development of collective farm-and-co-operative property and its approximation to state property.

Collective farms, like other land users, are obliged to make effective and thrifty use of the land and to increase its fertility.

Article 13

Earned income forms the basis of the personal property of Soviet citizens. The personal property of citizens of the USSR may include articles of everyday use, personal consumption and convenience, the implements and other objects of a small-holding, a house, and earned savings. The personal property of citizens and the right to inherit it are protected by the state.

Citizens may be granted the use of plots of land, in the manner prescribed by law, for a subsidiary small-holding (including the keeping of livestock and poultry), for fruit and vegetable growing or for building an individual dwelling. Citizens are required to make rational use of the land allotted to them. The state, and collective farms provide assistance to citizens in working their small-holdings.

Property owned or used by citizens shall not serve as a means of deriving unearned income or be employed to the detriment of the interests of society.

Article 14

The source of the growth of social wealth and of the well-being of the people, and of each individual, is the labour, free from exploitation, of Soviet people.

The state exercises control over the measure of labour and of consumption in accordance with the principle of socialism: "From each according to his ability, to each according to his work." It fixes the rate of taxation on taxable income.

Socially useful work and its results determine a person's status in society. By combining material and moral incentives and encouraging innovation and a creative attitude to work, the state helps transform labour into the prime vital need of every Soviet citizen.

Article 15

The supreme goal of social production under socialism is the fullest possible satisfaction of the people's growing material, and cultural and intellectual requirements.

Relying on the creative initiative of the working people, socialist emulation, and scientific and technological progress, and by improving the forms and methods of economic management, the state ensures growth of the productivity of labour, raising of the efficiency of production and of the quality of work, and dynamic, planned, proportionate development of the economy.

Article 16

The economy of the USSR is an integral economic complex comprising all the elements of social production, distribution, and exchange on its territory.

The economy is managed on the basis of state plans for economic and social development, with due account of the sectoral and territorial principles, and by combining centralised direction with the managerial independence and initiative of individual and amalgamated enterprises and other organisations, for which active use is made of management accounting, profit, cost, and other economic levers and incentives.

Article 17

In the USSR, the law permits individual labour in handicrafts, farming, the provision of services for the public, and other forms of activity based exclusively on the personal work of individual citizens and members of their families. The state makes regulations for such work to ensure that it serves the interests of society.

Article 18

In the interests of the present and future generations, the necessary steps are taken in the USSR to protect and make scientific, rational use of the land and its mineral and water resources, and the plant and animal kingdoms, to preserve the purity of air and water, ensure reproduction of natural wealth, and improve the human environment.

Chapter 3
SOCIAL DEVELOPMENT AND CULTURE

Article 19

The social basis of the USSR is the unbreakable alliance of the workers, peasants, and intelligentsia.

The state helps enhance the social homogeneity of society, namely the elimination of class differences and of the essential distinctions between town and country and between mental and physical labour, and the all-round development and drawing together of all the nations and nationalities of the USSR.

Article 20

In accordance with the communist ideal—"The free development of each is the condition of the free development of all"—the state pursues the aim of giving citizens more and more real opportunities to apply their creative energies, abilities, and talents, and to develop their personalities in every way.

Article 21

The state concerns itself with improving working conditions, safety and labour protection and the scientific organisation of work, and with reducing and ultimately eliminating all arduous physical labour through comprehensive mechanisation and automation of production processes in all branches of the economy.

Article 22

A programme is being consistently implemented in the USSR to convert agricultural work into a variety of industrial work, to extend the network of educational, cultural and medical institutions, and of trade, public catering, service and public utility facilities in rural localities, and to transform hamlets and villages into well-planned and well-appointed settlements.

Article 23

The state pursues a steady policy of raising people's pay levels and real incomes through increase in productivity.

In order to satisfy the needs of Soviet people more fully social consumption funds are created. The state, with the broad participation of public organisations and work collectives, ensures the growth and just distribution of these funds.

Article 24

In the USSR, state systems of health protection, social security, trade and public catering, communal services and amenities, and public utilities, operate and are being extended.

The state encourages co-operatives and other public organisations to provide all types of services for the population. It encourages the development of mass physical culture and sport.

Article 25

In the USSR there is a uniform system of public education, which is being constantly improved, that provides general education and vocational training for citizens, serves the communist education and intellectual and physical development of the youth, and trains them for work and social activity.

Article 26

In accordance with society's needs the state provides for planned development of science and the training of scientific personnel and organises introduction of the results of research in the economy and other spheres of life.

Article 27

The state concerns itself with protecting, augmenting and making extensive use of society's cultural wealth for the moral and aesthetic education of the Soviet people, for raising their cultural level.

In the USSR development of the professional, amateur and folk arts is encouraged in every way.

Chapter 4

FOREIGN POLICY

Article 28

The USSR steadfastly pursues a Leninist policy of peace and stands for strengthening of the security of nations and broad international co-operation.

The foreign policy of the USSR is aimed at ensuring international conditions favourable for building communism in the USSR, safeguarding the state interests of the Soviet Union, consolidating the positions of world socialism, supporting the struggle of peoples for national liberation and social progress, preventing wars of aggression, achieving universal and complete disarmament, and consistently implementing the principle of the peaceful coexistence of states with different social systems.

In the USSR war propaganda is banned.

Article 29

The USSR's relations with other states are based on observance of the following principles: sovereign equality; mutual renunciation of the use or threat of force; inviolability of frontiers; territorial integrity of states; peaceful settlement of disputes; non-intervention in internal affairs; respect for human rights and fundamental freedoms; the equal rights of peoples and their right to decide their own destiny; co-operation among states; and fulfilment in good faith of obligations arising from the generally recognised principles and rules of international law, and from the international treaties signed by the USSR.

Article 30

The USSR, as part of the world system of socialism and of the socialist community, promotes and strengthens friendship, co-operation, and comradely mutual assistance with other socialist countries on the basis of the principle of socialist internationalism, and takes an active part in socialist economic integration and the socialist international division of labour.

Chapter 5

DEFENCE OF THE SOCIALIST MOTHERLAND

Article 31

Defence of the Socialist Motherland is one of the most important functions of the state, and is the concern of the whole people.

In order to defend the gains of socialism, the peaceful labour of the Soviet people, and the sovereignty and territorial integrity of the state, the USSR maintains Armed Forces and has instituted universal military service.

The duty of the Armed Forces of the USSR to the people is to provide reliable defence of the Socialist Motherland and to be in constant combat readiness, guaranteeing that any aggressor is instantly repulsed.

Article 32

The state ensures the security and defence capability of the country, and supplies the Armed Forces of the USSR with everything necessary for that purpose.

The duties of state bodies, public organisations, officials, and citizens in regard to safeguarding the country's security and strengthening its defence capacity are defined by the legislation of the USSR.

II. The State and the Individual

Chapter 6

CITIZENSHIP OF THE USSR
EQUALITY OF CITIZENS' RIGHTS

Article 33

Uniform federal citizenship is established for the USSR. Every citizen of a Union Republic is a citizen of the USSR.

The grounds and procedure for acquiring or forfeiting Soviet citizenship are defined by the Law on Citizenship of the USSR.

When abroad, citizens of the USSR enjoy the protection and assistance of the Soviet state.

Article 34

Citizens of the USSR are equal before the law, without distinction of origin, social or property status, race or nationality, sex, education, language, attitude to religion, type and nature of occupation, domicile, or other status.

The equal rights of citizens of the USSR are guaranteed in all fields of economic, political, social, and cultural life.

Article 35

Women and men have equal rights in the USSR.

Exercise of these rights is ensured by according women equal access with men to education and vocational and professional training, equal opportunities in employment, remuneration, and promotion, and in social and political, and cultural activity, and by special labour and health protection measures for women; by providing conditions enabling mothers to work; by legal protection, and material and moral support for mothers and children, including paid leaves and other benefits for expectant mothers and mothers, and gradual reduction of working time for mothers with small children.

Article 36

Citizens of the USSR of different races and nationalities have equal rights.

Exercise of these rights is ensured by a policy of all-round development and drawing together of all the nations and nationalities of the USSR, by educating citizens in the spirit of Soviet patriotism and socialist internationalism, and by the possibility to use their native language and the languages of other peoples of the USSR.

Any direct or indirect limitation of the rights of citizens or establishment of direct or indirect privileges on grounds of race or nationality, and any advocacy of racial or national exclusiveness, hostility or contempt, are punishable by law.

Article 37

Citizens of other countries and stateless persons in the USSR are guaranteed the rights and freedoms provided by law, including the right to apply to a court and other state bodies for the protection of their personal, property, family, and other rights.

Citizens of other countries and stateless persons, when in the USSR, are obliged to respect the Constitutvn of the USSR and observe Soviet laws.

Article 38

The USSR grants the right of asylum to foreigners persecuted for defending the interests of the working people and the cause of peace, or for participation in the revolutionary and national-liberation movement, or for progressive social and political, scientific or other creative activity.

Chapter 7

THE BASIC RIGHTS, FREEDOMS, AND DUTIES OF CITIZENS OF THE USSR

Article 39

Citizens of the USSR enjoy in full the social, economic, political and personal rights and freedoms proclaimed and guaranteed by the Constitution of the USSR and by Soviet laws. The socialist system ensures enlargement of the rights and freedoms of citizens and continuous improvement of their living standards as social, economic, and cultural development programmes are fulfilled.

Enjoyment by citizens of their rights and freedoms must not be to the detriment of the interests of society or the state, or infringe the rights of other citizens.

Article 40

Citizens of the USSR have the right to work (that is, to guaranteed employment and pay in accordance with the quantity and quality of their work, and not below the state-established minimum), including the right to choose their trade or profession, type of job and work in accordance with their inclinations, abilities, training and education, with due account of the needs of society.

This right is ensured by the socialist economic system, steady growth of the productive forces, free vocational and professional training, improvement of skills, training in new trades or professions, and development of the systems of vocational guidance and job placement.

Article 41

Citizens of the USSR have the right to rest and leisure.

This right is ensured by the establishment of a working week not exceeding 41 hours, for workers and other employees, a shorter working day in a number of trades and industries, and shorter hours for night work; by the provision of paid annual holidays, weekly days of rest, extension of the network of cultural, educational and health-building institutions, and the development on a mass scale of sport, physical culture, and camping and tourism; by the provision of neighbourhood recreational facilities, and of other opportunities for rational use of free time.

The length of collective farmers' working and leisure time is established by their collective farms.

Article 42

Citizens of the USSR have the right to health protection.

This right is ensured by free, qualified medical care provided by state health institutions; by extension of the network of therapeutic and health-building institutions; by the development and improvement of safety and hygiene in industry; by carrying out broad prophylactic measures; by measures to improve the environment; by special care for the health of the rising generation, including prohibition of child labour, excluding the work done by children as part of the school curriculum; and by developing research to prevent and reduce the incidence of disease and ensure citizens a long and active life.

Article 43

Citizens of the USSR have the right to maintenance in old age, in sickness, and in the event of complete or partial disability or loss of the breadwinner.

This right is guaranteed by social insurance of workers and other employees and collective farmers; by allowances for temporary disability; by the provision by the state or by collective farms of retirement pensions, disability pensions, and pensions for loss of the breadwinner; by providing employment for the partially disabled; by care for the elderly and the disabled; and by other forms of social security.

Article 44

Citizens of the USSR have the right to housing.

This right is ensured by the development and upkeep of state and socially-owned housing; by assistance for co-operative and individual house building; by fair distribution, under public control, of the housing that becomes available through fulfilment of the programme of building well-appointed dwellings, and by low rents and low charges for utility services. Citizens of the USSR shall take good care of the housing allocated to them.

Article 45

Citizens of the USSR have the right to education.

This right is ensured by free provision of all forms of education, by the institution of universal, compulsory secondary education, and broad development of vocational, specialised secondary, and higher education, in which instruction is oriented toward practical activity and production; by the development of extramural, correspondence and evening courses; by the provision of state scholarships and grants and privileges for students; by the free issue of school textbooks; by the opportunity to attend a school where teaching is in the native language; and by the provision of facilities for self-education.

Article 46
Citizens of the USSR have the right to enjoy cultural benefits.

This right is ensured by broad access to the cultural treasures of their own land and of the world that are preserved in state and other public collections; by the development and fair distribution of cultural and educational institutions throughout the country; by developing television and radio broadcasting and the publishing of books, newspapers and periodicals, and by extending the free library service; and by expanding cultural exchanges with other countries.

Article 47
Citizens of the USSR, in accordance with the aims of building communism, are guaranteed freedom of scientific, technical, and artistic work. This freedom is ensured by broadening scientific research, encouraging invention and innovation, and developing literature and the arts. The state provides the necessary material conditions for this and support for voluntary societies and unions of workers in the arts, organises introduction of inventions and innovations in production and other spheres of activity.

The rights of authors, inventors and innovators are protected by the state.

Article 48
Citizens of the USSR have the right to take part in the management and administration of state and public affairs and in the discussion and adoption of laws and measures of All-Union and local significance.

This right is ensured by the opportunity to vote and to be elected to Soviets of People's Deputies and other elective state bodies, to take part in nationwide discussions and referendums, in people's control, in the work of state bodies, public organisations, and local community groups, and in meetings at places of work or residence.

Article 49
Every citizen of the USSR has the right to submit proposals to state bodies and public organisations for improving their activity, and to criticise shortcomings in their work.

Officials are obliged, within established time-limits, to examine citizens' proposals and requests, to reply to them, and to take appropriate action.

Persecution for criticism is prohibited. Persons guilty of such persecution shall be called to account.

Article 50

In accordance with the interests of the people and in order to strengthen and develop the socialist system, citizens of the USSR are guaranteed freedom of speech, of the press, and of assembly, meetings, street processions and demonstrations.

Exercise of these political freedoms is ensured by putting public buildings, streets and squares at the disposal of the working people and their organisations, by broad dissemination of information, and by the opportunity to use the press, television, and radio.

Article 51

In accordance with the aims of building communism, citizens of the USSR have the right to associate in public organisations that promote their political activity and initiative and satisfaction of their various interests.

Public organisations are guaranteed conditions for successfully performing the functions defined in their rules.

Article 52

Citizens of the USSR are guaranteed freedom of conscience, that is, the right to profess or not to profess any religion, and to conduct religious worship or atheistic propaganda. Incitement of hostility or hatred on religious grounds is prohibited.

In the USSR, the church is separated from the state, and the school from the church.

Article 53

The family enjoys the protection of the state.

Marriage is based on the free consent of the woman and the man; the spouses are completely equal in their family relations.

The state helps the family by providing and developing a broad system of child-care institutions, by organising and improving communal services and public catering, by paying grants on the birth of a child, by providing children's allowances and benefits for large families, and other forms of family allowances and assistance.

Article 54

Citizens of the USSR are guaranteed inviolability of the person. No one may be arrested except by a court decision or on the warrant of a procurator.

Article 55

Citizens of the USSR are guaranteed inviolability of the home. No one may, without lawful grounds, enter a home against the will of those residing in it.

Article 56

The privacy of citizens, and of their correspondence, telephone conversations, and telegraphic communications is protected by law.

Article 57

Respect for the individual and protection of the rights and freedoms of citizens are the duty of all state bodies, public organisations, and officials.

Citizens of the USSR have the right to protection by the courts against encroachments on their honour and reputation, life and health, and personal freedom and property.

Article 58

Citizens of the USSR have the right to lodge a complaint against the actions of officials, state bodies and public bodies. Complaints shall be examined according to the procedure and within the time-limit established by law.

Actions by officials that contravene the law or exceed their powers, and infringe the rights of citizens, may be appealed against in a court in the manner prescribed by law.

Citizens of the USSR have the right to compensation for damage resulting from unlawful actions by state organisations and public organisations, or by officials in the performance of their duties.

Article 59

Citizens' exercise of their rights and freedoms is inseparable from the performance of their duties and obligations.

Citizens of the USSR are obliged to observe the Constitution of the USSR and Soviet laws, comply with the standards of socialist conduct, and uphold the honour and dignity of Soviet citizenship.

Article 60

It is the duty of, and a matter of honour for, every able-bodied citizen of the USSR to work conscientiously in his chosen, socially useful occupation, and strictly to observe labour discipline. Evasion of socially useful work is incompatible with the principles of socialist society.

Article 61

Citizens of the USSR are obliged to preserve and protect socialist property. It is the duty of a citizen of the USSR to combat misappropriation and squandering of state and socially-owned property and to make thrifty use of the people's wealth.

Persons encroaching in any way on socialist property shall be punished according to the law.

Article 62

Citizens of the USSR are obliged to safeguard the interests of the Soviet state, and to enhance its power and prestige.

Defence of the Socialist Motherland is the sacred duty of every citizen of the USSR.

Betrayal of the Motherland is the gravest of crimes against the people.

Article 63

Military service in the ranks of the Armed Forces of the USSR is an honourable duty of Soviet citizens.

Article 64

It is the duty of every citizen of the USSR to respect the national dignity of other citizens, and to strengthen friendship of the nations and nationalities of the multinational Soviet state.

Article 65

A citizen of the USSR is obliged to respect the rights and lawful interests of other persons, to be uncompromising toward anti-social behaviour, and to help maintain public order.

Article 66

Citizens of the USSR are obliged to concern themselves with the upbringing of children, to train them for socially useful work, and to raise them as worthy members of socialist society. Children are obliged to care for their parents and help them.

Article 67

Citizens of the USSR are obliged to protect nature and conserve its riches.

Article 68

Concern for the preservation of historical monuments and other cultural values is a duty and obligation of citizens of the USSR.

Article 69

It is the internationalist duty of citizens of the USSR to promote friendship and co-operation with peoples of other lands and help maintain and strengthen world peace.

III. The National-State Structure
of the USSR

Chapter 8
THE USSR—A FEDERAL STATE

Article 70

The Union of Soviet Socialist Republics is an integral, federal, multinational state formed on the principle of socialist federalism as a result of the free self-determination of nations and the voluntary association of equal Soviet Socialist Republics.

The USSR embodies the state unity of the Soviet people and draws all its nations and nationalities together for the purpose of jointly building communism.

Article 71

The Union of Soviet Socialist Republics unites:

the Russian Soviet Federative Socialist Republic,
the Ukrainian Soviet Socialist Republic,
the Byelorussian Soviet Socialist Republic,
the Uzbek Soviet Socialist Republic,
the Kazakh Soviet Socialist Republic,
the Georgian Soviet Socialist Republic,
the Azerbaijan Soviet Socialist Republic,
the Lithuanian Soviet Socialist Republic,
the Moldavian Soviet Socialist Republic,
the Latvian Soviet Socialist Republic,
the Kirghiz Soviet Socialist Republic,
the Tajik Soviet Socialist Republic,
the Armenian Soviet Socialist Republic,
the Turkmen Soviet Socialist Republic,
the Estonian Soviet Socialist Republic.

Article 72

Each Union Republic shall retain the right freely to secede from the USSR.

Article 73

The jurisdiction of the Union of Soviet Socialist Republics, as represented by its highest bodies of state authority and administration, shall cover:

1) the admission of new republics to the USSR; endorsement of the formation of new autonomous republics and autonomous regions within Union Republics;

2) determination of the state boundaries of the USSR and approval of changes in the boundaries between Union Republics;

3) establishment of the general principles for the organisation and functioning of republican and local bodies of state authority and administration;

4) the ensurance of uniformity of legislative norms throughout the USSR and establishment of the fundamentals of the legislation of the Union of Soviet Socialist Republics and Union Republics;

5) pursuance of a uniform social and economic policy; direction of the country's economy; determination of the main lines of scientific and technological progress and the general measures for rational exploitation and conservation of natural resources; the drafting and approval of state plans for the economic and social development of the USSR, and endorsement of reports on their fulfilment;

6) the drafting and approval of the consolidated Budget of the USSR, and endorsement of the report on its execution; management of a single monetary and credit system; determination of the taxes and revenues forming the Budget of the USSR; and the formulation of prices and wages policy;

7) direction of the sectors of the economy, and of enterprises and amalgamations under Union jurisdiction, and general direction of industries under Union-Republican jurisdiction;

8) issues of war and peace, defence of the sovereignty of the USSR and safeguarding of its frontiers and territory, and organisation of defence; direction of the Armed Forces of the USSR;

9) state security;

10) representation of the USSR in international relations; the USSR's relations with other states and with international organisations; establishment of the general procedure for, and co-ordination of, the relations of Union Republics with other states and with international organisations; foreign trade and other forms of external economic activity on the basis of state monopoly;

11) control over observance of the Constitution of the USSR, and ensurance of conformity of the Constitutions of Union Republics to the Constitution of the USSR;

12) and settlement of other matters of All-Union importance.

Article 74

The laws of the USSR shall have the same force in all Union Republics. In the event of a discrepancy between a Union Republic law and an All-Union law, the law of the USSR shall prevail.

Article 75

The territory of the Union of Soviet Socialist Republics is a single entity and comprises the territories of the Union Republics.

The sovereignty of the USSR extends throughout its territory.

Chapter 9
THE UNION SOVIET SOCIALIST
REPUBLIC

Article 76

A Union Republic is a sovereign Soviet socialist state that has united with other Soviet Republics in the Union of Soviet Socialist Republics.

Outside the spheres listed in Article 73 of the Constitution of the USSR, a Union Republic exercises independent authority on its territory.

A Union Republic shall have its own Constitution conforming to the Constitution of the USSR with the specific features of the Republic being taken into account.

Article 77

Union Republics take part in decision-making in the Supreme Soviet of the USSR, the Presidium of the Supreme Soviet of the USSR, the Government of the USSR, and other bodies of the Union of Soviet Socialist Republics in matters that come within the jurisdiction of the Union of Soviet Socialist Republics.

A Union Republic shall ensure comprehensive economic and social development on its territory, facilitate exercise of the powers of the USSR on its territory, and implement the decisions of the highest bodies of state authority and administration of the USSR.

In matters that come within its jurisdiction, a Union Republic shall co-ordinate and control the activity of enterprises, institutions, and organisations subordinate to the Union.

Article 78

The territory of a Union Republic may not be altered without its consent. The boundaries between Union Republics may be altered by mutual agreement of the Republics concerned, subject to ratification by the Union of Soviet Socialist Republics.

Article 79

A Union Republic shall determine its division into territories, regions, areas, and districts, and decide other matters relating to its administrative and territorial structure.

Article 80

A Union Republic has the right to enter into relations with other states, conclude treaties with them, exchange diplomatic and consular representatives, and take part in the work of international organisations.

Article 81

The sovereign rights of Union Republics shall be safeguarded by the USSR.

Chapter 10

THE AUTONOMOUS SOVIET SOCIALIST REPUBLIC

Article 82

An Autonomous Republic is a constituent part of a Union Republic.

In spheres not within the jurisdiction of the Union of Soviet Socialist Republics and the Union Republic, an Autonomous Republic shall deal independently with matters within its jurisdiction.

An Autonomous Republic shall have its own Constitution conforming to the Constitutions of the USSR and the Union Republic with the specific features of the Autonomous Republic being taken into account.

Article 83

An Autonomous Republic takes part in decision-making through the highest bodies of state authority and administration of the USSR and of the Union Republic respectively, in matters that come within the jurisdiction of the USSR and the Union Republic.

An Autonomous Republic shall ensure comprehensive economic and social development on its territory, facilitate exercise of the powers of the USSR and the Union Republic on its territory, and implement decisions of the highest bodies of state authority and administration of the USSR and the Union Republic.

In matters within its jurisdiction, an Autonomous Republic shall coordinate and control the activity of enterprises, institutions, and organisations subordinate to the Union or the Union Republic.

Article 84

The territory of an Autonomous Republic may not be altered without its consent.

Article 85

The Russian Soviet Federative Socialist Republic includes the Bashkir, Buryat, Daghestan, Kabardin-Balkar, Kalmyk, Karelian, Komi, Mari, Mordovian, North Ossetian, Tatar, Tuva, Udmurt, Chechen-Ingush, Chuvash, and Yakut Autonomous Soviet Socialist Republics.

The Uzbek Soviet Socialist Republic includes the Kara-Kalpak Autonomous Soviet Socialist Republic.

The Georgian Soviet Socialist Republic includes the Abkhasian and Adzhar Autonomous Soviet Socialist Republics.

The Azerbaijan Soviet Socialist Republic includes the Nakhichevan Autonomous Soviet Socialist Republic.

Chapter 11

THE AUTONOMOUS REGION
AND AUTONOMOUS AREA

Article 86

An Autonomous Region is a constituent part of a Union Republic or Territory. The Law on an Autonomous Region, upon submission by the Soviet of People's Deputies of the Autonomous Region concerned, shall be adopted by the Supreme Soviet of the Union Republic.

Article 87

The Russian Soviet Federative Socialist Republic includes the Adygei, Gorno-Altai, Jewish, Karachai-Circassian, and Khakass Autonomous Regions.

The Georgian Soviet Socialist Republic includes the South Ossetian Autonomous Region.

The Azerbaijan Soviet Socialist Republic includes the Nagorno-Karabakh Autonomous Region.

The Tajik Soviet Socialist Republic includes the Gorno-Badakhshan Autonomous Region.

Article 88

An Autonomous Area is a constituent part of a Territory or Region. The Law on an Autonomous Area shall be adopted by the Supreme Soviet of the Union Republic concerned.

IV. Soviets of People's Deputies
and Electoral Procedure

Chapter 12
THE SYSTEM OF SOVIETS OF PEOPLE'S DEPUTIES AND THE PRINCIPLES OF THEIR WORK

Article 89

The Soviets of People's Deputies, i.e. the Supreme Soviet of the USSR, the Supreme Soviets of Union Republics, the Supreme Soviets of Autonomous Republics, the Soviets of People's Deputies of Territories and Regions, the Soviets of People's Deputies of Autonomous Regions and Autonomous Areas, and the Soviets of People's Deputies of districts, cities, city districts, settlements and villages shall constitute a single system of bodies of state authority.

Article 90

The term of the Supreme Soviet of the USSR, the Supreme Soviets of Union Republics, and the Supreme Soviets of Autonomous Republics shall be five years.

The term of local Soviets of People's Deputies shall be two and a half years.

Elections to Soviets of People's Deputies shall be called not later than two months before expiry of the term of the Soviet concerned.

Article 91

The most important matters within the jurisdiction of the respective Soviets of People's Deputies shall be considered and settled at their sessions.

Soviets of People's Deputies shall elect standing commissions and form executive-administrative, and other bodies accountable to them.

Article 92

Soviets of People's Deputies shall form people's control bodies combining state control with control by the working people at enterprises, collective farms, institutions, and organisations.

People's control bodies shall check on the fulfilment of state plans and assignments, combat breaches of state discipline, localistic tendencies, narrow departmental attitudes, mismanagement, extravagance and waste, red tape and bureaucracy, and help improve the working of the state machinery.

Article 93

Soviets of People's Deputies shall direct all sectors of state, economic and social and cultural development, either directly or through bodies instituted by them, take decisions and ensure their execution, and verify their implementation.

Article 94

Soviets of People's Deputies shall function publicly on the basis of collective, free, constructive discussion and decision-making, of systematic reporting back to them and the people by their executive-administrative and other bodies, and of involving citizens on a broad scale in their work.

Soviets of People's Deputies and the bodies set up by them shall systematically inform the public about their work and the decisions taken by them.

Chapter 13
THE ELECTORAL SYSTEM

Article 95

Deputies to all Soviets shall be elected on the basis of universal, equal, and direct suffrage by secret ballot.

Article 96

Elections shall be universal: all citizens of the USSR who have reached the age of 18 shall have the right to vote and to be elected, with the exception of persons who have been legally certified insane.

To be eligible for election to the Supreme Soviet of the USSR a citizen of the USSR must have reached the age of 21.

Article 97

Elections shall be equal: each citizen shall have one vote; all voters shall exercise the franchise on an equal footing.

Article 98

Elections shall be direct: Deputies to all Soviets of People's Deputies shall be elected by citizens by direct vote.

Article 99

Voting at elections shall be secret: control over voters' exercise of the franchise is inadmissible.

Article 100

The following shall have the right to nominate candidates: branches and organisations of the Communist Party of the Soviet Union, trade unions, and the All-Union Leninist Young Communist League; co-operatives and other public organisations; work collectives, and meetings of servicemen in their military units.

Citizens of the USSR and public organisations are guaranteed the right to free and all-round discussion of the political and personal qualities and competence of candidates, and the right to campaign for them at meetings, in the press, and on television and radio.

The expenses involved in holding elections to Soviets of People's Deputies shall be met by the state.

Article 101

Deputies to Soviets of People's Deputies shall be elected by constituencies.

A citizen of the USSR may not, as a rule, be elected to more than two Soviets of People's Deputies.

Elections to the Soviets shall be conducted by electoral commissions consisting of representatives of public organisations and work collectives, and of meetings of servicemen in military units.

The procedure for holding elections to Soviets of People's Deputies shall be defined by the laws of the USSR, and of Union and Autonomous Republics.

Article 102

Electors give mandates to their Deputies.

The appropriate Soviets of People's Deputies shall examine electors' mandates, take them into account in drafting economic and social development plans and in drawing up the budget, organise implementation of the mandates, and inform citizens about it.

Chapter 14

PEOPLE'S DEPUTIES

Article 103

Deputies are the plenipotentiary representatives of the people in the Soviets of People's Deputies.

In the Soviets, Deputies deal with matters relating to state, economic and social and cultural development, organise implementation of the decisions of the Soviets, and exercise control over the work of state bodies, enterprises, institutions and organisations.

Deputies shall be guided in their activities by the interests of the state, and shall take the needs of their constituents into account and work to implement their electors' mandates.

Article 104

Deputies shall exercise their powers without discontinuing their regular employment or duties.

During sessions of the Soviet, and so as to exercise their Deputy's powers in other cases stipulated by law, Deputies shall be released from their regular employment or duties, with retention of their average earnings at their permanent place of work.

Article 105

A Deputy has the right to address inquiries to the appropriate state bodies and officials, who are obliged to reply to them at a session of the Soviet.

Deputies have the right to approach any state or public body, enterprise, institution, or organisation on matters arising from their work as Deputies and to take part in considering the questions raised by them. The heads of the state or public bodies, enterprises, institutions or organisations concerned are obliged to receive Deputies without delay and to consider their proposals within the time-limit established by law.

Article 106

Deputies shall be ensured conditions for the unhampered and effective exercise of their rights and duties.

The immunity of Deputies, and other guarantees of their activity as Deputies, are defined in the Law on the Status of Deputies and other legislative acts of the USSR and of Union and Autonomous Republics.

Article 107

Deputies shall report on their work and on that of the Soviet to their constituents, and to the work collectives and public organisations that nominated them.

Deputies who have not justified the confidence of their constituents may be recalled at any time by decision of a majority of the electors in accordance with the procedure established by law.

V. HIGHER BODIES OF STATE AUTHORITY AND ADMINISTRATION OF THE USSR

Chapter 15

THE SUPREME SOVIET OF THE USSR

Article 108

The highest body of state authority of the USSR shall be the Supreme Soviet of the USSR.

The Supreme Soviet of the USSR is empowered to deal with all matters within the jurisdiction of the Union of Soviet Socialist Republics, as defined by this Constitution.

The adoption and amendment of the Constitution of the USSR; admission of new Republics to the USSR; endorsement of the formation of new Autonomous Republics and Autonomous Regions; approval of the state plans for economic and social development, of the Budget of the USSR, and of reports on their execution; and the institution of bodies of the USSR accountable to it, are the exclusive prerogative of the Supreme Soviet of the USSR.

Laws of the USSR shall be enacted by the Supreme Soviet of the USSR or by a nationwide vote (referendum) held by decision of the Supreme Soviet of the USSR.

Article 109

The Supreme Soviet of the USSR shall consist of two chambers: the Soviet of the Union and the Soviet of Nationalities.

The two chambers of the Supreme Soviet of the USSR shall have equal rights.

Article 110

The Soviet of the Union and the Soviet of Nationalities shall have equal numbers of deputies.

The Soviet of the Union shall be elected by constituencies with equal populations.

The Soviet of Nationalities shall be elected on the basis of the following representation: 32 Deputies from each Union Republic, 11 Deputies from each Autonomous Republic, five Deputies from each Autonomous Region, and one Deputy from each Autonomous Area.

The Soviet of the Union and the Soviet of Nationalities, upon submission by the credentials commissions elected by them, shall decide on the validity of Deputies' credentials, and, in cases in which the election law has been violated, shall declare the election of the Deputies concerned null and void.

Article 111

Each chamber of the Supreme Soviet of the USSR shall elect a Chairman and four Vice-Chairmen.

The Chairmen of the Soviet of the Union and of the Soviet of Nationalities shall preside over the sittings of the respective chambers and conduct their affairs.

Joint sittings of the chambers of the Supreme Soviet of the USSR shall be presided over alternately by the Chairman of the Soviet of the Union and the Chairman of the Soviet of Nationalities.

Article 112

Sessions of the Supreme Soviet of the USSR shall be convened twice a year.

Special sessions shall be convened by the Presidium of the Supreme Soviet of the USSR at its discretion or on the proposal of a Union Republic, or of not less than one-third of the Deputies of one of the chambers.

A session of the Supreme Soviet of the USSR shall consist of separate and joint sittings of the chambers, and of meetings of the standing commissions of the chambers or commissions of the Supreme Soviet of the USSR held between the sittings of the chambers. A session may be opened and closed at either separate or joint sittings of the chambers.

Article 113

The right to initiate legislation in the Supreme Soviet of the USSR is vested in the Soviet of the Union and the Soviet of Nationalities, the Presidium of the Supreme Soviet of the USSR, the Council of Ministers of the USSR, Union Republics through their higher bodies of state authority, commissions of the Supreme Soviet of the USSR and standing commissions of its chambers, Deputies of the Supreme Soviet of the USSR, the Supreme Court of the USSR, and the Procurator-General of the USSR.

The right to initiate legislation is also vested in public organisations through their All-Union bodies.

Article 114

Bills and other matters submitted to the Supreme Soviet of the USSR shall be debated by its chambers at separate or joint sittings. Where necessary, a bill or other matter may be referred to one or more commissions for preliminary or additional consideration.

A law of the USSR shall be deemed adopted when it has been passed in each chamber of the Supreme Soviet of the USSR by a majority of the total number of its Deputies. Decisions and other acts of the Supreme Soviet of the USSR are adopted by a majority of the total number of Deputies of the Supreme Soviet of the USSR.

Bills and other very important matters of state may be submitted for nationwide discussion by a decision of the Supreme Soviet of the USSR or its Presidium taken on their own initiative or on the proposal of a Union Republic.

Article 115

In the event of disagreement between the Soviet of the Union and the Soviet of Nationalities, the matter at issue shall be referred for settlement to a conciliation commission formed by the chambers on a parity basis, after which it shall be considered for a second time by the Soviet of the Union and the Soviet of Nationalities at a joint sitting. If agreement is again not reached, the matter shall be postponed for debate at the next session of the Supreme Soviet of the USSR or submitted by the Supreme Soviet to a nationwide vote (referendum).

Article 116

Laws of the USSR and decisions and other acts of the Supreme Soviet of the USSR shall be published in the languages of the Union Republics over the signatures of the Chairman and Secretary of the Presidium of the Supreme Soviet of the USSR.

Article 117

A Deputy of the Supreme Soviet of the USSR has the right to address inquiries to the Council of Ministers of the USSR, and to Ministers and the heads of other bodies formed by the Supreme Soviet of the USSR. The Council of Ministers of the USSR, or the official to whom the inquiry is addressed, is obliged to give a verbal or written reply within three days at the given session of the Supreme Soviet of the USSR.

Article 118

A Deputy of the Supreme Soviet of the USSR may not be prosecuted, or arrested, or incur a court-imposed penalty, without the sanction of the Supreme Soviet of the USSR or, between its sessions, of the Presidium of the Supreme Soviet of the USSR.

Article 119

The Supreme Soviet of the USSR, at a joint sitting of its chambers, shall elect a Presidium of the Supreme Soviet of the USSR, which shall be a standing body of the Supreme Soviet of the USSR, accountable to it for all its work and exercising the functions of the highest body of state authority of the USSR between sessions of the Supreme Soviet, within the limits prescribed by the Constitution.

Article 120

The Presidium of the Supreme Soviet of the USSR shall be elected from among the Deputies and shall consist of a Chairman, First Vice-Chairman, 15 Vice-Chairmen (one from each Union Republic), a Secretary, and 21 members.

Article 121

The Presidium of the Supreme Soviet of the USSR shall:
1) name the date of elections to the Supreme Soviet of the USSR;
2) convene sessions of the Supreme Soviet of the USSR;
3) co-ordinate the work of the standing commissions of the chambers of the Supreme Soviet of the USSR;
4) ensure observance of the Constitution of the USSR and conformity of the Constitutions and laws of Union Republics to the Constitution and laws of the USSR;
5) interpret the laws of the USSR;
6) ratify and denounce international treaties of the USSR;
7) revoke decisions and ordinances of the Council of Ministers of the USSR and of the Councils of Ministers of Union Republics should they fail to conform to the law;
8) institute military and diplomatic ranks and other special titles; and confer the highest military and diplomatic ranks and other special titles;
9) institute orders and medals of the USSR, and honorific titles of the USSR; award orders and medals of the USSR; and confer honorific titles of the USSR;

10) grant citizenship of the USSR, and rule on matters of the renunciation or deprivation of citizenship of the USSR and of granting asylum;

11) issue All-Union acts of amnesty and exercise the right of pardon;

12) appoint and recall diplomatic representatives of the USSR to other countries and to international organisations;

13) receive the letters of credence and recall of the diplomatic representatives of foreign states accredited to it;

14) form the Council of Defence of the USSR and confirm its composition; appoint and dismiss the high command of the Armed Forces of the USSR;

15) proclaim martial law in particular localities or throughout the country in the interests of defence of the USSR;

16) order general or partial mobilisation;

17) between sessions of the Supreme Soviet of the USSR, proclaim a state of war in the event of an armed attack on the USSR, or when it is necessary to meet international treaty obligations relating to mutual defence against aggression;

18) and exercise other powers vested in it by the Constitution and laws of the USSR.

Article 122

The Presidium of the Supreme Soviet of the USSR, between sessions of the Supreme Soviet of the USSR and subject to submission for its confirmation at the next session, shall:

1) amend existing legislative acts of the USSR when necessary;

2) approve changes in the boundaries between Union Republics;

3) form and abolish Ministries and State Committees of the USSR on the recommendation of the Council of Ministers of the USSR;

4) relieve individual members of the Council of Ministers of the USSR of their responsibilities and appoint persons to the Council of Ministers on the recommendation of the Chairman of the Council of Ministers of the USSR.

Article 123

The Presidium of the Supreme Soviet of the USSR promulgates decrees and adopts decisions.

Article 124

On expiry of the term of the Supreme Soviet of the USSR, the Presidium of the Supreme Soviet of the USSR shall retain its powers until the newly elected Supreme Soviet of the USSR has elected a new Presidium.

The newly elected Supreme Soviet of the USSR shall be convened by the outgoing Presidium of the Supreme Soviet of the USSR within two months of the elections.

Article 125

The Soviet of the Union and the Soviet of Nationalities shall elect standing commissions from among the Deputies to make a preliminary review of matters coming within the jurisdiction of the Supreme Soviet of the USSR, to promote execution of the laws of the USSR and other acts of the Supreme Soviet of the USSR and its Presidium, and to check on the work of state bodies and organisations. The chambers of the Supreme Soviet of the USSR may also set up joint commissions on a parity basis.

When it deems it necessary, the Supreme Soviet of the USSR sets up commissions of inquiry and audit, and commissions on any other matter.

All state and public bodies, organisations and officials are obliged to meet the requests of the commissions of the Supreme Soviet of the USSR and of its chambers, and submit the requisite materials and documents to them.

The commissions' recommendations shall be subject to consideration by state and public bodies, institutions and organisations. The commissions shall be informed, within the prescribed time-limit, of the results of such consideration or of the action taken.

Article 126

The Supreme Soviet of the USSR shall supervise the work of all state bodies accountable to it.

The Supreme Soviet of the USSR shall form a Committee of People's Control of the USSR to head the system of people's control.

The organisation and procedure of people's control bodies are defined by the Law on People's Control in the USSR.

Article 127

The procedure of the Supreme Soviet of the USSR and of its bodies shall be defined in the Rules and Regulations of the Supreme Soviet of the USSR and other laws of the USSR enacted on the basis of the Constitution of the USSR.

Chapter 16

THE COUNCIL OF MINISTERS
OF THE USSR

Article 128

The Council of Ministers of the USSR, i.e. the Government of the USSR, is the highest executive and administrative body of state authority of the USSR.

Article 129

The Council of Ministers of the USSR shall be formed by the Supreme Soviet of the USSR at a joint sitting of the Soviet of the Union and the Soviet of Nationalities, and shall consist of the Chairman of the Council of Ministers of the USSR, First Vice-Chairmen and Vice-Chairmen, Ministers of the USSR, and Chairmen of State Committees of the USSR.

The Chairmen of the Councils of Ministers of Union Republics shall be ex officio members of the Council of Ministers of the USSR.

The Supreme Soviet of the USSR, on the recommendation of the Chairman of the Council of Ministers of the USSR, may include in the Government of the USSR the heads of other bodies and organisations of the USSR.

The Council of Ministers of the USSR shall tender its resignation to a newly-elected Supreme Soviet of the USSR at its first session.

Article 130

The Council of Ministers of the USSR shall be responsible and accountable to the Supreme Soviet of the USSR and, between sessions of the Supreme Soviet of the USSR, to the Presidium of the Supreme Soviet of the USSR.

The Council of Ministers of the USSR shall report regularly on its work to the Supreme Soviet of the USSR.

Article 131

The Council of Ministers of the USSR is empowered to deal with all matters of state administration within the jurisdiction of the Union of Soviet Socialist Republics insofar as, under the Constitution, they do not come within the competence of the Supreme Soviet of the USSR or the Presidium of the Supreme Soviet of the USSR.

Within its powers the Council of Ministers of the USSR shall:

1) ensure direction of economic, social and cultural development; draft and implement measures to promote the well-being and cultural development of the people, to develop science and engineering, to ensure rational exploitation and conservation of natural resources, to consolidate the monetary and credit system, to pursue a uniform prices, wages, and social security policy, and to organise state insurance and a uniform system of accounting and statistics; and organise the management of industrial, constructional, and agricultural enterprises and amalgamations, transport and communications undertakings, banks, and other organisations and institutions of Union subordination;

2) draft current and long-term state plans for the economic and social development of the USSR and the Budget of the USSR, and submit them to the Supreme Soviet of the USSR; take measures to execute the state plans and Budget; and report to the Supreme Soviet of the USSR on the implementation of the plans and Budget;

3) implement measures to defend the interests of the state, protect socialist property and maintain public order, and guarantee and protect citizens' rights and freedoms;

4) take measures to ensure state security;

5) exercise general direction of the development of the Armed Forces of the USSR, and determine the annual contingent of citizens to be called up for active military service;

6) provide general direction in regard to relations with other states, foreign trade, and economic, scientific, technical, and cultural cooperation of the USSR with other countries; take measures to ensure

fulfilment of the USSR's international treaties; and ratify and denounce intergovernmental international agreements;

7) and when necessary, form committees, central boards and other departments under the Council of Ministers of the USSR to deal with matters of economic, social and cultural development, and defence.

Article 132

A Presidium of the Council of Ministers of the USSR, consisting of the Chairman, the First Vice-Chairmen, and Vice-Chairmen of the Council of Ministers of the USSR, shall function as a standing body of the Council of Ministers of the USSR to deal with questions relating to guidance of the economy, and with other matters of state administration.

Article 133

The Council of Ministers of the USSR, on the basis of, and in pursuance of, the laws of the USSR and other decisions of the Supreme Soviet of the USSR and its Presidium, shall issue decisions and ordinances and verify their execution. The decisions and ordinances of the Council of Ministers of the USSR shall be binding throughout the USSR.

Article 134

The Council of Ministers of the USSR has the right, in matters within the jurisdiction of the Union of Soviet Socialist Republics, to suspend execution of decisions and ordinances of the Councils of Ministers of Union Republics, and to rescind acts of ministries and state committees of the USSR, and of other bodies subordinate to it.

Article 135

The Council of Ministers of the USSR shall co-ordinate and direct the work of All-Union and Union-Republican ministries, state committees of the USSR, and other bodies subordinate to it.

All-Union ministries and state committees of the USSR shall direct the work of the branches of administration entrusted to them, or exercise inter-branch administration, throughout the territory of the USSR directly or through bodies set up by them.

Union-Republican ministries and state committees of the USSR direct the work of the branches of administration entrusted to them, or exercise inter-branch administration, as a rule, through the corresponding ministries and state committees, and other bodies of Union Republics, and directly administer individual enterprises and amalgamations of Union subordination. The procedure for transferring enterprises and amalgamations from Republic or local subordination to Union subordination shall be defined by the Presidium of the Supreme Soviet of the USSR.

Ministries and state committees of the USSR shall be responsible for the condition and development of the spheres of administration entrusted to them; within their competence, they issue orders and other acts on the basis of, and in execution of, the laws of the USSR and other decisions of the Supreme Soviet of the USSR and its Presidium, and of decisions and ordinances of the Council of Ministers of the USSR, and organise and verify their implementation.

Article 136

The competence of the Council of Ministers of the USSR and its Presidium, the procedure for their work, relationships between the Council of Ministers and other state bodies, and the list of All-Union and Union-Republican ministries and state committees of the USSR are defined, on the basis of the Constitution, in the Law on the Council of Ministers of the USSR.

VI. Basic Principles of the Structure
of the Bodies of State Authority and
Administration in Union Republics

Chapter 17

HIGHER BODIES OF STATE AUTHORITY AND
ADMINISTRATION OF A UNION REPUBLIC

Article 137

The highest body of state authority of a Union Republic shall be the Supreme Soviet of that Republic.

The Supreme Soviet of a Union Republic is empowered to deal with all matters within the jurisdiction of the Republic under the Constitutions of the USSR and the Republic.

Adoption and amendment of the Constitution of a Union Republic; endorsement of state plans for economic and social development, of the Republic's Budget, and of reports on their fulfilment; and the formation of bodies accountable to the Supreme Soviet of the Union Republic are the exclusive prerogative of that Supreme Soviet.

Laws of a Union Republic shall be enacted by the Supreme Soviet of the Union Republic or by a popular vote (referendum) held by decision of the Republic's Supreme Soviet.

Article 138

The Supreme Soviet of a Union Republic shall elect a Presidium, which is a standing body of that Supreme Soviet and accountable to it for all its work. The composition and powers of the Presidium of the Supreme Soviet of a Union Republic shall be defined in the Constitution of the Union Republic.

Article 139

The Supreme Soviet of a Union Republic shall form a Council of Ministers of the Union Republic, i.e. the Government of that Republic, which shall be the highest executive and administrative body of state authority in the Republic.

The Council of Ministers of a Union Republic shall be responsible and accountable to the Supreme Soviet of that Republic or, between sessions of the Supreme Soviet, to its Presidium.

Article 140

The Council of Ministers of a Union Republic issues decisions and ordinances on the basis of, and in pursuance of, the legislative acts of the USSR and of the Union Republic, and of decisions and ordinances of the Council of Ministers of the USSR, and shall organise and verify their execution.

Article 141

The Council of Ministers of a Union Republic has the right to suspend the execution of decisions and ordinances of the Councils of Ministers of Autonomous Republics, to rescind the decisions and orders of the Executive Committees of Soviets of People's Deputies of Territories, Regions, and cities (i.e. cities under Republic jurisdiction) and of Autonomous Regions, and in Union Republics not divided into regions, of the Executive Committees of district and corresponding city Soviets of People's Deputies.

Article 142

The Council of Ministers of a Union Republic shall co-ordinate and direct the work of the Union-Republican and Republican ministries and of state committees of the Union Republic, and other bodies under its jurisdiction.

The Union-Republican ministries and state committees of a Union Republic shall direct the branches of administration entrusted to them, or exercise inter-branch control, and shall be subordinate to both the Council of Ministers of the Union Republic and the corresponding Union-Republican ministry or state committee of the USSR.

Republican ministries and state committees shall direct the branches of administration entrusted to them, or exercise inter-branch control, and shall be subordinate to the Council of Ministers of the Union Republic.

Chapter 18

HIGHER BODIES OF STATE AUTHORITY AND ADMINISTRATION OF AN AUTONOMOUS REPUBLIC

Article 143

The highest body of state authority of an Autonomous Republic shall be the Supreme Soviet of that Republic.

Adoption and amendment of the Constitution of an Autonomous Republic; endorsement of state plans for economic and social development, and of the Republic's Budget; and the formation of bodies accountable to the Supreme Soviet of the Autonomous Republic are the exclusive prerogative of that Supreme Soviet.

Laws of an Autonomous Republic shall be enacted by the Supreme Soviet of the Autonomous Republic.

Article 144

The Supreme Soviet of an Autonomous Republic shall elect a Presidium of the Supreme Soviet of the Autonomous Republic and shall form a Council of Ministers of the Autonomous Republic, i.e. the Government of that Republic.

Chapter 19

LOCAL BODIES OF STATE AUTHORITY
AND ADMINISTRATION

Article 145

The bodies of state authority in Territories, Regions, Autonomous Regions, Autonomous Areas, districts, cities, city districts, settlements, and rural communities shall be the corresponding Soviets of People's Deputies.

Article 146

Local Soviets of People's Deputies shall deal with all matters of local significance in accordance with the interests of the whole state and of the citizens residing in the area under their jurisdiction, implement decisions of higher bodies of state authority, guide the work of lower Soviets of People's Deputies, take part in the discussion of matters of Republican and All-Union significance, and submit their proposals concerning them.

Local Soviets of People's Deputies shall direct state, economic, social and cultural development within their territory; endorse plans of economic and social development and the local budget; exercise general guidance over state bodies, enterprises, institutions and organisations subordinate to them; ensure observance of the laws, maintenance of law and order, and protection of citizens' rights, and help strengthen the country's defence capacity.

Article 147

Within their powers, local Soviets of People's Deputies shall ensure the comprehensive, all-round economic and social development of their area; exercise control over the observance of legislation by enterprises, institutions and organisations subordinate to higher authorities and located in their area; and co-ordinate and supervise their activity as regards land use, nature conservation, building, employment of manpower, production of consumer goods, and social, cultural, communal and other services and amenities for the public.

Article 148

Local Soviets of People's Deputies shall decide matters within the powers accorded them by the legislation of the USSR and of the appropriate Union Republic and Autonomous Republic. Their decisions shall be binding on all enterprises, institutions, and organisations located in their area and on officials and citizens.

Article 149

The executive-administrative bodies of local Soviets shall be the Executive Committees elected by them from among their Deputies.

Executive Committees shall report on their work at least once a year to the Soviets that elected them and to meetings of citizens at their places of work or residence.

Article 150

Executive Committees of local Soviets of People's Deputies shall be directly accountable both to the Soviet that elected them and to the higher executive-administrative body.

VII. JUSTICE, ARBITRATION, AND PROCURATOR'S SUPERVISION

Chapter 20
COURTS AND ARBITRATION

Article 151

In the USSR justice is administered only by the courts.

In the USSR there are the following courts: the Supreme Court of the USSR, the Supreme Courts of Union Republics, the Supreme Courts of Autonomous Republics, Territorial, Regional, and city courts, courts of Autonomous Regions, courts of Autonomous Areas, district (city) people's courts, and military tribunals in the Armed Forces.

Article 152

All courts in the USSR shall be formed on the principle of the electiveness of judges and people's assessors.

People's judges of district (city) people's courts shall be elected for a term of five years by the citizens of the district (city) on the basis of universal, equal and direct suffrage by secret ballot. People's assessors of district (city) people's courts shall be elected for a term of two and a half years at meetings of citizens at their places of work or residence by a show of hands.

Higher courts shall be elected for a term of five years by the corresponding Soviet of People's Deputies.

The judges of military tribunals shall be elected for a term of five years by the Presidium of the Supreme Soviet of the USSR and people's assessors for a term of two and a half years by meetings of servicemen.

Judges and people's assessors are responsible and accountable to their electors or the bodies that elected them, shall report to them, and may be recalled by them in the manner prescribed by law.

Article 153

The Supreme Court of the USSR is the highest judicial body in the USSR and supervises the administration of justice by the courts of the USSR and Union Republics within the limits established by law.

The Supreme Court of the USSR shall be elected by the Supreme Soviet of the USSR and shall consist of a Chairman, Vice-Chairmen, members, and people's assessors. The Chairmen of the Supreme Courts of Union Republics are ex officio members of the Supreme Court of the USSR.

The organisation and procedure of the Supreme Court of the USSR are defined in the Law on the Supreme Court of the USSR.

Article 154

The hearing of civil and criminal cases in all courts is collegial; in courts of first instance cases are heard with the participation of people's assessors. In the administration of justice people's assessors have all the rights of a judge.

Article 155

Judges and people's assessors are independent and subject only to the law.

Article 156

Justice is administered in the USSR on the principle of the equality of citizens before the law and the court.

Article 157

Proceedings in all courts shall be open to the public. Hearings in camera are only allowed in cases provided for by law, with observance of all the rules of judicial procedure.

Article 158

A defendant in a criminal action is guaranteed the right to legal assistance.

Article 159

Judicial proceedings shall be conducted in the language of the Union Republic, Autonomous Republic, Autonomous Region, or Autonomous Area, or in the language spoken by the majority of the people in the locality. Persons participating in court proceedings, who do not know the language in which they are being conducted, shall be ensured the right to become fully acquainted with the materials in the case; the services of an interpreter during the proceedings; and the right to address the court in their own language.

Article 160

No one may be adjudged guilty of a crime and subjected to punishment as a criminal except by the sentence of a court and in conformity with the law.

Article 161

Colleges of advocates are available to give legal assistance to citizens and organisations. In cases provided for by legislation citizens shall be given legal assistance free of charge.

The organisation and procedure of the bar are determined by legislation of the USSR and Union Republics.

Article 162

Representatives of public organisations and of work collectives may take part in civil and criminal proceedings.

Article 163

Economic disputes between enterprises, institutions, and organisations are settled by state arbitration bodies within the limits of their jurisdiction.

The organisation and manner of functioning of state arbitration bodies are defined in the Law on State Arbitration in the USSR.

Chapter 21
THE PROCURATOR'S OFFICE

Article 164

Supreme power of supervision over the strict and uniform observance of laws by all ministries, state committees and departments, enterprises, institutions and organisations, executive-administrative bodies of local Soviets of People's Deputies, collective farms, co-operatives and other public organisations, officials and citizens is vested in the Procurator-General of the USSR and procurators subordinate to him.

Article 165

The Procurator-General of the USSR is appointed by the Supreme Soviet of the USSR and is responsible and accountable to it and, between sessions of the Supreme Soviet, to the Presidium of the Supreme Soviet of the USSR.

Article 166

The procurators of Union Republics, Autonomous Republics, Territories, Regions and Autonomous Regions are appointed by the

Procurator-General of the USSR. The procurators of Autonomous Areas and district and city procurators are appointed by the procurators of Union Republics, subject to confirmation by the Procurator-General of the USSR.

Article 167

The term of office of the Procurator-General of the USSR and all lower-ranking procurators shall be five years.

Article 168

The agencies of the Procurator's Office exercise their powers independently of any local bodies whatsoever, and are subordinate solely to the Procurator-General of the USSR.

The organisation and procedure of the agencies of the Procurator's Office are defined in the Law on the Procurator's Office of the USSR.

VIII. The Emblem, Flag, Anthem, and Capital
of the USSR

Article 169

The State Emblem of the Union of Soviet Socialist Republics is a hammer and sickle on a globe depicted in the rays of the sun and framed by ears of wheat, with the inscription "Workers of All Countries, Unite!" in the languages of the Union Republics. At the top of the Emblem is a five-pointed star.

Article 170

The State Flag of the Union of Soviet Socialist Republics is a rectangle of red cloth with a hammer and sickle depicted in gold in the upper corner next to the staff and with a five-pointed red star edged in gold above them. The ratio of the width of the flag to its length is 1:2.

Article 171

The State Anthem of the Union of Soviet Socialist Republics is confirmed by the Presidium of the Supreme Soviet of the USSR.

Article 172

The Capital of the Union of Soviet Socialist Republics is the city of Moscow.

IX. The Legal Force of the Constitution of
the USSR and Procedure for Amending
the Constitution

Article 173

The Constitution of the USSR shall have supreme legal force. All laws and other acts of state bodies shall be promulgated on the basis of and in conformity with it.

Article 174

The Constitution of the USSR may be amended by a decision of the Supreme Soviet of the USSR adopted by a majority of not less than two-thirds of the total number of Deputies of each of its chambers.

LAW ON THE USSR COUNCIL OF MINISTERS

Passed by the Supreme Soviet of the U.S.S.R. on July 5, 1978

(Excerpts)

Article 1

The Council of Ministers of the U.S.S.R.—the Government of the U.S.S.R.—is the supreme executive and administrative organ of state power of the U.S.S.R.

The Constitution of the U.S.S.R., on the basis of Leninist ideas and principles, defines the role and tasks of the Council of Ministers of the U.S.S.R. in implementing the functions of the socialist state of the entire people.

The Council of Ministers of the U.S.S.R. is empowered to resolve all questions of state administration conferred upon the jurisdiction of the U.S.S.R., so long as they are, according to the Constitution of the U.S.S.R., not within the jurisdiction of the Supreme Soviet of the U.S.S.R. and the Presidium of the Supreme Soviet of the U.S.S.R.

In its activity the Council of Ministers of the U.S.S.R. shall be guided by the Constitution of the U.S.S.R. and by the laws of the U.S.S.R.

The Council of Ministers of the U.S.S.R. on the basis of and in implementation of the laws of the U.S.S.R. and of other decisions of the Supreme Soviet of the U.S.S.R. and of its Presidium issues resolutions and orders and verifies their execution. Resolutions and orders of the Council of Ministers are compulsory and must be executed throughout the entire territory of the U.S.S.R. by all organs, organizations, state officials and citizens.

Article 23

The All-Union Ministries of the U.S.S.R. are
Aviation Industry
Automobile Industry
Foreign Trade
Gas Industry
Civil Aviation
Machine Building
Machine Building for Animal Husbandry and Fodder Production

Machine Building for Light and Food Industries and for Household
  Appliances
Medical Industry
Merchant Marine
Petroleum Industry
Defense Industry
Defense
General Machine Building
Instrument Making, Means of Automation and Control Systems
Communications Equipment Industry
Radio Industry
Medium Machine Building
Machine Tool and Instrument Industry
Construction Machinery, Road-building Machinery and Civil En-
  gineering Machinery
Construction of Petroleum and Gas Industry Enterprises
Shipbuilding Industry
Tractor and Agricultural Machinery Manufacture
Construction of Transportation
Heavy and Transport Machine Building
Chemical and Petroleum Machine Building
Chemical Industry
Paper and Pulp Industry
Electronic Industry
Electrotechnical Industry
Power Machinery Construction

Article 24

The Union-Republic Ministries of the U.S.S.R. are
Internal Affairs
Higher and Specialized Secondary Education
Geology
Grain Procurement
Public Health
Foreign Affairs
Culture
Light Industry
Lumber and Wood-processing Industry
Land Improvement and Irrigation
Assembly and Special Construction
Meat and Dairy Industry
Petroleum Refining and Petro-chemical Industry
Food Industry
Industrial Construction
Building Materials Industry
Education
Fisheries
Communications
Rural Construction

Agriculture
Construction
Construction of Heavy Industrial Enterprises
Trade
Coal Industry
Finance
Nonferrous Metallurgy
Ferrous Metallurgy
Power and Electrification
Justice

Article 25

The All-Union State Committees of the U.S.S.R. are
Science and Technology
Inventions and Discoveries
Standards
Foreign Economic Relations
Hydrometeorology and Environmental Control
Material Reserves

Article 26

The Union-Republic State Committees of the U.S.S.R. are
Planning
Construction
Material and Technical Supply
Labor and Social Questions
Prices
Vocational and Technical Education
Television and Radio Broadcasting
Cinematography
Publishing, Printing and the Book Trade
Forestry
State Security
Production and Technical Supply to Agriculture

Article 27

Other organs subordinate to the Council of Ministers of the U.S.S.R. are the State Bank of the U.S.S.R. and the Central Statistical Administration of the U.S.S.R., whose heads are included with the Government of the U.S.S.R. according to established procedures.

Also subordinate to the Council of Ministers of the U.S.S.R. are the Committee for Supervision of Industrial Safety and for Mine Inspection, the Committee for Physical Culture and Sport and other Committees, Chief Administrations and Departments under the Council of Ministers of the U.S.S.R. for economic, social-cultural and defense construction and other agencies, in accordance with legislation of the U.S.S.R.

To resolve economic disputes between enterprises, institutions and organizations State Arbitration of the U.S.S.R. operates under the Council of Ministers of the U.S.S.R.

PROGRAM OF THE COMMUNIST PARTY
OF THE SOVIET UNION

Adopted by the Twenty-second Party Congress, October 31, 1961

(Excerpts)

III
THE TASKS OF THE PARTY IN THE SPHERES OF
STATE DEVELOPMENT AND THE FURTHER PROMOTION OF SOCIALIST
DEMOCRACY

The dictatorship of the proletariat, born of the socialist revolution, has played an epoch-making role by ensuring the victory of socialism in the U.S.S.R. In the course of socialist construction, however, it underwent changes. . . . The socialist state has entered a new period of its development. . . . Proletarian democracy is becoming more and more a socialist democracy of the people as a whole . . . , the dictatorship of the proletariat has fulfilled its historic mission and has ceased to be indispensable in the U.S.S.R. from the point of view of the tasks of internal development. The state, which arose as a state of the dictatorship of the proletariat has become in the new contemporary period a state of the entire people, an organ expressing the interests and will of the people as a whole. Since the working class is the foremost and best organized force of Soviet society, it plays a leading role also in the period of the full scale construction of communism. The working class will have completed its role of leader of society after communism is built and classes disappear. . . . As socialist democracy develops the organs of state power will gradually be transformed into organs of public self-government. . . .

The role of the Soviets, which are an all-inclusive organization of the people, the embodiment of their unity, will grow as communist construction progresses . . . the participation of social organizations and associations of the people in the legislative activity of the representative bodies of the Soviet state will be extended. . . . The Party holds that democratic principles in administration must be developed further. . . . An effort should be made to ensure that the salaried government staffs be reduced, that ever larger sections of the people learn to take part in administration and that work on government staffs eventually cease to constitute a profession. . . .

The further promotion of socialist law and order and the improvement of legal rules governing economic organization, cultural and educational work and contributing to the accomplishment of the tasks of communist construction and to the all-round development of the individual are very important. The transition to communism means the fullest extension of personal freedom and the rights of Soviet citizens. . . . The Party calls for enforcing strict observance of socialist legality, for eradication of all violations of law and order, for the abolition of crime and the removal of the causes of crime. . . . There should be no room for law breakers and criminals in a society building communism. But as long as there are criminal offenses, it is necessary severely to punish those who commit crimes dangerous to society, violate the rules of the socialist community and refuse to live by honest labor. Attention should be focussed mainly on crime prevention. Higher standards of living and culture, and greater social consciousness of the people will pave the way to the abolition of crime and the ultimate replacement of judicial punishment by measures of public influence and education. . . .

Historical development inevitably leads to the withering away of the state. To ensure that the state withers away completely, it is necessary to provide both internal conditions—the building of a developed communist society—and external conditions—the victory and consolidation of socialism in the international arena. . . .

IV
THE TASKS OF THE PARTY IN
THE FIELD OF NATIONAL RELATIONS

Under socialism the nations flourish and their sovereignty grows stronger. . . . The boundaries between the constituent republics of the U.S.S.R. are increasingly losing their former significance, since all the nations are equal, their life is based on a common socialist foundation, the material and spiritual needs of every people are satisfied to the same extent, and they are all united in a single family by common vital interests and are advancing together to the common goal—communism. . . . Full-scale communist construction constitutes a new stage in the development of national relations in the U.S.S.R. in which the nations will draw closer together until complete unity is achieved. . . . However, the obliteration of national distinctions, and especially of language distinctions, is a considerably longer process than the obliteration of class distinctions. . . . The historical experience of socialist states shows that national forms do not ossify; they change, advance and draw closer together, shedding all outmoded traits that contradict the new living conditions. An international culture common to all the Soviet nations is developing. . . . The Party will promote . . . the formation of a single world-wide culture of communist society. . . .

VII
THE PARTY IN THE PERIOD OF
FULL-SCALE COMMUNIST CONSTRUCTION

As a result of the victory of socialism in the U.S.S.R. and the consolidation of the unity of Soviet society, the Communist Party of the working class has become the vanguard of the Soviet people, a Party of the entire people, and extended its guiding influence to all spheres of social life. The Party is the brain, the honor and the conscience of our epoch. . . . The period of full-scale communist construction is characterized by a further enhancement of the role and importance of the Communist Party as the leading and guiding force of Soviet society. . . . Being the vanguard of the people building a communist society, the Party must also be in the van in the organization of internal Party life and serve as an example and model in developing the most advanced forms of public communist self-government. . . .

The people are the decisive force in the building of communism. . . . The Party considers it its duty always to consult the working people on the major questions of home and foreign policy, to make these questions an object of nationwide discussion, and to attract the more extensive participation of non-members in all its work. The more socialist democracy develops, the broader and more versatile the work of the Party among the working people must be, and the stronger will be its influence among the masses. . . .

RULES OF THE COMMUNIST PARTY
OF THE SOVIET UNION

*Adopted by the Twenty-second Party Congress, October 31, 1961,
and Amended by the Twenty-third Party Congress, April 8, 1966,
and by the Twenty-fourth Party Congress, April 9, 1971*

The Communist Party of the Soviet Union (CPSU) is the tried and tested militant vanguard of the Soviet people, which unites, on a voluntary basis, the more advanced, the politically more conscious section of the working class, collective-farm peasantry and intelligentsia of the U.S.S.R.

Founded by V. I. Lenin as the vanguard of the working class, the Communist Party has traveled a glorious road of struggle, and brought the working class and the working peasantry to the victory of the Great October Socialist Revolution and to the establishment of the dictatorship of the proletariat in the U.S.S.R. Under the leadership of the Communist Party, the exploiting classes were abolished in the Soviet Union, and the moral and political unity of Soviet society has taken shape and grown in strength. Socialism has triumphed completely and finally. The Communist Party, the party of the working class, has today become the party of the Soviet people as a whole.

The Party exists for, and serves, the people. It is the highest form of socio-political organization, and is the leading and guiding force of Soviet society. It directs the great creative activity of the Soviet people, and imparts an organized, planned, and scientifically based character to their struggle to achieve the ultimate goal, the victory of communism.

The CPSU bases its work on the unswerving adherence to the Leninist standards of Party life—the principle of collective leadership, the promotion, in every possible way, of inner-party democracy, the activity and initiative of the Communists, criticism and self-criticism.

Ideological and organizational unity, monolithic cohesion of its ranks, and a high degree of conscious discipline on the part of all Communists are an inviolable law of the CPSU. All manifestations of factionalism and group activity are incompatible with Marxist-Leninist Party principles, and with Party membership. The Party rids itself of persons infringing the program and rules of the CPSU and compromising by their conduct the high calling of a Communist.

In all its activities, the CPSU is guided by Marxist-Leninist theory and the Program based on it, which defines the fundamental tasks of the Party for the period of the construction of communist society.

In creatively developing Marxism-Leninism, the CPSU vigorously combats all manifestations of revisionism and dogmatism, which are profoundly alien to revolutionary theory.

The Communist Party of the Soviet Union is an integral part of the international communist and working-class movement. It firmly adheres to the tried and tested Marxist-Leninist principles of proletarian internationalism; it actively promotes the unty of the international communist and workers' movement as a whole, and of the fraternal ties with the great army of the Communists of all countries.

I

PARTY MEMBERS, THEIR DUTIES
AND RIGHTS

1. Membership in the CPSU is open to any citizen of the Soviet Union who accepts the Program and Rules of the Party, takes an active part in communist construction, works in one of the Party organizations, carries out all Party decisions, and pays membership dues.

2. It is the duty of a Party member:

a) To work for the creation of the material and technical basis of communism; to serve as an example of the communist attitude toward labor; to raise labor productivity; to take the initiative in all that is new and progressive; to support and propagate advanced methods; to master techniques, to improve his skills; to protect and increase socialist social property, the mainstay of the might and prosperity of the Soviet country;

b) To put Party decisions firmly and steadfastly into effect; to explain the policy of the Party to the masses; to help strengthen and multiply the Party's bonds with the people; to be considerate and attentive to people; to respond promptly to the needs and requirements of the working people;

c) To take an active part in the political affairs of the country; in the administration of state affairs, and in economic and cultural development; to set an example in the fulfilment of his public duty; to assist in developing and strengthening communist social relations;

d) To master Marxist-Leninist theory, to improve his ideological knowledge, and to contribute to the molding and education of the man of communist society; to combat decisively all manifestations of bourgeois ideology, religious prejudices, remnants of a private-property psychology, and other survivals of the past; to observe the rules of communist morality, and to give public interests precedence over his own;

e) To be an active proponent of the ideas of socialist internationalism and Soviet patriotism among the masses of the working people; to combat survivals of nationalism and chauvinism; to contribute by word and by deed to the consolidation of the friendship of the peoples of the U.S.S.R. and the fraternal bonds linking the Soviet people with the peoples of the socialist countries, with the proletarians and other working people in all countries;

f) Vigorously to strengthen the ideological and organizational unity of the Party; to safeguard the Party against the infiltration of people unworthy of the lofty name of Communist; to be truthful and honest with the Party; to display vigilance, to guard Party and state secrets;

g) To develop criticism and self-criticism, boldly to lay bare shortcomings and strive for their removal; to combat ostentation, conceit, complacency and parochial tendencies; firmly to rebuff all attempts at suppressing criticism; to resist all actions injurious to the Party and the state, and to give information about them to Party bodies, up to and including the Central Committee of the Communist Party of the Soviet Union (CC CPSU).

h) To implement undeviatingly the Party's policy with regard to the proper selection of personnel according to their political and professional qualifications; to be uncompromising whenever the Leninist principles of the selection and education of personnel are infringed on;

i) To observe Party and state discipline, which is equally binding on all Party members. The Party has one discipline, one law, for all Communists, irrespective of their past services or the positions they occupy;

j) To assist in every way with the strengthening of the defensive power of the U.S.S.R., and conduct unceasing struggle for peace and friendship among peoples.

3. A Party member has the right:

a) To elect and be elected to Party bodies;

b) To discuss freely questions of the Party's policies and practical activities at Party meetings, conferences, and congresses, at the meetings of Party committees and in the Party press; to table motions; openly to express and uphold his opinion as long as the organization concerned has not adopted a decision;

c) To criticize any Communist, irrespective of the position he holds, at Party meetings, conferences, and congresses and at the plenary meetings of Party committees. Those who commit the offense of suppressing criticism or victimizing anyone for criticism are responsible to and will be penalized by the Party, to the point of expulsion from the CPSU.

d) To attend in person all Party meetings and all bureau and committee meetings that discuss his activities or conduct;

e) To address any question, statement, or proposal to any Party body, up to and including the CC CPSU, and to demand an answer on the substance of his address.

4. Applicants are admitted to Party membership only individually. Membership in the Party is open to politically conscious and active

workers, peasants, and representatives of the intellectuals, devoted to the communist cause. New members are admitted from among the candidate members who have passed through the established probationary period. Persons may join the Party on attaining the age of eighteen. Young people up to the age of twenty-three may join the Party only through the Young Communist League (YCL).

The procedure for the admission of candidate members of full Party membership is as follows:

a) Applicants for Party membership must submit recommendations from three Party members who have a Party standing of not less than five years and who know the applicants from having worked with them, professionally and socially, for not less than one year.

Note 1. In the case of members of the YCL applying for membership in the Party, the recommendation of a county and city committee of the YCL is equivalent to the recommendation of one Party member.

Note 2. Members and alternate members of the CC CPSU shall refrain from giving recommendations.

b) Applications for Party membership are discussed and a decision is taken by the general meeting of the primary Party organization; the decision of the latter is considered as having been adopted if two-thirds of the Party members present at the meeting voted for it, and it takes effect after endorsement by the county or borough Party committee, or by the city Party committee in cities with no borough divisions.

The presence of those who have recommended an applicant for Party membership at the discussion of the application concerned is optional;

c) Citizens of the U.S.S.R. who formerly belonged to the Communist or Workers' Party of another country are admitted to membership of the Communist Party of the Soviet Union in conformity with the rules established by the CC CPSU.

Former members of other parties are admitted to membership of the CPSU in conformity with the regular procedure, except that their admission must be endorsed by a regional or territorial committee or the CC of the Communist Party of a union republic.

5. Communists recommending applicants for Party membership are responsible to Party organizations for the impartiality of their description of the political, professional, and moral qualifications of those they recommend.

6. The Party standing of those admitted to membership dates from the day when the general meeting of the primary Party organization decides to accept them as full members.

7. The procedure of registering members and candidate members of the Party, and their transition from one organization to another is determined by the appropriate instructions of the CC CPSU.

8. The matter of a member or candidate member who fails to pay membership dues for three months in succession without sufficient reason shall be discussed by the primary Party organization. If it is revealed as a result that the Party member or candidate member in question has virtually lost contact with the Party organization, he shall be regarded as having ceased to be a member of the Party; the primary Party organiza-

tion shall pass a decision thereon and submit it to the county, borough, or city committee of the Party for endorsement.

9. A Party member who fails to fulfill his duties as laid down in the Rules, or commits other offenses, shall be called to account, and may be subjected to the penalty of admonition, reprimand (or severe reprimand), or censure (or severe censure) with entry in the registration card. The highest Party penalty is expulsion from the Party.

In the case of insignificant offenses, measures of Party education and influence should be applied—in the form of comradely criticism, Party censure, warning, or reproof.

When the question of expelling a member from the Party is discussed, the maximum prudence and attention must be shown, and the grounds for the charges preferred against a Communist must be thoroughly investigated.

10. The decision to expel a Communist from the Party is made by the general meeting of a primary Party organization. The decision of the primary Party organization expelling a member is regarded as adopted if not less than two-thirds of the Party members attending the meeting have voted for it, and it shall be endorsed by a county, borough, or city committee of the Party.

Until such time as the decision to expel him is endorsed by a provincial or territorial Party committee or the CC of the Communist Party of a union republic, the Party member retains his membership card and is entitled to attend closed Party meetings.

An expelled Party member retains the right to appeal, within the period of two months, to the higher Party bodies, up to and including the CC CPSU.

11. The question of calling a member or alternate member of the CC of the Communist Party of a union republic, of a territorial, provincial, area, city, county, or borough Party committee, or of an auditing commission, to account before the Party is discussed by primary Party organizations.

Party organizations pass decisions imposing penalties on members or alternate members of the said Party committees, or on members of auditing commissions, in conformity with the regular procedure.

A Party organization which proposes expelling a Communist from the CPSU communicates its proposal to the Party committee of which he is a member. A decision to expel from the Party a member or alternate member of the CC of the Communist Party of a union republic or a territorial, provincial, area, city, county, or borough Party committee, or a member of an auditing commission, is taken at the plenary meeting of the committee concerned by a majority of two-thirds of the membership.

The decision to expel from the Party a member or alternate member of the CC CPSU, or a member of the Central Auditing Commission, is made by the Party congress, and in the interval between two congresses, by a plenary meeting of the Central Committee, by a majority of two-thirds of the membership.

12. Should a Party member commit an indictable offense, he shall be expelled from the Party and prosecuted in conformity with the law.

13. Appeals against expulsion from the Party or against the imposition of a penalty, as well as the decisions of Party organizations on expulsion from the Party, shall be examined by the appropriate Party bodies within not more than one month from the date of their receipt.

II
CANDIDATE MEMBERS

14. Persons joining the Party must pass through a probationary period as candidate members in order to familiarize themselves with the Program and Rules of the CPSU and prepare for admission to full membership in the Party. Party organizations must assist candidates to prepare for admission to full membership in the Party, and test their personal qualities. Probationary membership shall be one year.

15. The procedure for the admission of candidate members (individual admission, submission of recommendations, decision of the primary organization as to admission, and its endorsement) is identical with the procedure for the admission of Party members.

16. On the expiration of a candidate member's probationary period the primary Party organization discusses and passes a decision on his application for admission to full membership. Should a candidate member fail, in the course of his probationary period, to show his worthiness, including his personal qualities, he may not be admitted to membership in the CPSU, and the party organization shall pass a decision rejecting his admission to membership in the party; after endorsement of that decision by the county or city Party committee, he shall cease to be considered a candidate member of the CPSU.

17. Candidate members of the Party must participate in all the activities of their Party organizations; they shall have a consultative voice at Party meetings. They may not be elected to any leading Party body, nor may they be elected delegates to a Party conference or congress.

18. Candidate members of the CPSU pay membership dues at the same rate as full members.

III

ORGANIZATIONAL STRUCTURE OF THE PARTY
INNER-PARTY DEMOCRACY

19. The guiding principle of the organizational structure of the Party is democratic centralism, which signifies:

a) Election of all leading Party bodies, from the lowest to the highest;

b) Periodic reports of Party bodies to their Party organizations and to higher bodies;

c) Strict Party discipline and subordination of the minority to the majority;

d) That the decisions of higher bodies are obligatory for lower bodies.

20. The Party is built on the territorial-industrial principle: Primary organizations are established wherever Communists are employed, and are associated territorially in county, city, etc., organizations. An organization serving a given area is higher than any Party organization serving part of that area.

21. All Party organizations are autonomous in the decision of local questions, unless their decisions conflict with Party policy.

22. The highest leading body of a Party organization is the general meeting (in the case of primary organizations); the conference (in the case of county, borough, city, area, provincial or territorial organizations); or the congress (in the case of the Communist Parties of union republics and the Communist Party of the Soviet Union).

23. The general meeting, conference, or congress elects a bureau or committee which acts as its executive body and directs all the current work of the Party organization.

24. The election of Party bodies shall be effected by secret ballot. In an election, all Party members have the unlimited right to challenge candidates and to criticize them. Each candidate shall be voted upon separately. A candidate is considered elected if more than one half of those attending the meeting, conference or congress has voted for him.

The principle of systematic renewal of the composition of Party bodies and of continuity of leadership shall be observed in the election of all Party bodies from primary organizations to the CC CPSU.

25. A member or alternate member of the CC CPSU must by his entire activity justify the great trust placed in him by the Party. A member or alternate member of the CC CPSU who does not uphold his honor and dignity may not remain a member of the Central Committee. The question of the removal of a member or alternate member of the CC CPSU from that body shall be decided by a plenary meeting of the Central Committee by secret ballot. The decision is regarded as adopted if not less than two-thirds of the membership of the CC CPSU vote for it.

The question of the removal of a member or alternate member of the CC of the Communist Party of a union republic, or of a territorial, provincial, area, city, county, or borough Party committee from the Party body concerned is decided by a plenary meeting of that body. The decision is regarded as adopted if not less than two-thirds of the membership of the committee in question vote for it by secret ballot.

A member of the Central Auditing Commission who does not justify the great trust placed in him by the Party shall be removed from that commission. This question shall be decided by a meeting of the Central Auditing Commission. The decision is regarded as adopted if not less than two-thirds of the membership of the Central Auditing Commission vote by secret ballot for the removal from that body of the member or alternate member concerned.

The question of the removal of a member from the auditing commission of a republican, territorial, provincial, area, city, county, or borough

Party organization shall be decided by a meeting of the appropriate commission according to the procedure established for members and alternate members of Party committees.

26. The free and business-like discussion of questions of Party policy in individual Party organizations or in the Party as a whole is the inalienable right of every Party member and is an important principle of inner-Party democracy. Only on the basis of inner-Party democracy is it possible to develop criticism and self-criticism and to strengthen Party discipline, which must be conscious and not mechanical.

Discussion of controversial or insufficiently clear issues may be held within the framework of individual organizations or the Party as a whole.

Party-wide discussion is necessary:

a) If the necessity is recognized by several Party organizations at provincial or republican level;

b) If there is not a sufficiently solid majority in the Central Committee on major questions of Party policy;

c) If the CC CPSU considers it necessary to consult the Party as a whole on any particular questions of policy.

Wide discussion, especially discussion on a countrywide scale, of questions of Party policy must be held so as to ensure for Party members the free expression of their views and preclude attempts to form factional groupings, destroying Party unity, attempts to split the Party.

27. The highest principle of Party leadership is collectivism, which is an absolute requisite for the normal functioning of Party organizations, the proper education of personnel, and the promotion of the activity and initiative of Communists. The cult of the individual and the violations of inner-Party democracy resulting from it must not be tolerated in the Party; they are incompatible with the Leninist principles of Party life.

Collective leadership does not exempt persons in office from their responsibility for the job entrusted to them.

28. The Central Committees of the Communist Parties of union republics, and territorial, provincial, area, city, county, and borough Party committees in the interval between congresses and conferences shall systematically inform Party organizations of their work.

29. Meetings of the most active members of borough, county, city, area, provincial, and territorial Party organizations and of the Communist Parties of union republics shall be held to discuss major decisions of the Party and to work out practical measures for their execution, as well as to examine questions of local significance.

IV

HIGHER PARTY ORGANS

30. The supreme organ of the CPSU is the Party congress. Congresses are convened at least once in five years. The convocation of a Party

congress shall be announced at least six weeks before the congress. Extraordinary congresses are convened by the Central Committee of the Party on its own initiative or on the demand of not less than one-third of the total membership represented at the preceding Party congress. Extraordinary congresses shall be convened within two months. A congress is considered properly constituted if not less than one-half of the total Party membership is represented at it.

The rates of representation at a Party congress are determined by the Central Committee.

31. Should the Central Committee of the Party fail to convene an extraordinary congress within the period specified in Article 30, the organizations which demanded it have the right to form an organizing committee which shall enjoy the powers of the Central Committee of the Party with respect to the convocation of the extraordinary congress.

32. The congress:

a) Hears and approves the reports of the Central Committee, of the Central Auditing Commission, and of the other central organizations;

b) Reviews, amends, and endorses the Program and the Rules of the Party;

c) Determines the line of the Party in matters of home and foreign policy, and examines and decides the most important questions of communist construction;

d) Elects the Central Committee and the Central Auditing Commission.

33. The number of members to be elected to the Central Committee and to the Central Auditing Commission is determined by the congress. In the event of vacancies occurring in the Central Committee, they are filled from among the alternate members of the CC CPSU elected by the congress.

34. Between congresses the CC CPSU directs the activities of the Party, the local Party bodies, selects and appoints leading functionaries, directs the work of central government bodies and social organizations of working people through the Party groups in them, sets up various Party organs, institutions, and enterprises and directs their activities, appoints the editors of the central newspapers and journals operating under its control, and distributes the funds of the Party budget and controls its execution.

The Central Committee represents the CPSU in its relations with other parties.

35. The CC CPSU shall keep the Party organizations regularly informed of its work.

36. The Central Auditing Commission supervises the expeditious and proper handling of business by the central bodies of the Party, and audits the accounts of the treasury and the enterprises of the CC CPSU.

37. The CC CPSU shall hold not less than one plenary meeting every six months. Alternate members of the Central Committee shall attend its plenary meetings with consultative voice.

38. The CC CPSU elects a Politburo to direct the work of the CC between plenary meetings and a Secretariat to direct current work,

chiefly the selection of personnel and the verification of the fulfillment of Party decisions. The CC elects a General Secretary of the CC CPSU.

39. The CC CPSU organizes the Party Control Committee of the CC. The Party Control Committee of the CC of the CPSU:

a) Verifies the observance of Party discipline by members and candidate members of the CPSU, and takes action against Communists who violate the program and the Rules of the Party, and Party or state discipline, and against violators of Party ethics;

b) Considers appeals against decisions of Central Committees of the Communist Parties of union republics or of territorial and provincial Party committees to expel members from the Party or impose Party penalties upon them.

40. In the interval between Party congresses the CC CPSU may convene when necessary an All-Union Party conference to discuss questions of Party policy which have come to the fore. The rules for conduct of the All-Union Party conference shall be established by the CC CPSU.

V

REPUBLICAN, TERRITORIAL, PROVINCIAL, AREA, CITY, COUNTY, AND BOROUGH ORGANIZATIONS OF THE PARTY

41. The republican, territorial, provincial, area, city, county, and borough Party organizations and their committees take guidance in their activities from the Program and the Rules of the CPSU, conduct all work for the implementation of Party policy and organize the fulfillment of the directives of the CC CPSU within the republics, territories, provinces, areas, cities, counties, and boroughs concerned.

42. The basic duties of republican, territorial, provincial, area, city, county, and borough Party organizations, and their leading bodies, are:

a) Political and organizational work among the masses, mobilization of the masses for the fulfillment of the tasks of communist construction, for the maximum development of industrial and agricultural production, for the fulfillment and overfulfillment of state plans; solicitude for the steady improvement of the material and cultural standards of the working people;

b) Organization of ideological work, propaganda of Marxism-Leninism, promotion of the communist awareness of the working people, guidance of the local press, radio, and television, control over the activities of cultural and educational institutions;

c) Guidance of Soviets, trade unions, the YCL, the co-operatives and other public organizations through the Party groups in them, and increasingly broader enlistment of working people in the activities of these organizations, development of the initiative and activity of the masses as an essential condition for the gradual transition from socialist statehood to public self-government under communism.

Party organizations must not act in place of government, trade union, co-operative, or other public organizations of the working people; they must not allow either the merging of the functions of Party and other bodies or undue parallelism in work;

d) Selection and appointment of leading personnel, their education in the spirit of communist ideas, honesty and truthfulness, and a high sense of responsibility to the Party and the people for the work entrusted to them;

e) Large-scale enlistment of Communists in the conduct of Party activities as non-staff workers, as a form of social work;

f) Organization of various institutions and enterprises of the Party within the bounds of the respective republic, territory, region, area, city, county, or borough, and guidance of their activities; distribution of Party funds within the given organization; systematic information of the higher Party body and accountability to it for their work.

LEADING BODIES OF REPUBLICAN, TERRITORIAL, AND PROVINCIAL PARTY ORGANIZATIONS

43. The highest body of provincial, territorial, and republican Party organizations is the respective provincial or territorial Party conference or the congress of the Communist Party of the union republic, and in the interim between their meetings the provincial committee, territorial committee, or the Central Committee of the Communist Party of the union republic.

44. Provincial and territorial Party conferences are convened by the respective provincial or territorial committees once every two or three years. An ordinary Party congress of a union republic is convened by the CC of the Communist Party of the union republic not less often than once in five years. Extraordinary conferences and congresses are convened by decision of provincial or territorial committees, or the CC of the Communist Parties of union republics, or on the demand of one-third of the total membership of the organizations belonging to the provincial, territorial, or republican Party organization.

The rates of representation at provincial and territorial conferences and at congresses of Communist Parties of union republics are determined by the respective Party committees.

Provincial and territorial conferences and congresses of the Communist Parties of union republics hear and act upon the reports of the respective provincial or territorial committee, or the CC of the Communist Party of the union republic, and of the Auditing Commission; discuss at their own discretion other matters of Party, economic and cultural development, and elect the Provincial or territorial committee, the Central Committee of the union republic, the Auditing Commission and the delegates to the congress of the CPSU.

In the intervals between Party congresses of the union republics the CC of the Communist Party of a union republic may convene when necessary a republic Party conference to discuss the most important questions of activity of Party organizations. The rules for conduct of republic Party conferences shall be established by the CC's of the Communist Parties of the union republics.

45. The provincial and territorial committees, and the Central Committees of the Communist Parties of union republics elect bureaus, which also include secretaries of the committees. The secretaries must have Party standing of not less than five years. The plenary meetings of the committees also confirm the chairmen of Party commissions, heads of departments of these committees, editors of Party newspapers and journals.

Provincial and territorial committees and the Central Committees of the Communist Parties of union republics may set up secretariats to examine current business and verify the execution of decisions.

46. The plenary meetings of provincial and territorial committees and the Central Committees of the Communist Parties of union republics shall be convened at least once every four months.

47. The provincial and territorial committees and the Central Committees of the Communist Parties of union republics direct the activities of area, city, county, and borough Party organizations, inspect their work and regularly hear reports of area, city, county, and borough Party committees.

Party organizations in autonomous republics, and in autonomous and other provinces forming part of a territory or union republic, function under the guidance of the respective territorial committees or Central Committees of the Communist Parties of union republics.

LEADING BODIES OF AREA, CITY, COUNTY, AND BOROUGH PARTY ORGANIZATIONS

48. The highest body of an area, city, county, or borough Party organization is the area, city, county, and borough Party conference or the general meeting of Communists convened by the area, city, county, or borough committee at least once in two years, and the extraordinary conference convened by decision of the respective committee or on the demand of one-third of the total membership of the Party organization concerned.

The area, city, county, or borough conference (general meeting) hears reports of the committee and auditing commission, discusses at its own discretion other questions of Party, economic and cultural development, and elects the area, city, county, and borough committee, and the auditing commission and delegates to the provincial and territorial conference or the congress of the Communist Party of the union republic. The rate of representation at provincial, city, county, and borough conferences shall be established by the corresponding party committee.

49. The area, city, county, or borough committee elects a bureau, including the committee secretaries, and confirms the appointment of

heads of committee departments and newspaper editors. The secretaries of the area, city, county, and borough committees must have a Party standing of at least three years. The committee secretaries are confirmed by the respective regional or territorial committee, or the Central Committee of the Communist Party of the union republic.

50. The area, city, county, and borough committee organizes and confirms the primary Party organizations, directs their work, regularly hears reports concerning the work of Party organizations, and keeps a register of Communists.

51. The plenary meeting of the area, city, county, and borough committee is convened at least once in three months.

52. The area, city, county, and borough committee has non-staff instructors, sets up standing or ad hoc commissions on various aspects of Party work and uses other ways to draw Communists into the activities of the Party committee on social lines.

VI
PRIMARY PARTY ORGANIZATIONS

53. The primary Party organizations are the basis of the Party.

Primary Party organizations are formed at the places of work of Party members—in factories, on state farms and at other enterprises, collective farms, units of the Soviet Army, offices, educational establishments, etc., wherever there are not less than three Party members. Primary Party organizations may also be organized on the residential principle in villages and at house administrations.

In individual situations with consent of the provincial committee, the territorial committee, the Central Committee of the Communist Party of a union republic, Primary Party organizations may be established within the structures of several enterprises which have been joined together within a production association and which are situate as a rule on the territory of one county or several boroughs of a single city.

54. Shop, sectional, farm, team, departmental, etc., Party organizations may be formed as units of the general primary Party organization, with the sanction of the area, City, county, or borough committee, at enterprises, collective farms, and institutions with over 50 Party members and candidate members.

Within shop, sectional, etc., organizations, and also within primary Party organizations having less than 50 members and candidate members, Party groups may be formed in the teams and other production units.

55. The highest organ of the primary Party organization is the Party meeting, which is convened at least once a month. In Party organizations having shop organizations the general Party meeting shall be convened not less often than once in two months.

In large Party organizations with a membership of more than 300

Communists a general Party meeting is convened when necessary at times fixed by the Party committee or on the demand of a number of shop or departmental Party organizations.

56. For the conduct of current business the primary, shop, or departmental Party organization elects a bureau for the term of one year. The number of its members is fixed by the Party meeting. Primary, shop, and departmental Party organizations with less than 15 Party members do not elect a bureau. Instead, they elect a secretary and deputy secretary of the Party organization.

Secretaries of primary, shop, and departmental Party organizations must have a Party standing of at least one year.

Primary Party organizations with less than 150 Party members shall have, as a rule, no salaried functionaries released from their regular work.

57. In large factories and offices with more than 300 members and candidate members of the Party, and in exceptional cases in factories and offices with over 100 Communists by virtue of special production conditions and territorial dispersion, subject to the approval of the provincial committee, territorial committee, or Central Committee of the Communist Party of the union republic, Party committees may be formed, the shop and departmental Party organizations at these factories and offices being granted the status of primary Party organizations.

The Party organizations of collective and state farms may set up Party committees if they have a minimum of 50 Communists.

In Party organizations numbering more than 500 Communists, or in individual situations with the consent of the provincial committee, the territorial committee, and the Central Committee of the Communist Party of a union republic, Party committees may be established in large shops, and the right of a Primary Party organization may be conferred on Party organizations of production subdivisions.

The Party committees are elected for the term of two or three years. Their numerical composition is fixed by the general Party meeting or conference.

58. The Party committee of a primary organization with over 1000 Communists may be given, with the consent of the CC of the Communist Party of a union republic the rights of county Party committee in matters of admission to the CPSU, of keeping a register of members and candidates of the Party, and of examining the personal affairs of Communists.

59. In its activities the primary Party organization takes guidance from the Program and the Rules of the CPSU. It conducts its work directly among the working people, rallies them around the Communist Party of the Soviet Union, organizes the masses to carry out the Party policy and to work for the building of communism.

The Primary Party organization:

a) Enrolls new members to the CPSU;

b) Educates Communists in a spirit of loyalty to the Party cause, ideological staunchness, and communist ethics;

c) Organizes the study by Communists of Marxist-Leninist theory in close connection with the practice of communist construction and opposes all attempts to introduce revisionist distortions into Marxism-Leninism and its dogmatic interpretation;

d) Ensures the vanguard role of Communists in the sphere of labor and in socio-political and economic activities of enterprises, collective farms, institutions, educational establishments, etc.;

e) Acts as the organizer of the working people for the performance of the current tasks of communist construction; heads the socialist emulation movement for the fulfillment of state plans and undertakings of the toilers; rallies the masses to disclose and make the best use of untapped resources at enterprises and collective farms, and on a broad scale to apply in production the achievements of science, engineering, and the experience of front-rankers; works for the strengthening of labor discipline, the steady increase of labor productivity and improvement of the quality of production, and shows concern for the protection and increase of social wealth at enterprises, state farms, and collective farms;

f) Conducts agitational and propaganda work among the masses, educates them in the communist spirit, helps the working people to acquire proficiency in administering state and social affairs;

g) On the basis of extensive criticism and self-criticism, combats cases of bureaucracy, parochialism, and violations of state discipline, thwarts attempts to deceive the state, acts against negligence, waste, and extravagance at enterprises, collective farms, and offices;

h) Assists the area, city, county, and borough committees in their activities and is accountable to them for its work.

The Party organization must see to it that every Communist should observe in his own life and cultivate among working people the moral principles set forth in the Program of the CPSU—in the moral code of the builders of communism:

—loyalty to the communist cause, love of his own socialist country, and of other socialist countries;

—conscientious labor for the benefit of society: He who does not work, neither shall he eat;

—concern on everyone's part for the protection and increase of social wealth;

—a lofty sense of public duty, intolerance of violations of public interests;

—collectivism and comradely mutual assistance: one for all, and all for one;

—humane relations and mutual respect among people: man is to man a friend, comrade and brother;

—honesty and truthfulness, moral purity, unpretentiousness, and modesty in public and personal life;

—mutual respect in the family circle and concern for the upbringing of children;

—intolerance of injustice, parasitism, dishonesty, careerism, and greed;

—friendship and fraternity among all peoples of the U.S.S.R., intolerance of national and racial hostility;

—intolerance of the enemies of communism, the enemies of peace and those who oppose the freedom of the peoples;

—fraternal solidarity with the working people of all countries, with all peoples.

60. Primary Party organizations of enterprises of industry, transport, communication, construction, material-technical supply, trade, public dining rooms, communal-cultural servicing, collective farms, state farms, and other agricultural enterprises, drafting organizations, construction offices, scientific research institutes, educational institutions, cultural-educational and curative health establishments shall enjoy the right to audit the work of the administration.

The Party organization at ministries, state committees, and other central and local soviet and economic agencies and administrative departments shall exercise the right of audit over the work of the administrative apparatus in executing the directives of the Party and government and in conforming to Soviet laws. They must actively promote improvement of the apparatus, cultivate among the personnel a high sense of responsibility for work entrusted to them, work for the strengthening of state discipline and for the better servicing of the population, firmly combat bureaucracy and red tape, inform the appropriate Party bodies in good time of shortcomings in the work of the respective offices and individuals, regardless of what posts the latter may occupy.

VII
THE PARTY AND THE YCL

61. The Leninist YCL of the Soviet Union is a voluntary social organization of young people, an active helper and reserve of the Party. The YCL helps the Party educate the youth in the communist spirit, draws it into the work of building a new society, trains a rising generation of harmoniously developed people who will live and work and administer public affairs under communism.

62. YCL organizations enjoy the right of broad initiative in discussing and submitting to the appropriate Party organizations questions related to the work of enterprises, collective farms and offices. They must be really active in the implementation of Party directives in all spheres of communist construction, especially where there are no primary Party organizations.

63. The YCL conducts its activities under the guidance of the Communist Party of the Soviet Union. The work of the local YCL organizations is directed and controlled by the appropriate republican, territorial, provincial, area, city, county, and borough Party organizations.

In their communist educational work among the youth, local Party organs and primary Party organizations rely on the support of the YCL organizations, and uphold and promote their useful undertakings.

64. Members of the YCL accepted as members of the CPSU cease to

belong to the YCL the moment they join the Party, provided they do not hold leading posts in YCL organizations.

VIII
PARTY ORGANIZATIONS IN THE SOVIET ARMY

65. Party organizations in the Soviet Army take guidance in their work from the Program and the Rules of the CPSU and operate on the basis of instructions issued by the Central Committee.

The Party organizations of the Soviet Army carry through the policy of the Party in the Armed Forces; rally servicemen around the Communist Party; educate them in the spirit of Marxism-Leninism and boundless loyalty to the socialist homeland; actively further the unity of the army and the people; work for the strengthening of discipline; rally servicemen to carry out the tasks of military and political training and acquire skill in the use of new techniques and weapons, and irreproachably to perform their military duty and the orders and instructions of the command.

66. The guidance of Party work in the Armed Forces is exercised by the Central Committee of the CPSU through the Chief Political Administration of the Soviet Army and Navy, which functions as a department of the CC CPSU.

The chiefs of the political administrations of military areas and fleets, and chiefs of the political administrations of armies must be Party members of five years' standing, and the chiefs of political departments of military formations must be Party members of three years' standing.

67. The Party organizations and political bodies of the Soviet Army maintain close contact with local Party committees and keep them informed about political work in the military units. The secretaries of military Party organizations and chiefs of political bodies participate in the work of local Party committees.

IX
PARTY GROUPS IN NON-PARTY ORGANIZATIONS

68. At congresses, conferences, and meetings and in the elective bodies of Soviets, trade unions, co-operatives, and other mass organizations of the working people, having at least three Party members, Party groups are formed for the purpose of strengthening the influence of the Party in every way and carrying out Party policy among non-Party people, strengthening Party and state discipline, combating bureaucracy, and verifying the fulfillment of Party and government directives.

69. The Party groups are subordinate to the appropriate Party bodies:

CC CPSU, the Central Committees of the Communist Parties of union republics, territorial, provincial area, city, county, or borough Party committees.

In all matters the groups must strictly and unswervingly abide by decisions of the leading Party bodies.

X
PARTY FUNDS

70. The funds of the Party and its organizations are derived from membership dues, income from Party enterprises and other revenue.

71. The monthly membership dues for Party members and candidate members are as follows:

Monthly Earnings	Dues	
Up to 50 rubles	10 kopeks	
From 51 to 100 rubles	0.5 per cent	
From 101 to 150 rubles	1.0 per cent	
From 151 to 200 rubles	1.5 per cent	of the
From 201 to 250 rubles	2.0 per cent	monthly
From 251 to 300 rubles	2.5 per cent	earnings
Over 300 rubles	3.0 per cent	

72. An entrance fee of 2 per cent of monthly earnings is paid on acceptance into the Party as a candidate member.

ANNOTATED BIBLIOGRAPHY

As publications in English on the Soviet system of government are now so numerous as to fill entire multi-volume bibliographies, only a few are listed here as an aid to students wishing to have a guide to monographs especially suited to the preparation of course papers developing in some depth the topics covered by each chapter. Sources of a generalized character are listed at the end of the listings by chapter; these being general bibliographies, collections of documents, biographical studies, symposia, and periodicals specializing in studies devoted to the U.S.S.R. Individual articles are listed in the general bibliographies as well as in the usual periodical indexes available in all libraries. None have been listed here. General introductory texts are also omitted.

Chapter 1. In the Name of Democracy

BEER, SAMUEL H. (ed.). *Marx and Engels: The Communist Manifesto.* Northbrook, Ill.: AHM Publishing Corporation, 1955. Reprinted 1975. xxix+96 pp.

Includes selections from the *Eighteenth Brumaire* and *Capital*, as well as a helpful introduction summarizing and assessing Marx.

CHRISTENSON, REO M.; ENGELS, ALAN S.; JACOBS, DAN N.; REJAI, MUSTAFA; WALZER, HERBERT. *Ideologies and Modern Politics.* New York and Toronto: Dodd Mead and Co., 1971. vi+320 pp.

Historical development, principal tenets and relevancy of contemporary policy formulation of various theorists, including Marx. May be supplemented by Dan N. Jacobs, *From Marx to Mao and Marchais* (New York: Longman, 1978), tracing Marx's thought in the works of other prominent contemporary theorists.

DRACHKOVITCH, MILORAD M. (ed.). *Marxist Ideology in the Contemporary World: Its Appeals and Paradoxes.* New York: Frederick A. Praeger, 1966. xvii+192 pp.

Concise statements by specialists defining Marxism and suggesting the degree to which Marx's heirs have revised him; concludes that Marxism is losing its persuasive power.

HAIMSON, LEOPOLD H. *The Russian Marxist and the Origins of Bolshevism.* Cambridge, Mass.: Harvard University Press, 1956. 246 pp.

A clarification of the various trends among revolutionary Russian intellectuals from 1880 to 1905. Profiles of the leaders. Helpful in identifying political influences on the Russian Revolution.

MEYER, ALFRED G. *Leninism.* Cambridge, Mass.: Harvard University Press, 1957. 324 pp.

A philosophical discussion in highly readable form of Lenin's theories and their relation to classical Marxist doctrine.

NOVE, ALEC. *Stalinism and After.* New York: Crane, Russak & Co., 1975. 208 pp.

A British economist's examination of the Soviet system in terms of Stalin's impact upon its development. Post-Stalin personalities and Communist party potential in a de-Stalinized era are also assessed.

TUCKER, ROBERT C. (ed.). *The Lenin Anthology.* New York: W. W. Norton & Co., 1975. xiv+764 pp.

Selection from 65 papers written by Lenin before and after the revolution and introduced by an extensive explanation of the setting of each. May be supplemented by the same editor's *Stalinism: Essays in Historical Interpretation* (New York: W. W. Norton & Co., 1977).

VON RAUGH, GEORGE. *A History of the Soviet Union.* New York: Frederick A. Praeger, 1957. xiii+423 pp.

A brief readable history of events from the 1880's to the beginning of the post-Stalin reforms, constituting the minimum necessary to a political scientist's understanding of the historical component in the evolution of Soviet politics. May be updated by Alec Nove's *Stalinism and After,* listed above.

Chapter 2. The Hard Core of the System

ARMSTRONG, JOHN A. *The Politics of Totalitarianism: The Communist Party of the Soviet Union from 1934 to the Present.* New York: Random House, 1961. xvi+459 pp.

Treatment by a political scientist of the era of purge, war, and party post-Stalin revolution with much on personalities and intrigue. May be updated with the same author's *Ideology, Politics and Government in the Soviet Union* (New York: Praeger Publishers, 4th edition, 1978).

FARRELL, R. BARRY (ed.). *Political Leadership in Eastern Europe and the Soviet Union.* Chicago: Aldine Publishing Co., 1970. xi+359 pp.

Sophisticated essays using quantitative data to determine leadership patterns in Communist parties.

GEHLEN, MICHAEL P. *The Communist Party and the Soviet Union: A Functional Analysis.* Bloomington, Ind.: University of Indiana Press, 1969. 161 pp.

Using behavioral techniques of analysis the study examines Soviet statistics to determine functions of the Communist party: recruitment, socialization, and goals, with special emphasis on the impact of technicians and specialists on policy as they are coopted into the governing élite. May be compared with Darrell P. Hammer, *U.S.S.R.: The Politics of Oligarchy* (Hinsdale, Ind.: The Dryden Press, 1974), emphasizing group rather than individual leadership and considering pluralization of Soviet society.

HOUGH, JERRY F. *The Soviet Perfects: The Local Party Organs in Industrial Decision Making.* Cambridge, Mass.: Harvard University Press. 1969. xii+416 pp.

A study of the role of middle-range Communist party secretaries in guiding industrial managers toward minimizing production. Draws on Soviet press for evidence.

MEDVEDEV, ROY A. *Let History Judge: The Origins and Consequences of Stalinism.* New York: Vintage Books, 1973. xxxiv+566 pp.

A perceptive insider's reflection on the politics of the Stalin years. Valuable not only for its revelations but also for the insight it provides into a Soviet citizen's reaction.

PLOSS, SIDNEY I. (ed.). *The Soviet Political Process: Aims, Techniques and Examples of Analysis.* Waltham, Mass., Toronto and London: Ginn and Company, 1971. viii+304 pp.

Soviet leadership problems, analyzed often in terms of personalities and power struggles: the Kremlinological approach.

SCHAPIRO, LEONARD. *The Communist Party of the Soviet Union.* New York: Random House, 1960. xiv+631 pp.

A British political scientist's objective account of the ever-changing Communist party's policies within their historical setting.

SKILLING, H. GORDON, and GRIFFITHS, FRANKLYN (eds.). *Interest Groups in Soviet Politics.* Princeton: Princeton University Press, 1971. vii+433 pp.

A pioneering study using group theory to assess the extent to which various professional groups within the Communist party endeavor to further their interests. Chapters discuss each group's status and position.

Chapter 3. Radiating Influence

BEZUGLOV, A. *Soviet Deputy.* Moscow: Progress Publishers, 1973. 155 pp.

The nomination, election, status, role, and accountability of the representatives of electoral districts under the post-Stalin conditions of emphasis upon popular participation in state administration, as seen by a Soviet author.

FISHER, RALPH TALCOTT, JR. *Pattern for Soviet Youth: A Study of the Congresses of the Komsomol, 1918–1954.* New York: Columbia University Press, 1959. xvii+452 pp.

The disciplining of Soviet youth to develop a leadership corps in preparation for Communist party duties.

GREGORYAN, L., and DOLGOPOLOV, Y. *Fundamentals of Soviet State Law.* Moscow: Progress Publishers, 1971. 328 pp.

Soviet constitutional law as seen by two Soviet specialists concerned with federal relationships with republics, state relationships with individuals, and the structure of Soviet institutions.

TUCKER, ROBERT C. *The Soviet Political Mind: Studies in Stalinism and Post-Stalin Change.* New York: Frederick A. Praeger, 1963. 250 pp.

Analysis of motivation in Soviet leadership by a long-term resident in the American colony in Moscow.

Chapter 4. Controlled Mass Participation

BARGHOORN, FREDERICK C. *Politics in the U.S.S.R.* Boston: Little Brown, 1966. xii+418 pp.

A general text fitting Soviet data into the Gabriel Almond categories designed for analysis in comparative politics. Especially strong on political indoctrination and the shaping of public opinion.

BROWN, EMILY CLARK. *Soviet Trade Unions and Labor Relations.* Cambridge, Mass.: Harvard University Press, 1966. ix+394 pp.

An economist's analysis of the trade unions' role; includes information on structure and function. May be updated with Kahan, Arcadus and Ruble, Blair (eds.). *Industrial Labor in the U.S.S.R.* Elmsford, N.Y.: Pergamon Press. 1979.

INKELES, ALEX. *Public Opinion in Soviet Russia: A Study in Mass Persuasion.* Cambridge, Mass.: Harvard University Press, 1950. xviii+379 pp.

Soviet press controls and mass propaganda techniques as seen by a sociologist, using materials from interviews with Soviet refugees now in the West.

MOTE, MAX E. *Soviet Local and Republic Elections.* Stanford: Hoover Institution, Stanford University Press, 1965. 193 pp.

A field study of the 1963 elections in Leningrad, including interview materials as well as documentary sources. May be updated with Friedgut, Theodore H., *Political Participation in the U.S.S.R.* Princeton, N.J.: Princeton University Press. 1979.

POTICHNYJ, PETER J. *Soviet Agricultural Trade Unions 1917–70.* Toronto: University of Toronto Press, 1972. xxx+258 pp.

A pioneering study of the extension to agricultural workers of the trade union system. Helpful in understanding the farm structures and the difference between collective farmers and farm workers on state farms.

SORENSON, JAY B. *The Life and Death of Soviet Trade Unions.* New York: Atherton, 1969. viii+283 pp.

A political scientist's examination of the revolutionary role of trade unions and their evolution during the 1930's into a structure of the Soviet state.

SHARLET, ROBERT. *The New Soviet Constitution of 1977: Analysis and Text.* Brunswick, Ohio: Kings Court Communications, 1978. vii+132 pp.

The discussions preceding adoption of the Constitution and speculation as to what political trends they and the document itself indicate.

TAUBMAN, WILLIAM. *Governing Soviet Cities: Bureaucratic Politics and Urban Development in the U.S.S.R.* New York: Praeger Publishers, 1973. xvii+166 pp.

The dynamics of urban soviets, as seen by a political scientist using documentary and interview sources.

Chapter 5. The Heritage of Terror

DALLIN, ALEXANDER, and BRESLAUER, GEORGE W. *Political Terror in Communist Systems.* Stanford: Stanford University Press, 1970. xi+163 pp.

A balanced assessment of terror as an instrument of politics, and of alternative control mechanisms that may permit its abatement or abandonment. Compares several Communist-led systems.

LENIN, V. I. *The State and Revolution.* Revised translation. New York: International Publishers, 1934. 104 pp.

The official justification for proletarian dictatorship from which the rationalization of terror as an instrument of dictatorship was developed. The volume is a handbook for Soviet political theorists.

MOORE, BARRINGTON, JR. *Terror and Progress, U.S.S.R.: Some Sources of Change and Stability in the Soviet Dictatorship.* Cambridge, Mass.: Harvard University Press, 1964. xvii+261 pp.

An argument that Soviet leaders use terror as a political instrument to achieve economic and social progress.

REDDAWAY, PETER (ed.). *Uncensored Russia: Protest and Dissent in the Soviet Union. The Unofficial Moscow Journal. A Chronical of Current Events.* New York: American Heritage Press, 1972. 499 pp.

Translation of the first eleven issues of the noted underground newspaper recounting the police measures taken to silence dissenters.

SAKHAROV, ANDREI D. *Progress, Coexistence and Intellectual Freedom.* New York: W. W. Norton & Co., 1970. 204 pp.

A prominent Soviet scientist, noted for his dissent, argues that democratization of the Soviet political system is in its own interest. He believes that dictatorship and mass myths, including narrow-minded ideologies, ossified dogmatism, and ideological censorship have created impediments to effective development.

WOLIN, SIMON, and SLUSSER, ROBERT M. (eds.). *The Soviet Secret Police.* New York: Frederick A. Praeger, 1957. ix+408 pp.

A documentary chronology from 1917 to 1956, with commentary, by former Soviet citizens on various aspects of the work of the security police.

Chapter 6. The Federal System

ALLWORTH, EDWARD et al. *Soviet Nationality Problems.* New York: Columbia University Press. xiv+296 pp.

Essays by West European and North American specialists on the continuing impact upon Soviet politics of ethnic groups. Helps to explain why federalism still triumphs over the unitary state structure preferred by Marxist theorists.

ALLWORTH, EDWARD (ed.). *The Nationality Question in Soviet Central Asia.* New York: Praeger Publications, 1973. xiv+217 pp.

A team effort to assess the possibility that the U.S.S.R.'s many ethnic minorities will eventually converge into one culture because of migrations and self-Russification. An eye-opener for those thinking a study of Soviet minorities unimportant for a study of Soviet politics.

BARGHOORN, FREDERICK C. *Soviet Russian Nationalism.* New York: Oxford University Press, 1956. ix+330 pp.

Exhaustive examination of the printed record to determine the place of the Great Russians and their culture within the Soviet federation and Stalin's attempt to create a new chauvinistic national pride for the U.S.S.R. as a whole.

COLE, J. P. *Geography of the U.S.S.R.* Baltimore: Penguin Books, 1967. 328 pp.

Particularly strong on population, natural resources, agriculture, and industry. Statistical tables and outline maps. No color plates.

PIPES, RICHARD. *The Formation of the Soviet Union: Communism and Nationalities, 1917–1922.* Rev. ed. Cambridge, Mass.: Harvard University Press, 1964. xii+365 pp.

Soviet concepts of federalism and the steps taken to create the federation of the U.S.S.R.

POTICHNYJ, PETER J. (ed.). *Ukraine in the Seventies.* Oakville, Ontario: Mosaic Press, 1975. 355 pp.

Exhaustive coverage of economic, political, and sociological aspects of the Ukraine as a republic of the U.S.S.R. The material on party, state, and society is especially valuable to political scientists. Authors are prominent scholars from Canada, the United Kingdom, and the United States.

SHEVTSOV, V. S. *National Sovereignty and the Soviet State.* Moscow: Progress Publishers, 1974. 176 pp.

The status of the republics within the U.S.S.R., explained by a Soviet specialist in constitutional law. Emphasizes the historical and legal features.

Chapter 7. Popularizing Administration

AZRAEL, JEREMY. *Managerial Power and Soviet Politics.* Cambridge, Mass.: Harvard University Press, 1966. 258 pp.

A study in some depth of Soviet industrial management and its political implications, suggesting that absolute monolithism under Communist party generalists is currently unattainable.

BERLINER, JOSEPH S. *Factory and Manager in the U.S.S.R.* Cambridge, Mass.: Harvard University Press, 1957. xv+386 pp.

An economist's evaluation of the role of the industrial manager, utilizing materials from emigré interviews as well as conventional sources.

CONYNGHAM, WILLIAM J. *Industrial Management in the Soviet Union: The Role of the CPSU in Industrial Decision-making, 1917–1970.* Stanford: Hoover Institution Press, Stanford University, 1973. xxxvi+378 pp.

A perceptive analysis of the Communist party's leadership role as seen in the industrial management field. Valuable not only for detail on the Khrushchev era but for its historical perspective. Considers possible evolution of relations between party and state bureaucracies.

NOVE, ALEC. *The Soviet Economy: An Introduction.* Rev. ed. New York: Frederick A. Praeger, 1966. xiii+354 pp.

A British economist's explanation of Soviet motivation and the institutions utilized to maximize production.

RYAVEC, KARL W. *Implementation of Soviet Economic Reforms: Political, Organizational and Social Processes.* New York: Praeger Publications, 1975. xiii+361 pp.

A thorough account of the Soviet search for efficiency in production through incessant reorganization of structures. May be supplemented by the same author's *Soviet Society and the Communist Party* (Amherst, Mass.: University of Massachusetts Press, 1978) containing papers from a round table on administration.

Chapter 8. Fostering the Community Spirit

MILLAR, JAMES R. (ed.). *The Soviet Rural Community.* Urbana: University of Illinois Press, 1971. xv+420 pp.

Essays touching many phases of Soviet rural life and organization, agricultural, and non-agricultural, beginning with pre-revolutionary structures. Thoroughly interdisciplinary.

OSOFSKY, STEPHEN. *Soviet Agricultural Policy: Toward the Abolition of Collective Farms.* New York: Praeger Publications, 1974. xi+300 pp.

The panorama of Soviet agricultural organizational structures anticipating the triumph of the state farm. Exhaustive examination of Soviet specialized literature.

SOLOMON, SUSAN GROSS. *The Soviet Agrarian Debate: A Controversy in Social Science, 1923–1929.* Boulder, Colorado: Westview Press, 1977. 240 pp.

An antidote for those who believe collectivization was inevitable: a review of contending views during the formative years of agricultural policy.

STUART, ROBERT C. *The Collective Farm in Soviet Agriculture.* Lexington, Mass.: D. C. Heath & Co., 1972. xx+254 pp.

The collective farm structure with emphasis upon its role in economic development. Based on the author's extensive residence in Moscow as a Canadian student.

Chapter 9. State Intervention in Private Affairs

BERMAN, HAROLD J. *Justice in the U.S.S.R.: An Introduction.* Rev. ed. New York: Vintage Books, 1963. 450 pp.

Relevant to "intervention" since it interprets Soviet law as "parental," in contrast to Western approaches focussed on *laissez-faire.*

CURTISS, JOHN S. *The Russian Church and the Soviet State, 1917–1950.* Boston: Little Brown & Co., 1953. x+387 pp.

A history of the measures taken by the government to discourage the Church and the Church's response. Includes the wartime relaxation to gain political support.

INKELES, ALEX, and BAUER, RAYMOND (eds.). *Soviet Socialism: Daily Life in a Totalitarian Society.* New York: Athenaeum, 1968. xix+533 pp.

Two sociologists examine the Soviet way of earning a living, getting an education, obtaining information, and raising a family.

TAUBMAN, WILLIAM. *The View from Lenin Hills: Soviet Youth in Ferment.* New York: Coward McCann, Inc., 1967. 249 pp.

A readable report by an American political scientist based on his student days in Moscow. Revealing on extent of student indoctrination.

Chapter 10. The Army and Politics

BERMAN, HAROLD J., and KERNER, MIROSLAV. *Soviet Military Law and Administration.* Cambridge, Mass.: Harvard University Press, 1955. xiv+208 pp.

Details not only on military law, but on the means used by the Communist party and police to penetrate the armed forces. One author served in the army.

BIALER, SEWERYN (ed.). *Stalin and His Generals: Soviet Military Memoirs of World War II.* New York: Pegasus, 1969. 644 pp.

Engaging accounts of the war by Soviet officers, providing insight into the education, structure, and functions of the armed forces. Also treats the control system and the great purge. Explains why military coups have never occurred.

KOLKOWICZ, ROMAN. *The Soviet Military and the Communist Party.* Princeton: Princeton University Press, 1967. xvi+429 pp.

A Rand study of controls and also of the military's impact on policy. For an updating, see Deane, *Political Control of the Soviet Armed Forces* (New York: Crane Russak, 1977).

LEE, ASHER (ed.). *The Soviet Air and Rocket Forces.* London: Weidenfeld & Nicolson, 1959. 311 pp.

Communist party and police controls are exposed in one chapter.

Chapter 11. Enforcement of Law

BARRY, DONALD D.; BUTLER, WILLIAM E.; and GINSBURGS, GEORGE. *Contemporary Soviet Law.* The Hague: Martinus Nijhoff, 1974. xxvi+242 pp.

Eleven Western specialists examine law on crime, political dissent, civil relationships, environmental protection, labor relations, computer science, international trade and relations, and the educational role of court procedure.

CHALIDZE, VALERY. *To Defend These Rights: Human Rights in the Soviet Union.* New York: Random House, 1974. viii+340 pp.

The deficiencies of the Soviet legal system as seen by a Soviet scientist who, before emigration, attempted to work within permissible limits in order to protect colleagues from bureaucratic restraints and tyrannical procedures.

CONNOR, WALTER D. *Deviance in Soviet Society: Crime, Delinquency, and Alcoholism.* New York: Columbia University Press, 1972. 327 pp.

A sociologist presents a depressing picture to those expecting socialist structures to eliminate crime. Conclusion: that Marxism-Leninism hampers basic scientific research because of focus on social causes of crime.

FEIFER, GEORGE. *Justice in Moscow.* New York: Simon & Schuster, 1964. 353 pp.

The most widely read of all books on Soviet law: an American student's account of the trials he witnessed and the explanations he heard during a year's residence in Moscow.

HAZARD, JOHN N. *Settling Disputes in Soviet Society: The Formative Years of Legal Institutions.* Reprinted with new preface. New York: Octagon Books, Farrar, Straus, and Giroux, 1978. xiv+534 pp.

Explains the transition from a simple legal system to the contemporary complex one, utilizing reports on debates of the early years and judicial practice.

MORGAN, GLEN G. *Soviet Administrative Legality: The Role of the Attorney General's Office.* Stanford: Stanford University Press, 1962. x+281 pp.

The institution designed to protect the Constitution and minimize bureaucratic excesses. Study based on reported practice.

SOLOMON, PETER H., JR. *Soviet Criminologists and Criminal Policy: Specialists in Policy Making.* New York: Columbia University Press, 1978. x+253 pp.

Reveals the extent to which legal specialists participate with Communist party generalists in formulating law. Throws light also on limitations created by technicians generally on Communist party domination of technical fields.

TEREBILOV, V. *The Soviet Court.* Moscow: Progress Publishers, 1973. 181 pp.

The U.S.S.R.'s Minister of Justice gives his authoritative statement of what should be understood as the history, structure, and procedure of courts.

Chapter 12. Employment by the State

BEREDAY, GEORGE Z., and PENNAR, JAAN (eds.). *The Politics of Soviet Education.* New York: Frederick A. Praeger, 1960. vi+217 pp.

A symposium by educators describing educational institutions. Strong on Communist party control, classroom conduct, teaching syllabi, and extracurricular activities.

YANOWITCH, MURRAY, and FISHER, WESLEY A. (eds.). *Social Stratification and Mobility in the U.S.S.R.* White Plains, N.Y.: International Arts & Sciences Press, 1973. xxxi+402 pp.

A selection by an economist and sociologist from Soviet literature depicting class and strata differences in income, prestige, access to education, and life styles. Indicates extent to which Soviet conditions create variations in status.

ULAM, ADAM B. *The Russian Political System.* New York: Random House, 1974. vii+180 pp.

A prominent historian's survey of the Soviet system, which finds that contradictions inherent in communism are being sharpened by increasing popular desire for consumer goods and the freedoms that usually accompany an improving standard of living.

General Symposia

HENDEL, SAMUEL (ed.). *The Soviet Crucible: The Soviet System in Theory and Practice.* North Scituate, Mass.: Duxbury Press, 4th edition. 1973. xvi+436 pp.

A popular collection of previously published essays touching history, theory, political and economic structures, and minorities' problems. Contains useful selected bibliography.

KANET, ROGER E. (ed.). *The Behavioral Revolution and Communist Studies.* New York: The Free Press, 1971. xv+376 pp.

Trends within the Communist party, testing the effectiveness of an empirical approach to the study of a relatively inaccessible society.

MORTON, HENRY W., and TÖKES, RUDOLPH (eds.). *Soviet Politics and Society in the 1970's.* New York: The Free Press, Macmillan Publishing Co., 1974. xxvi+401 pp.

A "post behavioral" study by ten Western specialists combining behavioral and area techniques in analysis of stability and change in the Soviet system.

Documentation

BERMAN, HAROLD J., and SPINDLER, JAMES W. *Soviet Criminal Law and Procedure: The R.S.F.S.R. Codes.* Cambridge, Mass.: Harvard University Press, 2nd ed. 1972. ix+599 pp.

Translation of the criminal code and code of criminal procedure with analysis of them in light of the history, interpretation, and functioning of Soviet legal institutions.

BUTLER, WILLIAM E. (compiler and translator). *The Soviet Legal System: Selected Contemporary Legislation and Documentation.* Dobbs Ferry, N.Y.: Oceana Publications, 1978. x+733 pp.

A miniature library of Soviet statutes establishing political structures and fundamental principles of all branches of law. May be supplemented by translations of judicial decisions in all fields arranged systematically in J. N. Hazard, W. E. Butler, and P. B. Maggs, *The Soviet Legal System* (Third ed., Dobbs Ferry, N.Y.: Oceana Publications, 1977).

BOIM, LEON, and MORGAN, GLEN G. (eds.). *The Soviet Procuracy Protests: 1937–1973.* Vol. 21, Law in Eastern Europe. Leiden: Sijthoff & Noordhoff, 1978. 620 pp.

Translations of all Procuratorial protests in defense of the Constitution and of Soviet legality generally. Provides insight into the functions of this unfamiliar institution.

GRULIOW et al. *Current Soviet Policies: The Documentary Record of the Communist Party Congresses.* Columbus, Ohio: Current Digest of the Soviet Press, The Ohio State University, 7 vols. 1953–76.

TRISKA, JAN F. (ed.). *Soviet Communism: Program and Rules, Lenin—Khrushchev, 1961–1952–1919.* San Francisco: Chandler Publishing Co., 1962. 196 pp.

Biography

Prominent Personalities in the U.S.S.R.: A Biographic Directory. Compiled by the Institute for the Study of the U.S.S.R. Munich, Germany. Metuchin, N.J.: The Scarecrow Press, 1965. x+782 pp.

SIMMONDS, GEORGE W. (ed.). *Soviet Leaders: Biographies of 42 Prominent Figures in Government, Science and the Arts.* New York: Thomas Y. Crowell Co., 1967. xi+405 pp.

Periodicals

Current Digest of the Soviet Press. (Weekly.) The Ohio State University, Columbus, Ohio, 43210.

Thorough coverage in translation of major news items and articles in the Soviet press as selected by a staff of American specialists. No comment or explanation provided. Sponsored by the American Association for the Advancement of Slavic Studies. Fully indexed quarterly since founding in 1949.

Problems of Communism. (Bimonthly.) United States Information Agency, U.S. Government Printing Office, Washington, D.C. 20005.

Interpretive articles, notes, book reviews, cartoons, published primarily for scholars outside the U.S.A., but available to all.

Reprints from the Soviet Press. (Biweekly.) Compass Publications, 115 East 87 Street, Box 12-F., New York, N.Y. 10028.

Official translations received from Novosti Press Agency, Moscow. Articles, documents, speeches, selected for distribution in the U.S.A.

The Russian Review. (Quarterly.) The Hoover Institution, Stanford, California 94305.

Edited by scholars of the Hoover Institution. Relatively brief but meaty articles on Russian history, literature, economics, and politics. Book reviews.

Slavic Review. (Quarterly.) American Association for the Advancement of Slavic Studies. James R. Millar, editor, University of Illinois, Champaign, Ill. 61820.

Articles, symposia, book reviews. A major source for interpretive articles by prominent scholars.

Soviet Life. (Monthly.) 1706 Eighteenth Street N.W., Washington, D.C. 20009.

Illustrated popularization by Soviet authors of the political, economic, and social system of their country.

Soviet Law and Government: Translations from Original Soviet Sources. (Quarterly.) M.E. Sharpe, Inc., 108 Grand Street, White Plains, N.Y. 10601.

Translations selected by knowledgeable American scholars to supplement classroom materials. No newspaper coverage.

Soviet Studies. (Quarterly.) Basil Blackwood, Oxford, England. Edited by the University of Glasgow, Scotland, U.K.

Timely scholarly analysis of contemporary events of political, economic, sociological concern. Book reviews.

A Chronicle of Current Events. Routledge Journals, 9 Park Street, Boston, Mass. 02108.

An English translation of the Russian language periodical originally published in Moscow by dissenters and now prepared from *Samizdat* materials by Khronika Press, 505 Eighth Avenue, New York, N.Y. 10018. Appears irregularly as materials warrant.

Bibliographies

American Bibliography of Slavic and East European Studies. 5 vols. (1968–69, 1970–72, 1973, 1974, 1975). Columbus, Ohio: American Association for the Advancement of Slavic Studies, Inc., The Ohio State University, 1970–1976. New volumes annually.

A nearly complete record of North American publications (books and articles) prepared at the Library of Congress, Washington, D.C. since the 1973 volume.

HORECKY, PAUL L. (ed.). *Russia and the Soviet Union: A Bibliographic Guide to Western Language Publications.* Chicago: University of Chicago Press, 1965. xxiv+473 pp.

Two thousand entries, annotated, prepared by authorities in Soviet politics, economics, history, literature, international relations, and law. A companion volume to *Basic Russian Publications: A Selected Bibliography on Russia and the Soviet Union, 1962.*

Encyclopedia

Great Soviet Encyclopedia: A Translation of the Russian Edition of 1970. New York and London: The Macmillan Co., 1973.

An index volume indicates location of articles, which appeared in the Soviet edition according to the Cyrillic alphabet, and are placed in the same order in the English translation.

INDEX

Administration, 112–34; of justice, 193–94; under Khrushchev, 122–23, 126–27, 128, 133; Lenin's concept of, 112–13, 129–30; and minorities, 115–16, 120–22; and nationalization, problem of, 116–17; and policy-making, 39; under Stalin, 39, 118, 119, 121, 132–33; in stateless society, 6

Administrative tribunals, 192

Age groups, and family attitudes, 168–69; in Komsomols, 41–42; and party membership, 35–36; and religious belief, 161, 164

Agnosticism, 161, 162

Agriculture, 112–34; administration of, 121; collectivization of, 141–43. See also Collective farm; State farm

Agriculture, Ministry of, 148, 149–50, 151, 153

Alexander II, Tsar, 89, 136

All-Russian Bureau of Military Commissars, 177, 178

All-Union Council of National Economy, 116–17

All-Union Farm Machinery Association, 149

All-Union ministries, 117–18

American Bar Association, 198

Appeal, right to, 186, 201–2

Armenian national group, 29, 94, 95, 100, 110–11

Armenian Republic, 97, 216

Army, 175–90; and commissar system, 177–83; defections from during World War II, 179; as interest group, 187–90, 238–39, 240; officers, 181, 182–83, 184–86; and party membership, 24, 25, 177, 180–81; in Revolu-

tion, 175–77; and security police, 183–84

"Artel," 139, 141, 145–46

Artisans, 68, 210–11, 233, 234

Assassination, 201, 203, 208

Assembly, right of, 66

Association, right of, 66, 231–32. See also Trade unions

Atheism, 157, 161, 162

Authoritarianism of parents, 168–69

Authors' certificates, 131

Automation, 36

Automobiles, ownership of, 173

Autonomous Republics, 101, 104; and status elevation question, 108–11

Azerbaidjanian national group, 95, 100, 110

Azerbaidjan Republic, 97

Baltic peoples, 95

Baltic states, 78

Banishment, 89–90, 91

Bashkirs, 95, 100; and status elevation question, 108–11

Berliner, Joseph S., 225

Bill of rights, 9–10, 99, 157, 160

Birth records, 157–58

Bolsheviks, 46–48; and army, 175–76; and industrial plant organization, 128–29; and justice, 191; and minorities, 94–95, 96; and peasants, 138; and trade unions, 68

Brest Litovsk, Treaty of, 96, 175

Brezhnev, Leonid I., 33, 36, 39, 43–44

Broken homes, and divorce, 167, 169–70

Budget, national, 107–8; committees, 61–62; and party dues, 30–31

Bulganin, Nikolai A., 61